ORATORY SCHOOL
LIBRARY

———:———

CLASS ....942.061.............

BOOK No. ....10771.............

D1491904

942 C61
16771

The Making of an English Revolutionary

The Making
of an English Revolutionary

The Early Parliamentary Career of John Pym

William W. MacDonald

Rutherford • Madison • Teaneck
Fairleigh Dickinson University Press
London and Toronto: Associated University Presses

© 1982 by Associated University Presses, Inc.

Associated University Presses, Inc.
4 Cornwall Drive
East Brunswick, N.J. 08816

Associated University Presses Ltd
69 Fleet Street
London EC4Y 1EU, England

Associated University Presses
Toronto M5E 1A7, Canada

Library of Congress Cataloging in Publication Data

MacDonald, William W.
   The making of an English revolutionary.

   Bibliography: p.
   Includes index.
   1. Pym, John, 1584-1643. 2. Great Britain—Politics and government—
1603-1649. 3. Statesman—Great Britain—Biography. I. Title.
DA396.P9M3   942.06′1′0924 [B]   80-65867
ISBN 0-8386-3018-9   AACR2

Printed in the United States of America

For my Mother and Paul

Contents

The Making of an English Revolutionary

1. John Pym: English Parliamentary Leader

All men of history are divisible into two classes: the men of the hour and the men of all time. Beyond all question John Pym belongs in the latter category, for he worked hard and created for himself a reputation that essentially remains unchallenged 300 years after his death. To many historians[1] he was the chief architect of that great political revolution of 1640–42 and therefore one of the most remarkable intellects in the constitutional history of England. By the titanic will of his phenomenal drive and his resourcefulness, and by the practicality of his mind and his actions, and by his admirable mastery of political timing, he welded together, against incredible odds and over incredible handicaps, a program and a party that not only dominated Parliament for three years but most certainly reshaped the government of England.

John Pym was the most popular man in England during the early years of the English Civil War. It was not simply that he was the foremost man in Parliament and the preeminent parliamentarian of his generation who possessed a profound knowledge of the strengths and weaknesses of the individual members of the House of Commons—it was much more than that. John Pym had his hand on the pulse of the nation, and he understood fully the ideals and aspirations of most Englishmen during that troubled era. His success was the result of several diverse factors: his political agility, his unmatched ability to get things done, his capacity to obtain the maximum from the most unpromising raw material, his genius as a political tactician, and his thoroughly realistic approach to government. It is said that he believed in everything that worked,[2] and like all historical generalizations, this belief contains a kernel of truth. For Pym politics was the art of the possible; a half-dead good cause was infinitely more valuable than the best dead one. When one contemplates the enormity of Pym's accomplishments and understands how little time he had for his labors, one cannot help but be awed by his achievements. The eventual triumph of Parliament over Charles I owed less to Oliver Cromwell than to the often drab ordinances that John Pym engineered through the Commons in his years of power. Cromwell might indeed have led the forces that brought the king down, but it was Pym who fashioned the machinery by which that fall took place. And one is on firm foundations when one accepts the thesis of Goldwin Smith, who wrote that the "greatest member of Parliament that ever lived, the greatest master of the convictions and feelings of the House of Commons was not Robert Peel, but John Pym."[3]

It is important and highly desirable, however, to say more than just that John Pym performed great acts and uttered great thoughts simply because he was a great man, and this tribute itself has not remained unchallenged. To some historians Pym represented all that was evil in a popular parliamentarian. To some he was intolerant, refusing to accept any ideas that were contrary to his own. To others he lacked the vision and foresight of an intelligent statesman, because he destroyed all that existed and failed to construct a responsible substitute, because he left the crown a hollow power and the government in the hands of the London mob, and because he was the leader of an unprincipled and destructive opposition that would neither formulate an alternative policy nor form an alternative government. To still others Pym was absolutely ruthless, a demagogue who helped mold and influence the opinions of the masses in order to accomplish his wicked will; he believed in mobocracy and fully foreshadowed the totalitarian methods of twentieth-century dictators.[4] Finally, he has been accused of being an opportunist. Clarendon wrote that Pym's

> power of doing shrewd turns was extraordinary, and no less in doing good offices for particular persons; and that he did preserve many from censure who were under the severe displeasure of the Houses and looked upon as eminent delinquents; and that the quality of many of them made it believed that he sold that protection for valuable considerations.[5]

But these attacks are both erroneous and deceiving. To argue that Pym was intolerant of other's ideas illustrates a rather superficial knowledge of his parliamentary career. To declare that he was a destructive statesman who had no policy or program is an extraordinary admission of total misinterpretation of John Pym's policies and of the political revolution of 1640–42. To state that he was a demagogue, a man who cultivated the political passions of the amoral masses, is to admit to a rather cursory understanding of Pym's stylistic habits. John Pym had, as will be revealed, the admirable faculty of giving logic and intellect to the ideas of the ordinary man; but he also had common sense and it was this common sense that the people of London understood and fully appreciated. To declare, moreover, that Pym was an opportunist and to equate this opportunism with evilness is to admit to a rather naïve interpretation of power politics. To get things done, to accomplish one's program, to succeed where others have failed, politicians must resort to compromise, and if compromise is opportunism, then John Pym was an opportunist and proud of it. Even Clarendon was cognizant of the higher political motives of John Pym:

> No man had more to answer to for the miseries of the kingdom, or had his hand or head deeper in their contrivance; and yet, I believe they grew much higher even in his life than he designed.... Besides the exact knowledge of the forms and orders of [Parliament], which few men had, he had a very comely and grave way of expressing himself, with great volubility of words, natural and proper; and understood the temper and affections of the kingdom as well as any man, and had observed the errors and mistakes in government, and knew well how to make them appear greater than they were .... He seemed to all men to have the greatest influence upon the House of Commons of any man; and, in truth, I think he was ... the most popular man, and the most able to do hurt, that hath lived in any time.[6]

Posterity had fully recognized the talents of John Pym, and it is in essential agreement that he was one of the ablest and wisest statesmen in English history.

But just who was this "greatest member of Parliament" who went under the name of John Pym? There was absolutely none of the glamor attached to his personality that shone from such leaders of Parliament as Walpole or Pitt. If he had a private life at all, or personal feelings, hardly the faintest hint survives of them. John Pym was one of those many men who made themselves public without making themselves known. The political Pym we know fairly well; the private Pym we know only in the most shallow sense. We can only guess at the various elements that made John Pym a living, human being and all that was tender and sincere in him. We do know, however, his appearance from his portrait—a portly form, almost fat; a broad-browed, heavy-jowled man; a forehead so high that lampooners compared it to a shuttle; a man with small alert eyes, a straight nose and a full-lipped mouth framed by a curled moustache and Vandyke beard. He wore his hair brushed straight back from his forehead and long enough to conceal his ears. His dress was that of a gentleman of the time, respectable black set off by a plain white linen. His portrait is so deceptively bland that it supports the time-worn phrase that it is indeed more than fine feathers that make fine birds.

An outline of the life of John Pym is all that is required for the purposes of this study.[7] From the time of Magna Charta, Pyms or Pims or Pymmes or Pimmes had resided near Bridgewater, a small commercial town in Wiltshire. By judicious and numerous marriage alliances and undoubtedly profitable business transactions, the Pym family had acquired a considerable fortune of around thirty estates by the 1580s.[8] The Pyms' main estate was situated at Brymore, and it was there on May 20, 1584, that John Pym was born.[9] His father was Alexander Pym, who was an important country landowner, a justice of the peace, and a member of Parliament.[10] His mother was Phillippe Coles, heiress of a rather large fortune, whose father, Humphrey Coles, had become prominently wealthy through the sale of confiscated church properties at Bath and Taunton, both of which had been expropriated and sold during the reign of Henry VIII.[11]

Fate, however, often plays drastic tricks, for it would be John Pym who attained power and prestige for the family name of Pym. It was not Alexander Pym's fortune to be an important member of Parliament, for sudden death cut short a promising career less than a year after John Pym was born. His mother, faced with the unenviable task of raising and guiding three small children, did the practical thing. After a suitable assessment of her assets and a suitable period of mourning, she married Sir Anthony Rous. This man was the only father John Pym ever knew, and he was an extraordinarily interesting father. In kaleidoscopic sequence he was at various times, and quite often at the same time, an explorer in search of adventure and profit in America,[12] a sheriff, a member of Parliament, and the friend and neighbor of that most daring and dashing of all those daring and dashing Elizabethans, Sir Francis Drake.[13]

Anthony Rous, as Pym's stepfather, undoubtedly developed a strong paternal influence upon John Pym, and that dominant influence appears to be overwhelmingly religious. Rous and his wife were devout and active members of the Established Church. They kept morning and evening prayer hours, they wrote passages of the Bible in a notebook for the education of their numerous children, and they always attended Sunday services regardless of "distance of place, or distemper of weather."[14] Yet it was a rather particular religion of the Established Church which they followed. There is a hint that Rous and his family had essentially Calvinistic leanings, for he educated two of his natural sons at the rigidly Calvinistic University of Leiden.[15] Be that as it may, one cannot deny the fact that truly dominant theme of John Pym's youthful and maturing years was religion, and throughout the 1620s this influence was reflected in his numerous and impassioned speeches in the House of Commons.

Like many another youth of the gentry class of England, John Pym traveled the time-worn path to Oxford University. He was only fifteen when he matriculated from Broadgates Hall (now Pembroke College). The entry in the University Register reads as follows: "1599. 18 May. Broadgates Hall. Pim John. Sem., arm. 15."[16] At Oxford Pym became friendly with Digory Wheare, his principal tutor. In later years Wheare was to become the first Professor of History in the University of Oxford, and also Principal of Gloucester Hall.[17] Pym and Wheare conducted a long and amiable Latin correspondence for over twenty-one years. Pym loaned Wheare money and advised him in business matters, and when the tutor became head of Gloucester Hall, Pym contributed funds.[18] Moreover, when Pym's young son entered Oxford, it was at Gloucester Hall that John, Jr., matriculated.[19] Very little is known, however, of John Pym's life at Oxford, for he left the university without a degree and in 1602 he became a student at one of the Inns of Court.

At the Middle Temple Pym became something of a wit, spouting fashionable witticisms.[20] Furthermore, while there, he undoubtedly became acquainted with several important future members of Parliament—John Hampden, John Selden, and Benjamin Rudyard. But his most trusted friend was William Whitaker. Pym and Whitaker were admitted to the Middle Temple on the same day[21] and became so close that the latter served as co-trustee of Pym's estates and worked closely with Pym and Francis Rous, Pym's stepbrother, in the work of the Short and Long Parliaments.[22]

John Pym's schooling at the Middle Temple was never completed; he was never called to the bar. But in June 1605, through the interest of the Earl of Bedford, Pym secured for himself the receivorship of Hampshire, Wiltshire, and Gloucester.[23] The following three entries in the *Calendar of State Papers, Domestic* reveal Pym's activities during this period:

> 1613 November 6, Westminster. Warrant to John Pymme, Receivor of Wiltshire, to pay yearly to Geo. Hungerford, 132. 4d. per load, for eight loads of hay for the King's deer in Braydon Forest.

> 1614 July 9, Westminster. Grant to William Bowler of the office of Bailiff of the Hundreds of Halford, Gratton, and Kittsgae, co. Gloucester; with certificate of John Pymme, Receivor General of the County, of his fitness for the place.

> 1618 September 28, Egham. John Pymme to the Lords of the Treasury. Impossibility of raising at once £2000 by the sale of His Majesty's rent, Iron, and fines on leases of disforested grounds, Blackmore and Pewsham. Can get no sale for the iron at the price required, £12.10s. per ton, and has no offers save for part of one forest.[24]

It was during this period of his young life that John Pym met, courted, and married Anne Hooke, daughter of Anthony Rous's sister, Barbara, and her husband, John Hooke.[25] Again, knowledge of John Pym between his marriage and his entrance into Parliament is scant. Apparently he was away from home quite often, but not very far away, for he sired in rapid succession a daughter, a daughter, a son, a daughter, a daughter, a son, and a son. In addition to his treasury position, Pym served at various times as a member of the county commission for parks, forests, sewerage disposal, and depopulation. Occasionally, too, he acted in a semi-official capacity overseeing a will, aiding in a post-mortem inquisition, and certifying a local candidate for office.[26]

The year 1620 was an especially terrible one for John Pym, for he lost in quick succession his wife, his mother, and his eldest stepbrother. Perhaps it was these tragedies upon tragedies that determined Pym to seek election to Parliament, for in December of 1620 he stood for the Wiltshire borough of Calne and, by the choice of seventeen electors there, became a member of Parliament.[27] Having buried his wife and mother and having provided for his children's welfare, Pym devoted himself with austere concentration to the career of a self-made politician. Henceforth, he directed himself solely to the public good with unflinching devotion. Parliament and his parliamentary career became his meat, his drink, his work, his exercise, his recreation, his pleasure, his ambition, indeed his all.

During his years in the Parliaments of 1621, 1624, 1625, 1626, and 1628, Pym made important contributions and established a notable reputation. During the tense, personal rule of Charles I, he served as treasurer and chief administrator of the Providence Island Company, a joint-stock company chartered for the purpose of establishing an English settlement in the West Indies. Pym was a squire of great business ability, and the main burden of this organization rested entirely upon him. He was an efficient manager and administrator with a quick, resourceful mind, a good memory, and an astonishing capacity for acquiring, digesting, and using information. By his leadership of the Providence Company and his rather heavy investment in this and other colonial adventures, Pym became well known in commercial circles in London and elsewhere.[28]

With the meetings of the Short and Long Parliaments in 1640, Pym became the acknowledged leader of the House of Commons.

With studious moderation he set about to control royal irresponsibility. Calmly, yet so comprehensively, Pym became determined to bind the Stuart king to those principles that moderate
men had advocated even before the Scottish wars: England is first
and foremost a royal commonwealth, not a despotic monarchy;
Englishmen are born free, not slaves of the state; the will of the
ruler of the realm must be bound by law, else no man's freedom
or property could be secure. By hook or by crook John Pym set
about to enlighten the king to this occasion; he was determined to
make Charles I the servant of the law and not its master.

Pym's success was immense. In two short years he dramatically and drastically changed the government of England. He
brought forth the supremacy of the law and the right of Parliament, together with the king, to determine that law. He had the
great Strafford beheaded and the equally great Laud imprisoned.
He struck so hard at the bastions of the Stuart theory of divine
right and dismantled so effectively the structure of absolute
monarchy in England that at last the hesitant Charles acted. He
attempted to impeach Pym and four others, who escaped to the
heart of London. But the king's coup failed, and revolution and
civil war became the only solutions. While the king was raising
the standard at Nottingham, John Pym resided in London as a
conquering hero. Pym became the master of revolution. It was he
and he alone who held, during those years of frightful crises, the
frame of the executive together. He was not only the orator of his
party, but its very soul and center; he knew not only how to
propagate his opinions with words but also how to organize the
means of victory. He managed the war, kept together the discor-
dant and wavering parliamentarians, and sustained, by his vigor
and eloquence, the enthusiasm of London. He remained the most
popular man in England until his untimely death.

The royalists, quite naturally, utterly despised John Pym. *King
Pym* was the favorite term of royalist reproach:

> Ask me no more why Strafford's dead
> And why we aimed at so at his head.
> Faith, all the answer I can give,
> 'Tis thought he was too wise to live.

Ask me no more why in this age
I sing so sharp without a cage.
This answer I in brief do sing,
All things were thus when Pym was King.[29]

His life was often in danger. In October 1641, in the midst of a debate in the Commons, a messenger came with a letter for Pym. When Pym opened it, an infectious rag, which had been applied to a plague sore, fell to the floor; the sender wrote that he hoped Pym would die as a result of handling the rag.[30] Shortly after this a man, mistaken for Pym, was stabbed in Westminster Hall; and in 1642 Pym was assaulted by some women and only with very great difficulty escaped their furious beating.[31]

In December 1643, Pym fell fatally ill. John Donne wrote to Lady Graham that "Pym is most desperately sick, and they say of the lowsy disease."[32] John Rushworth wrote that it was not the "loathsome and ignorminious Disease [the] true natural cause of his Death seeming to be the great pains he took, joined with a competent Old Age, and but an infirm constitution."[33] Pym's death was a natural one; he died of cancer. Frail of body and so thoroughly exhausted that he often fainted, worn out by the fearful efforts of the war, by the exciting alternations of danger and success, of defeat and victory, he became an heir of history. The House of Commons showed a respect to his memory that was without precedent. A committee was appointed to consider his debts and estates, and it was ordered that he be interred in Westminster Abbey,[34] and that a sumptuous monument be erected to his memory.[35]

His death brought joy to the monarchists, and they delighted to spread the rumor that he had been carried off by the foul disease of Herod. His death comforted his royalist enemies and fortified their beliefs in their eventual triumph. The Venetian ambassador wrote:

John Pym is dead, a solicitor of Civil causes but the promoter of the present rebellion and the director of the whole machine. His body has been shown to the people in his own house for two days, and on Wednesday it was buried in West-

minster, in the presence of the two Houses and a great con-
course. This hydra is not therefore without a head, but so far
no one has appeared of equal application and ability. Indeed it
would seem that rivalry for the lead gives hope of division and
parties, which affords the easiest and safest means of restoring
the King to his former greatness.[36]

Edward Nicolas wrote that with the death of Pym the parliamentarians "have no hope left but in the Scots invading this Kingdom."[37]

Pym's death also caused deep regret. "Woe is me," declared
Stephan Marshall, the prominent Puritan[38] who delivered the fu-
neral oration, "for the good man hath perished out of this
earth."[39] Children did not weep in the streets at Pym's passing—there was none of that. But history could indeed have better
snatched another man. His death witnessed the disintegration of
that moderate party and the end of that fragile unity of Parliament
that Pym had struggled so desperately to maintain.[40] Said Marshall: "Our Parliament is weakened, our armies wasted, our treasure exhausted, our enemies increased."[41] And in August 1644,
Robert Baillie wrote that "since Pyme died, no state head
amongst them: Many very good and able spirits, but not any of so
great and comprehensive a braine, as to manage the multitude of
so weightie affaires as lyes on them. If God did not sit at their
helme for any good guiding of theirs, long ere this they had been
gone."[42]

John Pym was an active and singularly important participant in
the vitally significant early years of the English Revolution and
Civil War. His role has been adequately described. It is fairly
well established that Pym was at most a reluctant revolutionist, a
conservative driven by the desperate circumstances of the time
into revolution, a moderate man who for a brief time acted im-
moderately. His fundamental conservatism is reflected in the
historical analyses of his actions during that period: Pym and the
methods of moderation; Pym and revolution through moderation;
and Pym and the revolution of the middle party.[43] It is clear that
the English Revolution and Civil War, as well as the issues leading up to them, were significant events, and that John Pym's
activities in those occurrences are important and demand careful
analyses. But it is no less true that there is a rather prominent

need for a thorough examination of his early parliamentary career. There is a need to recognize the significance of his parliamentary apprenticeship and a need to understand the background, training, hard work, and experience of the 1620s that made John Pym a great parliamentary leader of the 1640s. There is, moreover, a fundamental need to study the John Pym of the 1620s as he grappled with the entangled constitutional, political, and religious policies of that decade, for these were, in reality, the very problems that reached their climax in the English Revolution, and that molded and influenced the John Pym of the revolutionary era.

John Pym was the acknowledged leader of the House of Commons in both the Short and Long Parliaments. But the essential question is why. The answer, of course, involves a variety of conclusions: the absence of any truly first-rate parliamentary rival, for the Eliots, Cokes and Wentworths were long gone from the House; his reputation as a man of integrity and his perseverance, and his ability to get things done; his genius in recognizing that practical politics consists in accommodating one's principles to the reality of facts, and not in ignoring them; and his cultivation of public opinion and his recognition of its power. But it is my contention that John Pym's leadership in the Parliaments of the 1640s was due above all to the training he received in the Parliaments of the 1620s. And it is the chief object of this study to narrate the early parliamentary career of John Pym, to analyze his speeches and interpret his actions, to describe his political, religious, and constitutional thoughts, and to attempt to make intelligible those things which made John Pym a living, human, feeling, and thinking individual. A truly great man is one who does something for the first time, and John Pym was the first great parliamentary leader in English history. The following pages examine the background, the training, the experience, and the hard work that were necessary to make Pym's parliamentary leadership a living reality.

Notes

1. See S. R. Gardiner, *History of England from the Accession of James I to the Outbreak of the Civil War, 1603–1642* (London, 1883–84), 10:43–105—hereafter cited as Gardiner; G. M. Trevelyan, *England Under the Stuarts* (London, 1925), pp.

162–85; Godfrey Davies, *The Early Stuarts* (Oxford, 1959), pp. 99–124; Christopher Hill, *The Century of Revolution* (Edinburgh, 1961), pp. 112, 176, 191.

2. J. H. Hexter, *The Reign of King Pym* (Cambridge, Mass., 1941), pp. 190–207.

3. Goldwin Smith, *Three English Statesmen: Pym, Cromwell, Pitt* (New York, 1867), p. 8.

4. See Esme Wingfield-Stratford, *King Charles and King Pym* (London, 1949), pp. 11, 98; F. M. C. Higham, *Charles I: A Study* (London, 1932), pp. 153–54; S. Reed Brett, "John Pym," *Fortnightly* 154: (December 1943): 405–6; Isaac D'Israeli, *Eliot, Hampden and Pym* (London, 1832), pp. 16, 21.

5. Edward, Earl of Clarendon, *The History of the Rebellion and Civil Wars in England*, edited by W. D. McCray (Oxford, 1888), 7:413—hereafter cited as Clarendon.

6. Clarendon, 7:409–11.

7. See S. Reed Brett, *John Pym, 1583–1643* (London, 1940); C. E. Wade, *John Pym* (London, 1912); Hexter; Ida A. Taylor, *Revolutionary Types* (London, 1904), pp. 1–28; Smith; Goodwin F. Berquist, Jr., "The Parliamentary Speaking of John Pym, 1621–1643," an unpublished doctoral dissertation, Pennsylvania State University, 1958; John Forster, *Lives of Eminent British Statesmen* (London, 1831–39), vol. 3.

8. Brett, *John Pym*, p. xxvii.

9. Goodwin F. Berquist, Jr., "John Pym: New Evidence on an Old Parliamentarian," *Notes and Queries*, New Series (1958), 5:101.

10. F. A. Crisp, ed., *Abstracts of Somerset Wills* (London, 1887–90), 4:54; *Return of the Names of Every Member Returned to Serve in Each Parliament* (London, 1878), 1:415—hereafter cited as O.R.

11. A. W. Vivian Neal, *The Story of Brymore* (Taunton, Eng., c. 1951), p. 4.

12. Richard Hakluyt, *The Principal Navigations, Voyages, Trafficies and Discoveries of the English Nation* (London, 1598–1600), 3: 251–54; A. L. Rouse, *The Expansion of Elizabethan England* (New York, 1955), p. 40.

13. O.R., 1: 415; Richard Carew, *The Survey of Cornwall* (London, 1602), pp. 64, 113–14; Lady Eliot-Drake, *The Family and Heirs of Sir Francis Drake* (London, 1911), 1: 124.

14. Charles Fitzgeffrey, *Deaths Sermons Unto the Living, Delivered at the Funerall of the Religious Ladie Phillippe, late wife unto the Right Worshippful Sr. Anthonie Rous of Halton in Cornwall* (London, 1620); Charles Fitzgeffrey, *Elisha, His Lamentations for His Owne, and all Israel's losse in Elijah* (London, 1622).

15. Berquist, "Parliamentary Speaking," p. 21.

16. Andrew Clark, ed., *Register of the University of Oxford* (Oxford, 1888), 2, part 2, p. 278.

17. Charles E. Mallet, *A History of the University of Oxford* (London, 1924), 2: 278.

18. *Historical Manuscripts Commission, Second Report* (London, 1874), p. 143—hereafter cited as *H.M.C.; H.M.C., Sixth Report* (London, 1877), p. 549.

19. Joseph Foster, ed., *Alumni Oxoniensis: The Members of the University of Oxford* (Oxford, 1892), 3: 1223.

20. John Manningham, *Diary, 1601–03*, edited by John Bruce Society (Westminster: Camden, 1868), pp. 104, 155.

21. Charles H. Hopwood, ed., *Middle Temple Records* (London, 1904), 1: 421.

22. Mary F. Keeler, *The Long Parliament, 1640–1641* (Philadelphia, 1954), p. 390.

23. *Calendar of State Papers, Domestic, 1603–1610* (James I), p. 223—hereafter cited as *C.S.P.D.*

24. *C.S.P.D., 1611–1618* (James I), pp. 205, 243, 578.

25. John Burke, *A Genealogical and Heraldic History of the Landed Gentry, of the Commoners of Great Britain and Ireland* (London, 1838), 1: 119; Frederick T. Colby, ed., *The Visitations of the County of Devon in the year 1620* (London, 1872), p. 350; W. Bruce Bannerman, ed., *The Visitation of the County of Sussex, 1530–1644* (London, 1905), p. 63.

26. *C.S.P.D., 1611–1618*, p. 243, 578; *H.M.C., Laing Manuscripts* (London, 1914), 1: 125; W. W. Capes, *Scenes of Rural Life in Hampshire Among the Manors of Bramshott* (London, 1901), p. 166.

27. *O.R.*, 1: 454; A. E. W. Marsh, *A History of the Borough and Town of Calne* (Calne, 1903), p. 341.

28. A. P. Newton, *The Colonizing Activities of the English Puritans* (New Haven, 1914), pp. 75, 83–84; *H.M.C., Seventh Report* (London, 1875), pp. 546, 549.

29. Forster, *Eminent Lives*, 3: 215.

30. *A Damnable Treason by a Contagious Plaster of a Plague Sore* (London, 1641).

31. *H.M.C., Bath Manuscripts* (London, 1904), 1: 17.

32. *H.M.C., Sixth Report*, p. 335.

33. John Rushworth, *Historical Collections of Private Passages of State, 1618–1649* (London, 1721), 5: 376—hereafter cited as Rushworth; *A Narrative of the Disease and Death of That Noble Gentleman John Pym* (London, 1643).

34. *Journals of the House of Commons* (London, 1803–63), 3: 336–37—hereafter cited as C.J.; David Laing, ed., *The Letters and Journals of Robert Baillie* (Edinburgh, 1841–42), 2: 118.

35. *C.S.P.D., 1643–1647* (Charles I), p. 58.

36. *Calendar of State Papers, Venetian, 1643–1647* (Charles I), p. 53—hereafter cited as *C.S.P.V.*

37. *H.M.C., Hastings Manuscripts* (London, 1930), 2: 105.

38. Thomas Fuller, *England's Worthies in Church and State* (London, 1684), p. 391; C. F. Richardson, *English Preachers and Preaching* (New York, 1928), p. 60; E. W. Kirby, "Sermons before the Commons, 1640–42," *American Historical Review* 44 (1938): 528–48.

39. Stephan Marshall, *The Churches Lamentation. A Sermon of the Two Houses of Parliament at the Funerall of John Pym* (London, 1643).

40. Hexter, *Reign of King Pym*, pp. 151–52.

41. Marshall, *The Churches Lamentations*.

42. Laing, 2: 216.

43. Hexter, *Reign of King Pym*; Lotte Glow, "Pym and Parliament: the Methods of Moderation," *Journals Modern History* 36 (December 1964): 373–97; Goodwin F. Berquist, Jr., "Revolution Through Moderation: John Pym's Appeal to the Moderates in 1640," *Quarterly Journal of Speech* 41 (February 1963): 23–30.

2. The Parliament of 1621: First Session

John Pym's passport to immortality lay essentially in his extraordinary career in Parliament. He sat in the House of Commons from 1621 to 1643, and in all but his first Parliament, he was a member for Tavistock. He began his parliamentary career in the third Parliament of James I, sitting as a member of the borough of Calne in Wiltshire, his fellow member being the inconspicuous John Duckett.[1] With him in the House of Commons sat a number of men whose reputations in future English history would be household names, and who were closely involved in John Pym's political life. There was, first of all, Sir Thomas Wentworth, who had sat in the Addled Parliament of 1614 as one of the members for Yorkshire and who was once again representing the same county.[2] Wentworth, the future Earl of Strafford, was an "ally" of Pym during most of the 1620s. He would end his career, however, as John Pym's chief political antagonist. Another notable member who, like Pym, was a newcomer to Parliament was John Hampden, who represented the borough of Grampound in Cornwall. Hampden was a close political ally of Pym, indeed perhaps the closest of all until his death in 1643.[3] Still another notable parliamentarian who began his illustrious career in the Parliament of 1621 was Sir Robert Phelips, the son of the speaker of James I's first Parliament. Phelips, who was defeated in the parliamentary election of 1614 as a member of the "king's party,"[4] was one of the most dynamic and vocal opponents of the crown during the 1620s.

The formal opening of Parliament took place on January 30 when James I spoke to the assembled houses. The king, who never missed an opportunity to instruct his subjects on their duty toward an absolute monarch, lectured on the functions of Parliament in general and the duties of this Parliament in particular. "A Parliament," he declared, "is a thing compounded of a head and a body; the head is the Monarch that calleth it, the body is as the three estates called together by that head." James believed that the functions of Parliament were simple. They were summoned to advise and deliberate with the king upon the urgent affairs of the kingdom; they were called to give their king the best advice on matters which the monarch might be pleased to place before them. The House of Commons, however, had very special functions, for since they knew best the "particular estate" of the country, they would make known to the king any mispractice of administration or miscarriage of justice. But, more importantly, it was the particular duty of the Commons to equip the crown with "supply and sustenance to his necessities."

James then proceededed to the reasons the Parliament of 1621 had been assembled, explaining carefully his desire for the passage of "good laws," the protection of "good religion," and the numerous subsidies he needed to solve "the miserable spectacle" of Christendom because of the beginning of the Thirty Years' War. The king warmed the hearts of his listeners by declaring that, if he could not negotiate a peaceful settlement of the war, his "Crown and my blood and the blood of my son shall not be spared for it." The king, with an active memory of his previous relations with Parliament, concluded his long speech, however, by warning the assembled parliamentarians that he "would not have you to meddle with complaints against the King, the Church, or the state matters, nor with Princes' prerogatives."[5]

Indeed, King James had been reluctant to summon this Parliament. As early as December 1619, the war party in the court, which in reality meant the vast majority of privy councillors, though opinion most certainly differed as to what a clash of arms might mean, had urged James to summon Parliament, without which, they argued, he could not possibly hope to speak effectively on European affairs.[6] Unfortunately, among James's chief hates were both war and Parliament, and it was not until the Spanish had invaded the Palatinate that James deigned even to consider the thought of calling Parliament.[7] And yet still the king hesitated, and the exasperated councillors had the frustrating dual task of persuading James to call Parliament and of keeping him to that resolution once it was taken. Privy Councillor Naunton took the initiative and it was above all his leadership that eventually brought success.[8] James later remarked, upon hearing of some especially disheartening news from Germany, that "I may well

thank Naunton, as were it not for him I should not have summoned Parliament.''[9] Yet as reluctant as James was to summon
this Parliament, he allowed it considerable latitude both in initiative and in attacking domestic abuses. On Monday, February 5,
the first day the House of Commons met for business, Sir Edward
Giles moved rapidly for a petition to the king for freedom of
speech. He made this motion, he said, so that those members who
spoke ''extravagantly'' in the House might be punished by the
House themselves and not after Parliament had been adjourned.
He argued that this motion was solely in relation to the king's
proclamation of December 24, 1620, which forbade any licentious speeches on matters of state.[10]

Secretary of State Sir George Calvert intervened and reminded
the Commons that freedom of speech had already been granted by
the king. He repeated the king's reasons for summoning Parliament and pressed strongly for an immediate passing of supplies.
But the Commons were not to be detoured, and several members
of the House, notably Sir Edward Coke, spoke for petitioning
James for a guarantee of freedom of speech in Parliament. Finally, the issue was referred to a committee of the whole house.[11]

Ten days later John Glanville made a report on what the committee on freedom of speech had recommended. It suggested an
appeal to the king and the introduction of a bill forbidding the
imprisonment of members of Parliament for words spoken in the
House of Commons. At the end of the report Calvert rose and
revealed to the House that the king had commanded him to tell
them that he gave freedom of speech as no king before him had
ever done, and that if one of the parliamentarians did violate the
liberty of speech, the king hoped ''that the House would see them
punished there.''[12] This settled the affair, for John Pym recorded
in his diary that ''this speech set an end to that matter and from
that tyme all other Proposicions concerning libertie of speeches
were layde aside.''[13]

On the same day that the Commons received the report on
freedom of speech, a bill was read for the second time concerning
''punishing of abuses on the Sabbath day commonly called Sunday.'' The first reading occurred on February 9, and was introduced by Thomas Clerk, who asked that justices of the peace be
given wide discretion in punishing those who were guilty of

abusing the Sabbath.[14] The *Book of Sports*, which King James had issued in 1618, permitted all Englishmen who attended church service to engage in Sunday archery, dancing, and Maypole displays,[15] and the new bill, which was opposed to such harmless merrymaking, seemed to be plainly directed against the royal permission. Such, at least, was the interpretation of a certain young lawyer of Lincoln's Inn, Thomas Shepard by name.

Shepard stated that the bill was both inconvenient and indiscreet. He took exception ot it on three points: to the title of it, to the matter of it, and to the occasion of it. The bill, he declared, was legally false, for the Sabbath was not Sunday but, under the law, Saturday. Moreover, the bill condemned dancing and other exercises which went against both the king's book and that of King David's practices. "Let Divines," he said, "first resolve what is lawfull and unlawfull. Modestie befitts our Complexion. The Kinge by his edict hath given leave to his subjects to daunce." Furthermore, Shepard proceeded to declare that the bill had a foul puritanical odor. The bill, he said, was the work of Puritan "Cattle" who refused to submit themselves to the ceremonies of the Anglican Church. The bill savored of the spirit of a Puritan, and Puritans were in reality nothing more than atheists; they were foxes tied together by their tails, while their heads were divided into hostile factions, and their cause was joined together to destroy all the "good corne." Was Parliament, he asked, to make all those "gins and snares" for catching Catholics, and not design a "Mousetrap" to catch a Puritan? This bill, he concluded, was indeed a disturber of the peace.[16]

Shepard's fiery and tactless speech taxed the patience and goodwill of the House of Commons. Pym, recorded in his diary that Shepard's oration was "spoken with a greate deal of scorn and Malepeirt gesture; and thowgh the mislike and mutteringe of the Howse troubled him often, yet he protested he would speake and if he did offend, his bodye and his Fortune would answere it." [17] The speaker reproached Shepard and the House called him to the bar. He was examined, questioned, and ordered to withdraw himself from the House. The Commons would then have proceeded to censure Shepard, but other business put it off till the next day.[18]

On that day John Pym delivered his first speech in Parliament.

His maiden speech was indeed in character, for in a well-prepared paper, he zealously defended the functions and privileges of the House of Commons and espoused a vigorous Protestant religion, the single most important influence in his early parliamentary career. It is important to quote this speech in its entirety, for it is an excellent illustration of Pym's speeches, of his stylistic habit of carefully expounding and applying fundamental principles to clearly determined headings, and of his marshaling his arguments in a logical formation:

It is at all tymes a burthen to my modestie to speake in this Honourable Assembly. At this tyme it doth more oppresse my disposicion to speake against one whoe is yet (thowgh suspended) a Member of the Howse. This Gentleman, as I conceave, hath committed fower great faults, yet not faults all of one nature but arisinge each above other by fower remarkable steps of Gradacion. The first is a perticular fault against that worthy Member of this Howse who preferr'd the Bill. The second, a generall fault against all the Justices of Peace. The third, against the whole bodye of this High Courte, which is the representative-body of the Commons. The fowrth, as I may call it general generallissimum against the flourishinge estate of the Kingdome. All theis appeare stamped in his owne words.

The first is those whereby he did traduce that worthie Knight who preferred the Bill, calling him a Perturbulator of the Peace.

The second in those which cast a slander upon the Justices as if they were ever ready to protect such as were refractorie to his Majesties laws. And (as nothing is soe apt to multiplie as evell). The other twoe are eache of them double in the expression.

The offence to the Howse: (1) by calling your lawes by names of scorne and contempt, Engines, Barracardo's Mousetraps; (2) by makinge Puritanisme to be the occasion of this Bill, which he knewe past the votes of this Howse the last Convencion, And more sutable to our desires to bee past wherein he did noe lesse than laye upon us the name of Puritans.

The offence to the State: (1) By seeking to bring us into the ill opinion of the Kinge, whose favour and good opinion begetts our greatest hope of the prosperities and reformacion of the Kingdome. This he endeavoured to bereave us of, saying that we went about to make a lawe in the face of his Majestie opposition to his Royall iudgements declared in printe. Secondly, as he would divide the Kinge from us soe would he divide us amongst our selves, exasperatinge one partie by that odious and factious name of Puritans; or at least would make the world believe we were divided, which as it may breede in the Comen adversarie boldnes to attempt soe it maynourish among us ieolosye and suspicion in defense of our selves. And it hath beene often seene that small seeds of tumult and sedition growe upp into greate dangers, even in the overthrowe of states.

Faults are not equal. Sinnes against God are infinite in respect of the obiect, they are finite, being acted by the facultyes of a finite creature, And soe receiveth severall degrees as theis faculties are more or lesse intent. Althowgh this Gentlemans offence be against the State, which is the highest obiect that Civil offences can reache unto, And was acted with the greatest earnestnes and ambition that might be, Yet my Censure shall not bee according to either of these measures, but suited rather accordinge to the propercion of your mercie than of his Desert. And if it be agreeable to the order of the Howse (which is practised in other Courts) That the meanest give their opinion first, I shall match his fower faults with fower punishments. In the heate and eagernes of his speech, perceivinge the dislike of the Howse, He protested he would speake And if he did otherwise than became him, his person and his estate would answere it. I will distreigne him (thowgh moderately) by both his pledges, His person by Imprisonment duringe pleasure, His estate by the Fine of £100. And I think him worthy to be expelled the Howse and excepted out of the Generall Pardon.[19]

Some observations can be made on Pym's maiden speech. It was, of course, a typical seventeenth-century speech: full of learning, full of scripture, full of philosophic passages. He combined the plain and practical with the profound and contemplative. Beauty of style and harmony and grace and good rhythm, however, depend upon simplicity. Pym's style was almost deliberately grave and laborious. His speeches during the 1620s were almost always clear and solid, but they were also always tedious and dull.

In at least two respects, however, the subject matter of this maiden speech is of particular interest as foreshadowing some principles which John Pym maintained to the day of his death. There were, first of all, the very real indignation and resentment against Shepard for labeling some members of the Commons odious and factious Puritans. Pym remained a member of the Established Church throughout his life. He was never a Puritan in the most rigid sense of the term; that is, although he was always closely allied with many members of Parliament who were Puritans, he himself never openly joined any Puritan sects. Nevertheless, John Pym was a Puritan in all but name, for his main interest throughout the 1620s was religion, and if one cannot state that he was a Puritan in the rigid sense, one can at least declare that he was most certainly a Puritan in the broadest concept of the term: that as an English Protestant he worked to "purify" the Established Church of "Popish" remnants and innovations.

The second significant note in the speech was the insistence that the "greatest hope of prosperitie and reformacion of the Kingdome" depended upon the favor and good opinion of the king. Pym was sincerely loyal to the English crown throughout the 1620s. This allegiance to the king and to English kingship was a consistent feature of John Pym's political thought. That the king in Parliament was Pym's political ideology is amply illustrated in his speeches and actions in the 1620s. And the peace of the kingdom, he believed, consisted in the "peace of this House." That, too, was a consistent concept of John Pym. The king in a united Parliament; the harmony of ideals and institutions. Although Pym's concept of government was both simple and constructive, it was very difficult to effectuate that belief during the reigns of James I and Charles I.

After Coke and several other members had made observations on the "irreligiousness" of Shepard's speech, and after Sir Jerome Horsey[20] reminded the Commons of an incident during Elizabeth's reign—upon a question of passing a bill for the Sabbath with the House divided, 140 being of each side, one gentleman who had given his vote for the bill was kept from going out, whereby the number became equal and after a time he fell down dead—the House of Commons declared its judgment against the unlamented Shepard. In his diary Pym wrote that the sentence was intended to be one of forgiveness rather than one of punishment and that Shepard was merely expelled. Pym's suggestions, however, were almost totally ignored, and he discharged the matter by tersely writing that Shepard was called in and "received his iudgment upon his Knee at the Barr, was discharged from the Howse, and a newe Writt awarded." [21]

Three days after the expulsion of the hapless Shepard, the House of Commons was led to consider another question that also was to provoke the consideration of Pym. On February 19, William Noy called the attention of the House to monopolies and to the abuses arising from them. [22] The history of monopolies in England was often a bitter clash between an enraged House of Commons and a rather hesitant monarchy. [23] The great Elizabeth was forced in her last Parliament to bow, but to bow graciously, to the will of Parliament and revoke several obnoxious letters patent and to issue a royal proclamation forcing all monopolies to submit themselves to the careful scrutiny of the common-law courts. [24] It did not take long for the courts to pass judgment on the problem of monopolies by letters patent. [25] According to the decision of the judges, there was only one instance in which letters patent could be legally granted. This occurred when any man through invention or industry brought a new trade or engine tending to further trade in England. [26] James I on his accession to the throne suspended all monopolies until the privy council could examine them. Despite all this, however, monopolies continued to multiply in numbers and abuses during the next two decades. [27]

There was little need for the Commons to go beyond the walls of their own house to discover obnoxious monopolists, for the individual primarily responsible for extortionist practices was a member of Parliament, Sir Gyles Mompesson, often sarcastically dubbed Sir Gyles Overreach. Mompesson held two patents, one for the making of gold and silver thread and the other for licensing inns and alehouses. [28] His manipulations in regard to the former were small in comparison to his scandalous proceedings in the latter. From all parts of the House came evidence of his fraudulent operations. [29] Pym in his diary adequately summarized the charges of the House against Mompesson as abusive and without precedent in the commonwealth. [30]

Futher examination of the widespread network of the patent for

alehouses revealed that the chief offender was Sir Francis
Michell, who used and abused his office as a justice of the peace
in a manner to enrich himself handsomely from those who
applied for licenses. The anger and frustrated outrage of the
House of Commons became heightened when the list of his
known offenses lengthened and many degrading punishments
were suggested. Coke would have him scourged of knighthood,
of being justice of the peace, of being a government commissioner, and would send him forthwith to the Tower. Christopher
Brooke suggested that a "paper might be set on his breast with
the offence, and so go through the streets." Still others suggested
fines, imprisonment, and degradation.[31] But, as Pym wrote, after
being informed by the Master of the Rolls that Michell's father
was a "religious gentleman," the House simply labeled him unfit
for any commission and ordered him to walk to the Tower and
there "remayne duringe pleasure."[32]

In dealing with Michell, who was not a member of the House
of Commons, the members of Parliament were exceeding their
parliamentary privileges.[33] Sir Robert Phelips, in fact, dissented
from fining Michell, arguing that the precedents cited were cases
which had offended the House of Commons, whereas "this
man's offence is against the country."[34] In any case, the immediate effect of their action was to frighten Mompesson, who
accordingly confessed to the House the error of his ways and
begged for mercy. The Commons, however, continued its investigation and on February 27, Coke reported officially to the
House the evidence collected by a committee.[35] A heated debate
followed in which Pym took an important part.

Pym followed Coke's report with a rather lengthy examination
of Mompesson's crimes. Pym contended that Mompesson's defense, that he had no grant of concealments, ironically manifested
his crimes, for it indicated that he had rented many lands clearly
not meant to yield rent. Pym suggested that a committee examine
Mompesson's practices in detail to "produce from us some provisions to secure the Commonwealth hereafter and work in him
such humiliation as may make him fitt for a greater degree of
mercye."[36]

On that same day Pym was appointed to the committee to examine further into Mompesson's misconduct.[37] A week later,

on March 6, Pym was appointed along with Coke as assistants to William Hakewill to make further inquiries into the matter of Mompesson's concealments.[38] It was, however, very much in vain. Indeed, the final act of this play had something of the melodramatic to it. Mompesson was arrested, but, as Pym recorded in his diary, when the officer took charge of Mompesson on the way home from the committee, Mompesson desired to "fetch some papers from his howse, whither the Sargeant went with him, and goeing into a Closset to speake with his Ladie got out a backe waye."[39] As soon as his escape was known, the ports were ordered closed, and at the request of the two Houses the Lords undertook to obtain the "Kings proclamation for apprehendinge him." It was too late, however, for Mompesson had already succeeded in crossing the Channel. England's gain was France's loss. The House of Commons had to content themselves with the expulsion of Mompesson from his seat in their House.[40]

The House of Commons's inquiry into the rather shady affairs of English monopolists cleared the road for the downward path of Sir Francis Bacon. Yet the details of the great drama of the impeachment of the famous statesman-philosopher do not really concern us here, because Pym was merely a silent spectator. In fact, Pym's diary is quite barren of the trial and tribulations of the unfortunate Bacon; he merely recorded the formal judgment of the House of Lords.[41]

John Pym did not, however, remain a silent spectator in still another famous case in English constitutional history, that of Edward Floyd. Floyd, like the tactless Shepard before him, was a barrister; like the expelled member of Parliament, he was far too free with his tongue; like Shepard, he brought the wrath of the House of Commons down upon his hapless head. But most importantly, unlike Shepard, Edward Floyd was not a member of Parliament; he could not possibly be because he was a Roman Catholic.

Floyd's chief problem lay in consistently speaking about sensitive things at the most insensitive times. The House of Commons, which mirrored the attitudes of the state and which logically reflected the temper of the nation, was in no mood for insults. On April 28, the Warden of the Fleet was ordered to bring Floyd to Parliament to hear the accusation of one Doctor Willet, who claimed that Floyd had exhibited un-English joy on the news that the English king's son-in-law, Frederick of the Palatinate, had been defeated at the battle of White Mountain. Floyd, it appeared, had sarcastically declared that he had waited a long time for a military rout of the King of Bohemia, and that "now good man palsgrave and goody palsgrave might trott." Sir John Strangeways, a member of the committee of the Fleet, ordered that Floyd and Willet be summoned. The speaker of the House argued that the Commons had no jurisdiction to send for a prisoner of the Fleet, but he was overruled.[42] Indeed, the mood of the House was far too heated to listen to moderation and reason. And John Pym quite accurately captured the feeling of the Commons when he wrote that, if there was no precedent in such a matter, the House should make one rather than let the offense slip from their hands.[43]

On Monday, April 30, Floyd was brought to the bar. It was reported that not only had he praised the defeat of the Protestant forces at Prague, but he had even claimed that he had as much right to the Kingdom of Bohemia as did the Elector Frederick. Floyd naturally denied the charges, whereupon it was ordered that his papers be seized and that witnesses be examined. On the following day the Commons examined several individuals; each readily related Floyd's outrageous remarks. Finally, a committee was selected and sent to the Fleet to examine Floyd's belongings. In the afternoon the committee reported that they had found beads, "friars girdles," a crucifix, and a silver box which contained "Divine relicks and popish trincketts."[44]

By this time the Commons had worked itself into a furor. It was not only hatred of Roman Catholics and anger at Floyd's slight of James I's daughter that raised the evil temper of the House of Commons to the boiling point, but also the dormant feeling of frustration within the House generated by the foreign policy of the king. James I's foreign diplomacy was, in truth, the saddest spectacle of his reign. Basically a personal policy which was neither understood nor supported by his people, it merely served to widen the gulf which separated the king from his subjects and to produce endless difficulties between crown and Commons. His fundamental aim was of itself an admirable vision: universal peace and goodwill to men. His fundamental mistake lay in the fallacy that he might promote, indeed champion, the cause of Protestantism while at the same time remaining on friendly and intimate terms with Catholic Spain. But as so often happened, his theory was hopelessly divorced from fact. It worked in times of peace, and his early rapprochement with Spain and France was not entirely in vain, but in times of stress it became impossible. When after 1618 the bitter contest between religions in Europe passed from words to weapons, it became a travesty. James's forte was words, not acts, and lacking any really firm foundation of national support or military power, his policy deteriorated into paper diplomacy, ridiculed by European realists, harangued at by the exasperated Commons. Unable to execute his commitments or to follow up his threats, James became a champion who could not champion, a defender who could not defend, while his failure, palpable to all, tempted Parliament to make for the first time a truly serious demand for a voice in shaping foreign diplomacy.[45] Indeed, chafing under the "self-imposed silence which had for many weeks restrained their tongues from even mentioning the name of the Palatinate, the Commons were in a temper to catch eagerly at the first opportunity which offered itself to give vent to the thoughts which were burning within."[46] The aged Roman Catholic barrister, Floyd, was indeed a convenient scapegoat.

What followed was the likes of which has seldom been exhibited in an English Parliament.[47] Floyd was most certainly a convenient scapegoat and the members of the House of Commons scraped the bottom of the barrel to declare punishments for him. Phelips would have Floyd carried from Westminster with his face to the "Horses breech," with a paper to signify a popish wretch punished for depraving his majesty's children, then "to the tower and there put into little ease." Sir George More would whip him. John Whitson would have hot grease dropped on him after every six lashes of the whip. Sir Francis Seymour would "have him goe from Westminster with his dublett off, and to have as many lashes as beades." Sir Edward Cecil would have a hole bored through his tongue, while Sir Jerome Horsey would have the tongue cut out altogether.[48] And John Pym? He was not much different from the rest, for he would "whipp him unless he redeeme it with 1000 li, within 10 days, *quia* his gentillity mistaken."[49]

Experience, however, is a wondrous teacher, the wisest counsellor of all, and nothing succeeds so successfully in over-whelming the irrational as an excess of irrationalism. It was Sir Edwin Sandys and not John Pym or even Sir Edward Coke who brought calm to an emotionally intoxicated Commons. He re-minded the House not to be overcome with affection so that "we punish illegally and irregularly." Sandys had struck that prover-bial nail. The members of Parliament had been gleefully dancing on a volcano. But with the wisdom that comes from the experi-ence of a veteran member of the Commons, Sandys informed the House that the real charge against Floyd was his religion and that if in his punishment his religion was touched, he would become a martyr.[50] Sandys was right, for Pym noted in his diary that all those who suggested degrading punishments aimed at such punishments and circumstances as "might make it most notable to the people, especially Marchant strangers."[51]

Sandys's speech had a very telling effect, for the final sentence of the Commons against Floyd was devoid of brandings and other humiliations. He was sentenced by the House to be pillored twice, to ride from pillory to pillory on a bare-backed horse with his face toward its tail, and to pay a fine of £1,000.[52]

The House of Commons was, however, waylaid in its deter-mined persecution of the unfortunate Floyd. King James, often described as the despot's despot, stood forth as the champion of law and liberty. On the following day the chancellor of the ex-chequer informed the House that James wished to know whether Parliament had the authority or jurisdiction over anyone who was not its member, or whether the members could punish anyone who had not offended any member of the Commons. Moreover the king challenged the Common's right to sentence a man who denied his crime without proving his guilt by oaths of witnesses against him.[53]

The king's pronouncement struck the Commons like a thun-derbolt. It was certain that the House had no jurisdiction over Floyd; indeed, during this Parliament the Commons had ex-pressly repudiated such rights in the case of Michell.[54] Coke, attempting to retain the dignity of the Commons, argued that, if the House of Commons did not have power for all things, it did have some, and certainly was a court of record: "He that saies that this is not a court of record, he wisheth his tongue may cleave to the roof of his mouth." Coke went on, however, to admit that jurisdiction lay with the House of Lords, and directed that the Commons go up to the Lords "and let them know that we hold that opinion of him as hath been delivered."[55]

Accordingly a long drawn-out series of negotiations took place, and John Pym played a rather significant role in the course of those negotiations. On May 5, he was selected as one of the representatives of the Lower House in a conference with the Lords.[56] Again, on May 7, he was once more a representative of the Commons in a conference with the Lords.[57] Moreover, on May 16, during a discussion of the charges brought against the Warden of the Fleet, Pym spoke clearly for the privileges of the House of Commons. After Sir Robert Heath had made a motion that the concealing of Floyd's insults might be added to the charges against the warden, Sir Thomas Wentworth replied that since the House had already referred the matter to the Lords, the Commons should not "meddle with the accessarye." Pym replied that the Commons had not referred the case to the Lords, but merely left it up to them. He concluded that because "wee made our title to that business as arisinge out of our inquirye into the Wardens offences, if wee showld not insert that it would bee thowght a kind of disclayme of that title."[58]

Pym reiterated his defense of the Commons' parliamentary privileges in still another speech involving Floyd. The Commons had ordered the examination of papers contained in a trunk belonging to Floyd; the trunk was then sealed. When Floyd's case came before the Lords, they sent a message to the Commons asking for the trunk "with power" to open it. Pym opposed this action and argued that since it was the Commons' privilege only to examine evidence, a precedent contrary to the Commons' own privileges would be established if they allowed the Lords to open the trunk.[59] Pym's cogently worded and logically presented contribution was, however, very much in vain, for he recorded in his diary that "notwithstandinge the Howse Order'd that the Trunke showld be delivered."[60]

Finally, to bring this famous case to a close, the House of Lords passed judgment on Floyd on May 28. Floyd had his fine raised from £1,000 to £5,000; he was declared an infamous person never to be received in a court of justice; he was to ride bare-back on a horse, face to its tail and tail in hand; and he was to be whipped at the Cart's Tail from London bridge to Westminster Hall.[61] King James, however, at the intercession of Prince Charles, had the whipping rescinded.[62]

Meanwhile, still another long drawn-out incident had arisen which also demanded negotiations and conferences with the House of Lords. This matter involved a fresh charge of corruption against a member of the House of Commons, and once again John Pym took an active role in exposing and punishing the offender.

Sir John Bennett was an ambitious man. He is said to have offered £30,000 for the chancellorship in succession to Ellesmere when Bacon obtained it. In addition to being a member of Parliament from Oxford, he had been in transitional sequence the chancellor to Queen Anne; a high commissioner; a judge in Admiralty, Delegates and Prerogative courts; and a master of Chancery. Moreover, he had been one of the commissioners in the infamous Essex divorce case and had done himself the honor of being in the minority of five with Archbishop Abbott when the majority gave a decision to please the court. But in this Parliament of 1621, honor was turned to dishonor and John Bennett was attacked by the House of Commons.

Shortly after the inquiry into Sir Francis Bacon's conduct had begun, Bennett presented a petition to the House from the masters in Chancery, relative to their fees. The judges, he said, desperately needed a greater increase of allowance because, as Pym recorded, "their ancient Fees [have been] monopolized and taken from them; that the Act of Parliament [1 Jac., C. 10] was made to prevent exaction, not establishment of Fees."[63] Before long, however, Bennett was hard put to defend himself, for he was accused of extorting large sums of money from those who had applied to him for letters of administration.

A subcommittee was created by the Commons to examine and report on the charges against Bennett. John Pym was a member of this subcommittee[64] and on April 13, he reported to the House its conclusions.[65] Witnesses were examined, a grand committee was created, and the counsel for the defense heard from. But the members of the Commons were pressed as to the procedure they should follow in prosecuting Bennett, and on April 20, this question was debated at great length. The problem was twofold. First, should the case against Bennett be given to the Lords immediately or should the Commons first inquire into the matter themselves? Second, and in correlation to the first, should the Commons expel Bennett from Parliament and then send him to the Lords for judgment? Coke wished "it to be set down in writing and then present it to the Lords. If it be found true, it will touch him near. If not, *beatus est*, for blessed is he that keepeth his hand from bribery." Sir Samuel Sandys desired the House to hear Bennett first and then to dispose of him accordingly. Sir Guy Palmes, on the other hand, was all for sending Bennett to the Lords immediately.[66]

Pym's views are clearly recorded. Parliament, he stated, is the great sentinel of the kingdom, whose purpose is to seek out and investigate all faults. The power to do this is divided into three areas: examination and inquisition, judgment, and execution. Execution, Pym said, is the sole province of the king. Judgment is the function of the House of Lords, although the Commons had upon occasion been called to judge; indeed, it had often examined members of the Upper House. Examination and inquisition are, however, the primary duties of the House of Commons, and the members of the Commons must fulfill these obligations thoroughly if they wished to reserve these areas exclusively for themselves. The House of Commons, therefore, must diligently examine anyone who would testify in Bennett's case and must do it thoroughly so that only the judging would be left to the House of Lords. Pym concluded his speech by stating that "God hath said of himself, that he is a searcher of all hearts," and, therefore, it is no derogation for the members of the Commons to be inquisitors.[67]

Pym's speech was obviously well received, for it was recorded at length by the diarists Barrington, Bolasye, Nicolas, and the anonymous X, a coverage which was quite unusual.[68] His interpretation that the nation rested upon the mutual relationship of the king and the two Houses of Parliament was a fundamental aspect of his political philosophy. The next day, Pym was selected as one of the twelve members added to the already existing committee to consider the matter further.[69] The Bennett case was, however, a long drawn-out affair and had not been settled when Parliament was hastily dissolved in January 1622. The Star Chamber finally took cognizance of the case and in November 1622 imposed upon Bennett a fine of £20,000, ordered him imprisoned during pleasure, and declared him to be perpetually debarred from office.

The members of the Parliament of 1621 were deeply interested in three great problems which had filled King James's reign. The first was that of foreign policy, which often involved religion. The nation was desperately eager to aid the unfortunate Elector Frederick and the Continental Protestants. King James, relying primarily on his diplomatic skills, had at first refused aid, and then, when his diplomacy had broken down and proved ineffectual, had consented. But with the return to intrigue of that master diplomatist, the Spanish ambassador to England, Count Gondomar, King James, with the prospect of a Spanish marriage, had drawn back once again. Balked at war, the House of Commons fell back upon the second great issue, corruption in government. They attacked monopolies, punishing the chief offenders; they impeached the lord chancellor, Sir Francis Bacon; and they exposed and attacked the exploitation of Sir John Bennett. Finally, and the last great issue, the Commons brought forth their right to debate general public policy, not just those matters which were put before them by the king, but those issues which touched the very foundations of the welfare of the nation. These three problems were those which dominated the minds of the members of the House of Commons; they are essentially the story of the Parliament of 1621.

The humiliating defeat of Frederick at the battle of White Mountain had unsettled King James; his utopian foreign policy and feeble dream of himself as the European peacemaker had crumbled with the flight of his son-in-law. Indeed, the king took a much more militant posture, and undoubtedly the only reason for the summoning of this Parliament of 1621 was to obtain money for war in Europe.[70] On the opening day of Parliament, James had explained his decision and asked for supplies to restore Frederick to the Palatinate. Several days later, Calvert reminded the House of the reasons for this Parliament and repeated the king's message for additional funds.

The House of Commons, however, was not to be rushed. After a debate which centered around the problem of whether supply should be granted immediately or whether the Commons should first gain satisfaction for their grievances, they decided to put the question to a committee of the whole house.[71] Ten days later the House granted James two subsidies. Apparently the Commons deliberately omitted the question of the Palatinate, for when Coke made the report to the House, he declared that the "two subsidies should be granted, neither for Defense of the Palatinate, nor yet for the releiving the King's wants, but only as a free gift and present of the love and duty of his Subjects."[72]

The subsidy bill was passed unanimously in the Commons on March 17 and was sent to the Lords. It was on March 12, when the bill was first engrossed, that Pym make his only speech on the subject. A question had arisen whether the bill should go to the king without grievances or whether some bills for the removal of abuses should accompany it. Pym said, "not to hinder the Subsidy: but yet to prepare some Bills to go with it."[73] Pym was right in paradoxical character. It seemed as if he were anxious to relieve the financial pressures upon James, but at the same time desiring to force the king to accept some bills that would effectuate various domestic reforms.

On April 20, King James again spoke to the assembled Houses of Parliament, explaining to them that the two subsidies were completely exhausted and that much more money was desperately needed.[74] The Commons, however, ignored the suggestion and continued to seek the redress of grievances. James, resenting both the Commons' failure to grant further subsidies and their rather independent attitude in domestic affairs, decided to give himself a rest from them. On May 28, the king sent a message to the Lower House informing them they should prepare for an early adjournment. His reasons were that the season of the year might bring a plague, and that the country gentlemen were needed in their own counties as justices of the peace.[75]

The House of Commons did not accept the king's message with joy. The order to adjourn was, in fact, received with much bitterness, for the Commons had much legislation to complete. Numerous speeches woefully lamenting the unexpected ending of Parliament followed the king's message, and a debate ensued as to what course the House should follow. Pym argued that the

Commons should do nothing at the moment, but should consult with the Lords, who were "as sensible of the generall good and as respective of us as may be, and so consider and conclude our best course."[76]

On the following day, May 29, Sir Edwin Sandys startled the assembled members by declaring that he would rather speak on the pressing problems of trade and religion than betray his country by silence, and that the Commons should that day debate and advise the king to remedy these problems.[77] On May 30, Phelips in a long, detailed speech used bolder language to attack the evils of the nation. Wentworth spoke directly after Phelips and pursued a more moderate path, arguing for a unanimous vote of confidence in the king's policy.[78] Pym followed Wentworth in advocating the equable position of making the most out of the days that remained to the Commons. Let not the House, he advised, run into disunity, but let them increasingly extend their functions of business because their time was very limited. The House of Commons, Pym declared, had done great work in this Parliament, for many good bills were passed, and the power of Parliament's justice which had been dormant for 300 years had at last been awakened to the terror of the guilty.[79] But Pym's speech was apparently disliked by numerous members of the Commons, and so he left the hall.[80]

The preceding took place in the morning of May 30. In the afternoon Pym changed his position. He desired, he said, no prorogation but a simple adjournment, which must be done by "consent of either Houses, for the Lords to adjourn theirs and we ours; but not by commission as once it was done."[81] It made no difference, of course, and Parliament was adjourned. Before they separated, however, the Commons rose and as one voice expressed their sentiments. Sir James Perrot, a privy councillor, moved that a declaration be made that the House of Commons would declare their lives and estates to the preservation of the true religion in the Palatinate. Perrot's motion was greeted with a general acclamation and the waving of hats.[82] After completion the declaration was finally read and enthusiastically accepted by the House of Commons.[83] John Pym wrote in his diary that was indeed a day of "jubilee."[84]

Notes

1. *Return of the Names of Every Member Returned to Serve in Each Parliament* (London, 1878), 1:454—hereafter cited as O.R.

2. O.R., 1:452; C. V. Wedgwood, *Thomas Wentworth, First Earl of Strafford* (London, 1961), pp. 36–37.

3. O.R., 1:450; H. R. Williamson, *John Hampden* (London, 1933), pp. 215, 282–87; Lord Nugent, *Some Memorials of John Hampden, His Party and His Times* (London, 1832), 1:291–375, 2:1–250.

4. N. E. McClure, ed., *The Letters of John Chamberlain* (Philadelphia, 1939), 1:518–24—hereafter cited as McClure; E. Farnham, "The Somerset Election of 1614," *English Historical Review* 46 (October 1931): 579–99; T. L. Moir, "The Parliamentary Election of 1614," *The Historian* (Spring 1954): 184.

5. Wallace Notestein, Francis H. Relf, and Hartley Simpson, ed., *Commons Debates 1621* (New Haven, 1935), 2:2–13, 4:1–6, 5:424–30, 6:281–82—hereafter cited as CD 1621; T. Tyrwritt, ed., *Proceedings and Debates of the House of Commons in 1620 and 1621* (London, 1766), 1:2–10—hereafter cited as P.D.

6. *Calendar of State Papers, Venetian, 1643–1647* (Charles I), p. 77—hereafter cited as *C.S.P.V.*; D. H. Willson, *The Privy Councillors in the House of Commons, 1604–1629* (Minneapolis, 1940), pp. 147–48.

7. D. H. Willson, "Summoning and Dissolving Parliament, 1603–1625," *American Historical Review* 45 (1940): 293.

8. Willson, *Privy Councillors*, p. 148; Willson, "Summoning and Dissolving Parliament," pp. 293–94.

9. *C.S.P.V., 1621–1623*, p. 64.

10. "A Proclamation against excisse of Lavish and Licentious Speech of Matters of State," James Spedding, ed., *The Letters and Life of Francis Bacon* (London, 1861–74, 7:156–57; CD 1621, 2:17–18, 4:11–12, 5:433, 6:437; *Journals of the House of Commons* (London, 1803–63), 1:508—hereafter cited as C.J.

11. CD 1621, 2:19–24, 4:13–16, 5:435–36; C.J., 1:508–10.

12. CD 1621, 2:83, 4:55, 5:256, 462–63, 7:575–76; C.J., 1:522.

13. CD 1621, 4:55.

14. CD 1621, 2:46, 82, 4:33, 52, 5:255, 6:376; P.D., 1:28, 45; C.J., 1:511, 514, 523.

15. James I, *The King's Majesties Declaration to his Subjects, Concerning Lawful Sports to be Used* (London, 1618).

16. CD 1621, 2:82, 4:52, 5:255; C.J., 1:522; P.D., 1:45.

17. CD 1621, 4:53.

18. CD 1621, 2:82, 4:53; P.D., 1:45–46; C.J., 1:523.

19. CD 1621, 4:62–64, 2:95, 5:12; P.D., 1:51–52; C.J., 1:524.

20. Pym in his diary gave Sir Edward Montague credit for Horsey's speech. CD 1621, 4:64. But he was mistaken. See CD 1621, 5:502; P.D., 1:52; C.J., 1:524. Moreover, Pym was mistaken on the year. He gave 26 Elizabeth, while Nicolas gave 35 Elizabeth. Horsey was probably referring to a vote which occurred in 43 Elizabeth. The vote was 106 to 105 for the negative; a Mr. Dale was kept from going out to the division. See Heywood Townshend, *Historical Collections* (London, 1680), pp.

371–21; Sir Simond D'Ewes, *The Journals of all the Parliaments During the Reign of Elizabeth* (London, 1682), pp. 682–83; J. E. Neale, *Elizabeth I and Her Parliaments* (London, 1953–54), 2:404–5.

21. CD 1621, 4:64–65.

22. CD 1621, 4:78–79, 6:249, 5:475–76; P.D., 1:63–65.

23. See W. H. Price, *The English Patents of Monopoly* (Cambridge, Mass., 1906); E. W. Hulme, "History of the Patent System Under the Prerogative and at Common Law," *Law Quarterly Review*, 12 (1896): 141–54; E. W. Hulme, "Elizabethan Patents of Monopoly," *Law Quarterly Review*, 16 (1900): 44–56; E. R. Foster, "The Procedure of the House of Commons against Patents of Monopolies," *Conflicts in Stuart England*, edited by W. A. Aiken and Basil Henning (New York, 1960), pp. 59–78.

24. Townshend, pp. 231–58; D'Ewes, pp. 644–56; Robert Steele, ed., *Tudor and Stuart Proclamations* (Oxford, 1910), 1, no. 921.

25. William Noy, *Reports and Cases, Kings Bench and Common Pleas, Taken in the time of Queen Elizabeth, King James and King Charles* (London, 1656), pp. 183–84; Sir Francis Moore, *Cases Collect and Report* (London, 1663), p. 675; Sir Edward Coke, *The Reports of Sir Edward Coke* (London, 1738), 2, part 11, pp. 87–88.

26. Noy, p. 182.

27. Steele, 1, no. 944; C.J., 1:316–18; *Journals of the House of Lords* (London, 1846), 2:447–48—hereafter cited as L.J.

28. *Historical Manuscripts Comission, Third Report* (London, 1875), pp. 16–18—hereafter cited as *H.M.C.*; CD 1621, 7:367–70, 379–86, 2:108, 4:84; *Calendar of State Papers, Domestic, 1611–1618* (James I), p. 449; McClure, 2:59.

29. CD 1621, 2:108–11, 6:254–57, 5:477–81; P.D., 1:71.

30. CD 1621, 4:84–85.

31. CD 1621, 2:128–32, 6:4–6, 4:94; P.D., 1:84–85.

32. CD 1621, 4:94.

33. Hakewill and Noy had vainly exerted their legal erudition to find a precedent to justify their action. CD 1621, 2:131; C.J., 1:530; P.D., 1:85.

34. CD 1621, 2:131, 5:486, 6:5.

35. CD 1621, 2:134, 145, 4:99, 110–11, 5:260, 6:7, 14, 301; C.J., 1:530; P.D., 1:89, 102–3.

36. CD 1621, 4:110–11; C.J., 1:530.

37. P.D., 1:124; CD 1621, 4:112, 2:146; C.J., 1:530.

38. P.D., 1:136; CD 1621, 4:126, 2:171, 6:32, 205.

39. CD 1621, 4:122.

40. CD 1621, 2:159–60, 5:22–33, 4:123, 202; P.D., 1:117–18; C.J., 1:530–33.

41. CD 1621, 4:296–97.

42. CD 1621, 3:109; C.J., 1:526.

43. CD 1621, 4:278.

44. CD 1621, 3:118, 120–21, 5:358–59, 6:118–19; C.J., 1:600; P.D., 1:368–69.

45. See D. H. Willson, *James VI and I* (New York, 1956), pp. 273–87, 357–76, 408–23; G. P. V. Akrigg, *Jacobean Pageant* (Cambridge, Mass., 1962), pp. 334–44; William McElwee, *The Wisest Fool in Christendom* (London, 1958), pp. 245–49, 253–74.

46. S. R. Gardiner, *History of England from the Accession of James I to the Outbreak of the Civil War, 1603–1642* (London, 1883–84), 4:119.

47. C. H. McIlwain, "The House of Commons in 1621," *Journal of Modern History* 9 (June 1937): 209–11.
48. CD 1621, 3:124–25, 5:359–60, 6:120–21; C.J., 1:601; P.D., 1:370–72.
49. CD 1621, 3:127; C.J., 1:602; P.D., 1:373.
50. CD 1621, 3:127, 5:361; C.J., 1:601–2; P.D., 1:373.
51. CD 1621, 4:286.
52. CD 1621, 4:287, 3:127–28, 5:130, 361, 6:122, 398, 2:335; C.J., 1:601; P.D., 1:374.
53. CD 1621, 3:136–37, 2:237–38, 4:290–91, 5:131–32, 362–63, 6:126, 398–99; C.J., 1:603; P.D., 1:5.
54. CD 1621, 2:148–49, 4:115–16, 5:264, 531, 6:302; C.J., 1:531; P.D., 1:108.
55. CD 1621, 6:127–28, 3:138–39, 4:292–93; C.J., 1:603–4; P.D., 1:2:6–7.
56. C.J., 1:610.
57. Ibid., p. 612.
58. CD 1621, 4:356, 3:275; C.J., 1:623.
59. CD 1621, 4:361, 3:287–88, 2:381, 6:165; C.J., 1:624.
60. CD 1621, 4:361.
61. *Journals of the House of Lords* (London, 1846), 3:134—hereafter cited as L.J.; CD 1621, 5:386, 6:404.
62. R. F. Williams, ed., *The Court and Times of James I* (London, 1848), 2:256—hereafter cited as *C&T James I*; CD 1621, 6:404.
63. CD 1621, 4:196.
64. Ibid., 5:330, 4:223, n. 9.
65. P.D., 1:256–57; CD 1621, 5:330.
66. CD 1621, 2:279–82, 302–3, 3:24–26, 28–32, 4:218–22, 238–39, 5:83, 329–30, 338–40; P.D., 1:282–83; C.J., 1:583.
67. CD 1621, 3:30, 5:83, 340; P.D., 1:283; C.J., 1:583.
68. See CD 1621, 3:30, n. 17.
69. C.J., 1:586.
70. Willson, "Summoning and Dissolving Parliaments," pp 292–93.
71. CD 1621, 2:20–24, 4:14–17, 5:249, 435–38, 6:439; C.J., 1:510; P.D., 1:15–16.
72. CD 1621, 5:465, 498, 4:58; P.D., 1:50.
73. C.J., 1:550.
74. CD 1621, 3:33–35, 2:303–6, 5:84, 342, 4:239–40; P.D., 1:285–87; L.J., 3:81.
75. CD 1621, 7:609–10, 3:325–26, 2:398, 4:382–83, 5:180, 387; C.J., 1:629; P.D., 1:110; *C.S.P.V., 1621–1623*, pp. 65–66.
76. CD 1621, 3:331, 2:399.
77. Ibid., 3:345, 2:406, 4:390–91, 5:185; P.D., 2:121–22, C.J., 1:631.
78. CD 1621, 3:348–50, 4:392, 6:178; C.J., 1:631; P.D., 2:125.
79. CD 1621, 2:353, 4:392; C.J., 1:631–32.
80. CD 1621, 3:353.
81. Ibid., 2:412, 3:360.
82. CD 1621, 2:428–29, 4:415–16, 5:200, 398; John Rushworth, *Historical Collections of Private Passages of State, 1618–1649* (London, 1721), 1:36—hereafter cited as Rushworth: P.D., 2:169.
83. CD 1621, 5:203–4; P.D., 2:172–73; C.J., 1:639.
84. CD 1621, 4:417.

3. The Parliament of 1621: Second Session

Before the Parliament of 1621 reconvened, certain events occurred which were notable in themselves and had rather grave consequences. On June 16, King James had the Earl of Southampton, Sir Edwin Sandys, and John Selden arrested. Selden was not a member of Parliament, but it was assumed that the chief offense of all three was that they had spoken too freely in connection with the events of the last session. Although the three men were soon released, no act could be better calculated to dampen the enthusiasm of the members of Parliament displayed in the declaration of the Commons issued on June 4.[1]

During the recess King James's attention was chiefly occupied by foreign diplomacy. The fortunes of the Elector Frederick deteriorated, for the Upper Palatinate was invaded and Frederick was forced to take refuge at The Hague, and, to climax events, the Holy Roman Emperor Ferdinand awarded to Maximilian of Bavaria the Electorate once possessed by Frederick. Protestantism appeared everywhere on the defensive and Catholicism appeared everywhere triumphant. King James, immediately after Parliament had been adjourned, sent Lord Digby to Vienna to negotiate on the hapless Frederick's behalf. But Digby's trip failed and upon his return to England and upon the news of the real danger of the Lower Palatinate to invasion, King James acted decisively. On November 3 a proclamation appeared summoning Parliament to meet on November 20. James was deeply moved as he listened to Digby's account, and he became determined to take some sort of action. Thirty thousand pounds was borrowed and sent to Frederick at The Hague, and more was to follow as soon as supplies had been voted by the House of Commons. Urging Frederick to put himself at the head of his armed forces, James wrote to the emperor demanding the restitution of his son-in-law's lands, intimating that Frederick would relinquish the crown of Bohemia and renounce any confederacy which would endanger the peace of the empire. James then sent a copy of this letter to Frederick, promising to support him fully if he would agree in writing to the Bohemia proposal.[2]

When the king's policy was known, the nation was swept up in a wave of general enthusiasm. For days Digby was the most popular man in England, and when Parliament reassembled in November 20, the House of Commons was given a message to meet with the Lords on the following day to hear the lord keeper speak on the king's policy. James's determined foreign policy, however, had degenerated into inaction and inertia. He had left London before the opening of Parliament and remained away during the entire session. His majesty, wrote the Venetian ambassador, "seems to hope that the Parliament will readily afford him every means of making war with little trouble on his part."[3] James feigned illness[4] and stayed at Newmarket, while Lord Keeper Williams opened the proceedings, asking the Commons to lay aside "importune Herangues" and "all malicious or Cunning Diversions," and to postpone all domestic business until the voting of supplies for the war in the Palatinate.[5] Digby then rose and explained to the assembled Houses his negotiations in Vienna: how he had obtained a temporary promise from the emperor that the Elector Frederick would be restored to his lands and titles; how Maximilian of Bavaria had persuaded the emperor to withdraw his promise; how Maximilian was in complete control of the Upper Palatinate and that the Lower Palatinate was safe from invasion only through the efforts of Sir Horace Vere and his English volunteers; how Count Mansfeld and his motley crew of mercenaries were forced to withdraw because of a lack of money. Digby concluded by asking the assembled Houses to confirm two propositions: first, to support the war effort with a grant of £900,000; second, to support the king in this effort and to "bless your consultations to the Kingdoms good [and] his glory."[6]

On November 26, the debate on the king's foreign policy began in the House of Commons. Phelips stood out alone as being opposed to the granting of subsidies. He argued that it was a dangerous precedent to grant supplies before any bills were passed, dangerous not only because it was against tradition and precedent, but also because it was thoroughly distasteful to the country. He believed, furthermore, that the war would be fought much more effectively by reuniting the Protestant German princes with the Netherlands. Calvert attempted to neutralize Phelips's speech by explaining the policy of the king. Referring to the Commons' delay in voting supplies, the secretary of state declared that "if the King have had his sword sheathed too long, letts not keep it in longer; letts remember our owne protestation and not fall of our owne offer."[7]

Thomas Crew, who followed Calvert, admirably reflected the attitudes of that faction in the Commons[8] which did not desire to supply the crown until the king explained his foreign policy and had settled parliamentary grievances. Crew stated that it was expedient to know and identify their enemies as well as their friends. If the West Indies were opened to the English, England could have as large an army as that of the King of Spain. All Englishmen, he said, would then contribute to the burdens of financing a European war with a swift and open hand. Indeed, Crew believed that England and Englishmen would gladly give more than enough money when all the Jesuits were banished and all papists were deposed, when all engrossed bills were signed by the king, and when all old debts were forgiven by the government. He concluded by stating that England could not wage a war against a concealed enemy. It was not Maximilian of Bavaria who was England's real enemy, he boldly declared, but the King of Spain.[9] But no decisions were reached, and the House adjourned, prepared to continue the discussion on the following morning.

On that day, November 27, John Pym emerged from a relatively unassuming position within the House of Commons to a position of influence. The activity within the House turned rapidly to the main issues. After some perfunctory matters, John Wilde rose and blatantly attacked the foreign policy of the king. He began by arguing that it was foolish for England to put any trust in Spain, because the Spaniards had broken their word countless times. King James, he said, was "deluded," and the Commons should promise to grant the king supplies only if Parliament had the right to declare who was England's chief adversary. "Let us be suitors," he concluded, "to his Majesty to set down who is the common enemy."[10] It appeared that Wilde's speech was much too strong an attack upon the king's policies, for Pym recorded in his diary that Wilde "began to speake too liberally of the House of Austria but was quickly stopt by the dislike of the Howse.''[11] Indeed, a privy councillor and treasurer of the household, Sir Thomas Edmondes, delivered a short admonition to Wilde and the House, telling them to leave the choice of the enemy and the direction of the war to the king, for the Commons' sole function consisted in debating the granting of supply.[12]

John Pym then rose and delivered a long speech. He argued, logically, that if the Commons failed to support the king with money, then the foreign policy of the king would collapse, for there would follow, in a natural sequence, discord between the king's allies, the fatal loss of the Palatinate, and the quiet discouragement of the king's son-in-law. On the other hand, if the Commons voted supplies and accomplished nothing else, then the members of the House would be guilty of failing to discharge their duties, because the commonwealth was not yet relieved of many burdens or satisfied to the condition of religion. He then "propounded," by means of three propositions, a middle position. First, in regard to war against Austria, Pym argued that in the extremely important matter of revenue, the enemy was far too strongly entrenched in Germany for England or English arms to do any good there: "Because warr by nature draws us to that kind of difficulty wherein our enemy is strongest and we weakest, for the great House of Austria hath both money and great power in Germany." Second, England was really not strong enough at home to wage war successfully, because the laws against Catholics had been suspended. Charity, declared Pym, must inevitably begin at home, and all Roman Catholics in England must be suppressed. Third, the House of Commons could best satisfy their king by having a session devoted solely to the voting of supply. This money, however, would be contingent on the fact that James would leave it to the Commons to provide some course of execution of the laws against the Catholics in England. Pym concluded his long speech by asking that every man be forced to take an oath of association in loyalty to the king before he be allowed into England.[13]

The debate continued. Wentworth urged compliance with the King's demands and policies. Sir Richard Weston, chancellor of the exchequer, and Sir Robert Heath enthusiastically supported

Wentworth's position. But then Sir Edward Coke rose and with a long speech went over the old quarrel between Elizabeth, Pius V, and the Spaniards. He concluded by stating that because a subsidy could not be collected until the end of a session, the Commons should continue with the business of the House, passing bills.[14] After many speeches, it was finally resolved that there would be a committee of the whole house to consider and debate three issues: "1, for the petitioning of his Majesty for the safety of religion and execution of the laws against Papists; 2, what was to be given for the Palatinate and when; 3, for petitioning the King to have bills passed and so to make it a session before Christmas."[15] It is significant to note that Pym's speech had been most effective, for his position in regard to the Catholics in England was accepted by the Commons.

The next morning, accordingly, the Commons went into a committee of the whole house. Perrot and Phelips were the first to speak. Perrot declared that it was the practice of the Catholics to destroy true religion in devious ways. The first was by their common and public propaganda, the second was by education, the third was by the printing and publishing of scandalous and superstitious books. He concluded by enjoining the members of the House to petition the king to banish all Catholics from London, "committing them to their lodging, and that there may be order, taken with those that are seducers to be severly punished." Phelips, in his turn, made a brief observation on the decay of the "Reformed Religion" within England and the increase of popery, and he concluded with a motion for a subcommittee to frame a petition to the king for redress of these misfortunes and for a thorough execution of the laws against Catholics.[16]

John Pym then rose and gave one of his most important speeches, undoubtedly his most important in this his first year in Parliament. He began by advising Phelips and his fellow members that the Roman Catholic problem was certainly not yet ready for a subcommittee, to whom only the order and frame were to be referred. On the contrary, the issues and written materials of such a petition could be prepared only by the House of Commons in a committee of the whole house. He then reminded the House that a petition similar to the one proposed had been presented to King James at the beginning of Parliament, but little had been accomplished, because James's "Royal disposition" was not yet "bent" toward that which the House of Commons desired.[17]

Apologizing for seeming in any way to question the king's reverence for religion, Pym then proceeded to give several reasons that Catholics had undermined the king's sincerity for their own evil purposes. First, the king, in his piety, had declared that he would not have any man "suffer for his conscience."[18] It is true, Pym noted, that heresies, which result above all from an ignorance of religion, could be righted only by persuasion and not by force. But if these heresies, however, break out into tumultuous plagues, they must be restrained by law, as mad men are restrained from committing outrages. The laws against Roman Catholics, argued Pym, had not been established to restrain their consciences, but to restrain their wealth and power that they may not "hurt us by it," and to restrain their persons that they may not "practice against us." Second, Pym continued, the papists had abused the king's leniency, that goodness of his nature which made him reluctant to hurt anyone. Let the House of Commons, asserted Pym, illustrate to the king, that he, the prince, and the nation should be the recipients of this virtue and not the papists, who would seek to use it as a means of absolute power. Similarly, the king's natural inclination for friendship had been abused to the disadvantage of religion in England. Friendship, Pym maintained, requires a mutual respect and a mutual giving and receiving, but the king had given far more to the papists than he had received from them. Foreign Catholic ambassadors, for example, had been able to prevail in England to the decay of the Protestant religion, but English ambassadors in foreign states had no such liberties. Finally, Pym argued that King James's wisdom, "and herein mistake me not, for I speak not of positives, that is, that things are so, but of probabilities that they may be so," was detrimental to the king's very own safety. James might think that by not enacting laws against the Catholics that he would win their hearts and procure his own safety. But Pym declared that the king was deluded if he thought any safety could be gained by this connivance, for though he might win their favors, he could never win their hearts. Pym asserted that Roman Catholics would never accept any compromise, but would always be active in the promulgation of their faith. Having gained favor Catholics would expect toleration, and after toleration they would demand equality; with equality they would scheme for superiority, and with superiority, they would seek to destroy any religion that differed from theirs. Perhaps some Englishmen, reasoned Pym, believed that James was now safe from religious or political assassination, because Catholics no longer had the hope that they once had in Queen Elizabeth's time of seizing the throne from the heirless queen and because James and his son were sincere Protestants. But this belief was, warned Pym, no more than wishful thinking, for Roman Catholic ambition would push them only further in their desire for self-preservation. Indeed, it was only natural for Roman Catholics to seek self-preservation, and it was this very fact which clearly illustrated the danger which the papists presented in England. Do not all kings, Pym asked, demand that all their subjects be wholly dependent upon them; but were not papists first and foremost dependent upon the pope? And must not all monarchs demand that they themselves be the most popular personage of their realm; but must not papists revere above all others the pope? Pym insisted that Roman Catholicism was too swollen with its own glory to be either suffered or tolerated.

Having thus stated these opinions, Pym again elaborated on the uncompromising nature of Catholicism. Prefacing his remarks with an acknowledgment that anything he might say would merely be a reflection of the king's own good judgment, and with a plea again not to appear offensive, Pym stated that the incompatibility of Catholicism with any other religion had set Europe and all of Christendom aflame. Moreover, the sparks from the flame had been "blown abroad by the Pope's own breath," who even now wrote letters to the King of France commending him for his brutal persecution of the Protestant Huguenots, an act which the pope equaled with St. Louis's attacks upon the Saracens. Furthermore, the pope was ardently enjoining the King of France to spread his policy across the ocean and to clean out that nest of heresies, England. Unfortunately, Pym regretted, the people of England would be like dry timber to those sparks, because of the government's failure to effectively enforce the laws against the Catholics.

Pym concluded his long speech by urging the king to take two steps against the threat of Catholicism in England. First, relating to the Elizabethan Bond of Association, he suggested that an oath of association be required of all Englishmen, for such an oath was already administered to the king's own servants. Second, he asked that a select commission for executing the laws against Catholics be appointed by the king. Such a commission, which Pym hoped would include some members of both Houses of Parliament, would be similar to those already appointed by the king for his navy, his debts, and his wards.[19]

What John Pym said was what most members of the House of Commons during the 1620s naturally and properly believed.[20] Catholicism, he had proclaimed, was an evil plague that sought to inflict every religion with its insidious doctrines. It had to be fought as a disease was fought or it would cause the death of a healthy religion. Roman Catholicism, and here was Pym's major thesis, was not to be attacked because it was an alien religion that naturally desired to win souls for its God, but simply because it undermined the constitution of the nation. Papists were to be persecuted above all because they threatened the security of the state.

Pym's speech, one of his most important, was exceedingly well received and had an immediate effect upon the House of Commons. John Chamberlain wrote to Dudley Carleton that he had heard of

> extraordinary commendation made of a neat speech by one Pyme, a receiver, wherein he laboured to show that the King's piety, clemency, justice, bounty, peaceable disposition and other his natural virtues, were by the adverse party turned and converted to a quite contrary course. And, though he were somewhat long in the explanation of these particulars, yet he had great attention, and was exceedingly commended, both in matter and manner.[21]

But Pym had challenged the king's policy and James was not slow to take up the challenge. Pym was eventually informed by the lord chancellor during the following days that James was displeased with his speech and commanded him to deliver a copy of his oration in writing. Pym answered that he could not possibly do this because he had not written the speech beforehand and had no notes except those that remained in his mind. He offered, however, to repeat his speech from memory in the presence of James. The king refused this request, and with a stricter command from the king, Pym proceeded to write a twelve-page letter enumerating the points he made in his memorable speech.

Pym's letter to James faithfully followed the context of his speech in Parliament. It was, however, far more conciliatory to the king and far more obvious in its anti-Catholicism. One short paragraph illustrates the tone and concept of the letter:

> The aim of the Laws in the Penalties and Restraint of papists, was not to punish them for believing and thinking; but that they may be disabled to do that which they think and believe they ought to do.

Pyme concluded his letter as he had begun it, with humility, modesty, and unabashed reverence for James I:

> As he [Pym] never consented to any thought contrary to his duty but in all his motions did labour to advance the confidence and love of your people to your Majesty, and those other honourable ends, for which this Parliament was summoned, without any declination to private respects; so will he ever, according to the obligation of his conscience and duty, wholly resign himself to your Majesty's service, with sincerity and estate, to obey your royal will, and with humility and modesty to submit myself to your pleasure.[22]

Pym spoke once again on the morning of November 28. His speech, concerning the supplies for the Palatinate, asked the Commons that "more be paid because it will be a long time before it can be paid." He concluded that one subsidy and two fifteenths be voted to be paid the following month of May.[23] After much debate, it was finally decided by the House that one subsidy should be granted for the support of troops in the Palatinate; the subsidy would be paid in February, and Catholics, because they were "strangers" and "aliens in hart," were assessed double the standard rate.[24]

On the same day, after the subsidy bill had been passed, the House voted to have a petition on religion presented to James I. A subcommittee was created with power to draw up the petition, and John Pym was selected as one of its members.[25] On December 3 the petition was presented to the Commons for discussion. It was a lengthy document, and one can clearly perceive the fine hand of John Pym in the petition. It was divided into "causes," "effects," and "remedies" of the Roman Catholic problem in England. The causes were the "vigilancy and ambition of the Pope of Rome and his dearest son: the one aiming at as large a temporal monarchy as the other at a spiritual." Their aggressive nature was revealed in the Roman Catholic ambassador's chapels, education of children by papists, dissemination of popish books, the disasters of Protestantism in Europe, and the proposed Spanish marriage at home. The effects of these Roman Catholic aggressions were, in Pym's phrase, clear: "If it once gets but a connivance, it will press for a toleration. If that shall be obtained they must have an equality, from thence they will aspire to superiority, and will never rest till they get a submission of true religion." As for the remedies, the petition asked King James to take his sword in hand, strike down his children's enemies abroad, and crush the papist faction at home by the vigorous execution of the penal laws. The petition concluded by asking King James to let his son "be married to one of our own religion."[26]

The debate that followed the reading of the petition turned almost exclusively upon the clause relating to the prince's marriage. Sir Edward Sackville rather unpopularly opposed the meddling of the Commons into this, the king's greatest prerogative, while others, such as Perrot, Weston, and Wentworth, supported the idea of advising the king on the matter. It was left to the impetuous Phelips, however, to state the most radical interpretation of the Commons' right to speak on state policies. He declared that there was neither honor nor safety in the marriage alliance with Spain, and that because all these issues were matters of general interest to the state, it was perfectly proper that they be handled in the House of Commons.[27]

How did John Pym interpret these fundamental constitutional issues? We do not really know, for Pym neither spoke nor recorded these speeches in his diary. Yet if one is careful to understand the decided limitations of such devices, one can surmise from his previous speeches in this Parliament his basic position. Pym was undoubtedly sympathetic to those members of the

House of Commons who opposed the king's policies, for he helped to compose the very petition under debate, and when one compares this petition with Pym's speech on religion, one can readily observe the similarities of thought and expression. In his long speech, moreover, Pym had systematically attacked the government, the king's policy of rapprochement with Spain, rampaging Catholicism in England, and the undesirability of a Spanish marriage. Parliament, Pym stated in the first session of the Parliament of 1621, was the nation itself, or, as Pym put it, "the great watch of the Kingdom."[28] And yet, although he himself might believe that the House of Commons had the right to debate English foreign policy, Pym would still leave to the king the right to execute that policy.

After much heated debate, which saw Brooke, Crew, Coke, and Noy citing precedents for the constitutional legality of the House of Commons' position, Solicitor Heath moved that the petition be a "mere declaration or remonstrance and no petition." This more moderate proposal was accepted by the House, and in the committee chamber there was added to the petition, or newly named remonstrance, the following words: "This is the sum and effect of our humble declaration (no way intending to press upon your Majesty's most undoubted and royal prerogative) we do with the fullness of our duty and obedience humbly submit to your most princely consideration."[29] This resolution was passed by the House, and twelve men,[30] some "of the Privy Council with some other courtiers," were selected to present the declaration to James.[31]

John Pym was not among those selected to carry the remonstrance to the king. Indeed, none of the committee members who had drawn up the declaration was selected, because Sir Nathaniel Rich had suggested that the House "spare all those which" drew up the petition. But Pym did, however, propose that the speaker should attend the session early next morning so that the "Remonstrance and Petition with the instruction fair written might be read to the House."[32] This was done the next day, Tuesday, December 4.

Meanwhile, back at Newmarket, King James sat burning with royal rage over the destiny of his country. It is said that when James first heard of the petition he cried out, "God give me patience!''[33] His rage was sharpened to a fine anger even more by a letter from the gifted and wily Spanish ambassador, Count Gondomar, who wrote to James that he would have left England already if he were not so confident that James would punish the seditious insolence of the House of Commons: "This it would have been my duty to do, as you would have ceased to be a King here, and as I have no army here at present to punish these people myself."[34] Without so much as waiting for the remonstrance to reach him, therefore, the king dashed off an angry letter to the speaker of the Commons. He had heard, James wrote, that his absence had "emboldened some fiery and popular spirits in our House of Commons to debate and argue publicly on matters far beyond their reach and capacity; and so tending to our high dishonour and to the trenching upon our prerogative royal." Commanding the House not to meddle in his son's match with the daughter of the Spanish king, James then mentioned that, although Sir Edwin Sandys had not been imprisoned for any infraction committed in Parliament, the crown felt very free and able to punish any misdemeanors in or out of Parliament and that thereafter punitive action would swiftly deal with any "man's insolent behavior."[35]

The king's letter gave "great discontentment to the House," for James had denied Parliament almost everything.[36] He had questioned the very essence of parliamentary privileges, asserting his right to punish any man's indiscretions in or out of Parliament. It would be convenient to have at our disposal the thoughts and feelings of the members of the House of Commons, especially of John Pym, as the king's message was read a second and still a third time. But we do not, for after a motion to recall the twelve messengers, the House adjourned until the next day to "consider of this great business."[37]

John Delbridge, "after a long silence in the House," began the debate the next day, December 5. He wished to petition over and over again until the king heard them. Phelips wished to uphold the stability of the nation and to maintain by precedents the privileges of the House of Commons. Sir Francis Seymour argued that the king was being misled by those close to him— "Yes, by some members of our own house," cried various members of Parliament. Hakewill stood forth for a committee to determine precedents, for satisfaction to the king by petition, and for proving and maintaining the privileges of Parliament.[38] John Pym then rose and cautioned moderation. Let us hope, he began, that the House of Commons "may not make the wound wider, but rather to lay balm on it and give satisfaction; and that those that have brought us into discredit, we may bring them into discredit, saving our reputations."[39] Did Pym here, when he mentioned those "that have brought us into discredit," mean those men who had the King's ear or certain members of Parliament? He obviously meant the former, for on the same day, after the Commons had transformed itself into a committee of the whole house, Pym reiterated his moderate position. He began by stating that the king's charges were grievous pronouncements, but that since the Commons had not questioned the charges, they therefore indicted the whole House. He asked the Commons to issue a petition to the king in order to discover those men who had misinformed the king. In this way, he proclaimed, the Commons "may justify ourselves and clear the House of those words." He concluded his brief speech by declaring that when any member of the House of Commons proposed any measure which the House desired, it was not the individual who proposed the measure that was at fault, but the whole House, for "when he is not punished, it is the public fault, and that the King would not deny that justice which he doth not deny to anyone."[40]

After much heated discussion, the Commons appointed a committee to draw up an "Explanatory Petition," which would explain to the king the fundamental meaning of the original petition and the reasons that the House of Commons had sent it.[41] Then the Commons, refusing to transmit any business until it was known how they stood in regard to their privileges, adjourned. Three days later the explanatory petition was completed. On the previous day, December 7, there was a long debate on whether the speaker should deliver the petition or whether it should be sent by the messengers already appointed. It was during this debate that John Pym delivered a rather curious and radical speech defending the honor and privileges of the House of Commons. The Commons' privileges, he said, are questioned by the king, but "if the speakinge in the defense of our privileges should offend, yet he would speake in the defense thereof." Let us not think, he continued, that a letter from the king could take away from the House of Commons their privileges, for the liberties of the Commons were but accessories. The true functions of the House, Pym concluded, were passing "Bills" and, therefore, let the Commons keep the care of preserving their privileges from hindering "the End for which we come hither."[42]

It was finally resolved that only the previously selected twelve messengers should accompany the petition. John Forster in his biography of Pym stated that Pym was one of the messengers.[43] This is wrong.[44] Forster undoubtedly desired to embellish his story into a more melodramatic setting and thus included Pym among the twelve in order to have one of his parliamentary heroes in a direct confrontation with the despotic king. Indeed, as we shall see, this error was not the only friction that Forster created. Yet though Pym was not one of the messengers and therefore not present when the king received the petition, he nevertheless had a considerable share in drawing up the declaration, for on December 8 there is the following terse statement in the Commons' *Journal*:

> The last Petition agreed upon Yesterday being found, by the Clerk, to be defective in the latter part and therefore left ingrossed; Mr. Pymme and some others, having perused it, and reformed it in a paper, the old and new were read over by Mr. Pymme: But the House not allowing it, divers gentlemen were appointed to retire into the Committee Chamber to perfect the same: Which accordingly was done: and being brought back and twice read by the Clerk was ordered to be ingrossed with the Residue.[45]

The language and content of the new petition were more conciliatory and more moderate than in the previous one. It began by qualifying the Commons' stated right to discuss openly questions connected with the penal laws and the Spanish marriage. The House of Commons, the petition declared, discussed these issues simply because they were deeply interested in the question of the defense of the Palatinate, which the king himself had publicly commanded to their attention and consideration. The Commons reverently acknowledged that it was certainly the king's prerogative and not theirs to decide upon peace and war and to select a wife for his son. They merely asked him to read their declaration, and they sought no answers to their petition except in regard to the penal laws and to the passing of bills. Then the petition came to the most sensitive topic of all, the Commons' privileges. Here the members humbly begged James to renew Parliament's ancient privileges of freedom of speech, jurisdiction, and just censure of the House, all of which his letter had seemed to abridge. The petition concluded that a wise and just king would realize that the members of the Commons would never transgress the bounds of loyal and dutiful subjects, and would reaffirm their right to free debate.[46]

King James received the deputation of twelve messengers on December 11 at Newmarket. The reception accorded the Commons' representatives was far better than expected. The king was in a jovial mood and received the messengers graciously, if not humorously. "Bring stools for the ambassadors!" he cried out as the deputation was introduced. The king was friendly, treating the messengers with great familiarity and sending them back to the Commons with another letter, which was read to the House of December 14.[47]

He had expected, James wrote, to hear nothing but expressions of gratitude for all his efforts to satisfy the Commons' desires, but he had to explain to them that the clause which they had added to the petition was contrary to the facts. Whatever the Commons proclaimed, there was no denying that they had infringed upon his prerogatives and had meddled with affairs that did not concern them, for to ask Parliament for supplies was not to ask it for advice on the Palatinate. Disclaiming the position that the King of Spain sought universal domination, James intelligently noted that the miserable war had been partly caused by the rashness of his son-in-law. As for the marriage alliance, which had already been negotiated beyond the point of cancellation with honor, James would see that it in no way dishonored England or the Protestant religion. In conclusion, the king returned to the subject of the House of Commons' privileges, and stated that he would rather the Commons had said that their liberties had been granted through the gracious permission of his royal ancestors, instead of having been inherited as a birthright. He would, however, protect these privileges as long as the Commons did not encroach upon his royal prerogatives.[48]

On the next day, December 15, the Commons discussed the king's letter. The debate indicated that nearly all members of the House of Commons recognized the justice of the king's statements on matters of foreign policy. Equally evident, however, is the fact that the House was not yet willing to allow James's claims about their privileges to pass unchallenged. Thomas Crew reflected the temper of the Commons when he declared that "our privileges are by law from our ancestors and our due," and more strongly, "our liberties must be maintained that they are by inheritance, and if we should yield that they are permissive, the walls would witness the contrary as in Magna Charta." Then, following a suggestion of Christopher Brooke, who had spoken before him, Crew moved that a protestation be written by a committee, clearly stating that the privileges of the Commons were recognized as inherited rights and not as royal favors. Crew was supported by Sackville, Noy, Digges, and Coke. In the end, the House decided to transform itself into a committee of the whole house to consider their parliamentary liberties.[49]

King James heard of the Commons' proposed plans and on Sunday, December 16, wrote still another letter to the House of Commons. Bishop Williams, the lord keeper, had previously written a letter to the Duke of Buckingham offering his advice on how to deal with the Commons. Cautioning moderation, Williams wrote that the privileges of the House of Commons were originally granted by the favors of princes, but they were now inalienable. If James, Williams concluded, "will be pleased to qualifie that Passage with some mild and noble exposition and require them strictly to prepare things for a Session, and to leave this needless dispute, his Majesty shall therefore make it appear to all wise and just men, that these persons are opposite to Common Ends."[50]

On Monday, December 17, Sir George Calvert read to the assembled members of the Commons the king's letter. He had heard, quoted Calvert from James's letter, that the House had decided to appoint a committee, and he therefore advised them not to "mispend their time which is so precious a thing." Most of the Commons' privileges, he argued, did indeed grow from precedents and thus it indicated a toleration of precedents, rather than in inheritance: "The plain truth is that we cannot with patience endure our subjects to use such anti-monarchial words to us concerning their liberties except they had subjoined that they were granted unto them by the Grace and favor of our predecessors." James then proceeded to acknowledge that he had no intention of infringing upon any of the liberties of the Commons; rather, he would preserve them in their integrity. He had absolutely no particular issue in mind when he said "to disallow of their liberties." The king concluded by asking the House to "go on cheerfully in their business, rejecting the curious wrangling of lawyers upon words and syllables."[51]

King James had bowed, however reluctantly, to parliamentary anger; he had declared that he anticipated no infringement of the liberties of the Commons. But he had not precisely defined just what those liberties were, and now that the question of the Commons' privileges had been raised, the House was not disposed to abandon it until they were clearly recognized. The House of Commons, the king's anger notwithstanding, was not to be deterred from its committee of the whole house. In fact, Pym, following Strode's motion that the proposed protestation be drawn up similar to that of James's first Parliament, moved that a search of the clerk's book be made to see "if the protestation made primo Jocobi be theare entered."[52]

Yet still another letter came from James the next morning. If the Commons, he wrote, wished to have the session ended by Christmas, they would have to get on with their business at once. If they did that, he would be willing to postpone the passing of the subsidy bill until the next session.[53] The Commons, however, was not to be either bribed or impeded. They sent a deputation to thank the king for his gracious letter, intimating that they would prefer a simple adjournment to a new session. Walter Earle then rose and demanded that the Commons continue the debate on their liberties. John Pym did not agree; in fact, he was opposed to such a move. The nation must come first, he declared, for when he considered the condition and necessities of the commonwealth and the reason Parliament had been summoned, "hee cannot without a great deale of horror looke upon the dissolution of this Parliament." He concluded his brief speech by stating that the House of Commons should "settle the good bills and articles nowe in agitacion and then if we have any more time to spend it about our privileges."[54] Notwithstanding Pym's admonition, the

Commons met that winter afternoon and by candlelight the famous and indeed revolutionary Protestation[55] was specifically written into the clerk's book and read to the members of the House.[56]

It took King James almost two weeks to decide what to do. He brooded over the problem during the Christmas holidays. He was indeed in a straitjacket of perplexity. To dissolve Parliament would mean no subsidies and poor James dearly needed money for his empty treasury. His privy councillors, almost to a man, were opposed to any dissolution of Parliament.[57] But to do nothing was simply impossible for King James I.[58] The Great Protestation had driven him into a protracted fury, and there is no fury like that of a humiliated king searching for lost dignity, and with the constant urging and backing of Count Gondomar, Buckingham, and probably Prince Charles as well,[59] James decided on a dissolution. On December 30, the king went to Whitehall, sent for the Commons' *Journal*, and there, as the privy councillors watched in spendid embarrassment, he tore out with his own hands the obnoxious page on which the Protestation was written.[60] One week later, on January 6, 1622, a proclamation appeared dissolving the Parliament of 1621.[61]

The dissolution of the Parliament of 1621, wrote D. H. Willson, the best biographer of the first Stuart king, marked the total eclipse of James as both a potent and a respected ruler. King James's name was never a tower of strength, and now completely cut off from his people, he could never hope to send assistance to the Palatinate. In fact, the king had been ridiculously reduced to the weakest possible position in foreign diplomacy—he could do nothing more than to ask Spain to be kind.[62] A wise man knows how to enforce with temper or conciliate with dignity; an honorable retreat is often as good as a successful advance. James knew neither. Instead of using restraint with power, James had proceeded rashly with impotence. Count Gondomar, on the other hand, who possessed the shrewd faculty of cultivating and harvesting the fertile soil of King James's vanity, was beside himself with joy. "It is certain," he wrote a day or two after the adjournment, "that the King will never summon another Parliament as long as he lives, or at least not another composed as this one was. It is the best thing that has happened in the interests of Spain and the Catholic religion since Luther began to preach heresy over a hundred years ago.''[63] And the truly ironic aspect of the whole affair is that James in his very next Parliament encouraged the House of Commons to discuss and debate those things he had just forbidden.

John Pym had inquisitively asked during Parliament who were those "fiery and popular spirits" that the king had indicted. He did not have to wait long to discover just who they were. King James, not yet satisfied with his mutilation of the Commons' *Journal*, moved rapidly to punish those parliamentarians whom he believed to be primarily responsible for parliamentary insolence. On December 27, several days before the king's Whitehall debacle, Sir Edward Coke was committed to the Tower. A few days later Robert Phelips and William Mallory followed him.[64] John Pym was also arrested, but he was merely ordered to consider himself a prisoner in his London lodgings.[65]

It is easy to comprehend Coke's imprisonment. That a privy councillor should do what he had done, and do it so magnificently, was a special irritation to James I. Robert Phelips's imprisonment is equally understandable. He had been a leader in the attack upon Spain and king's foreign policy. But the reason or reasons for William Mallory's imprisonment have long remained a mystery. He had neither distinguished himself in debate nor qualified himself in his opposition to the government.

The imprisonment of Pym is also somewhat enigmatic. Was he arrested for drawing up the petition on religion, or for his activity in writing the "explanatory petition," or for possibly helping to draw up the Great Protestation? All three motives seem very doubtful. One is more apt to conclude that Pym was arrested because of his important speech on religion, for he had committed a cardinal error—he had lectured the king. Pym had attacked the king's foreign and religious policies and indicated that they were untenable. It made very little difference that Pym had praised the king or emphatically declared that James was the "prime mover" of all things that occurred in England, or that the primary goal of Parliament lay in convincing James of the rightness of their arguments. In spite of all these considerations, the fact remained that John Pym had challenged the king's policy; he had attacked that most precious of all royal prerogatives, the right to be wrong.

Pym, tasting the bitter bread of imprisonment, remained confined to his house in London for more than four months. On April 20, 1622, however, he was allowed, for reasons of ill health, to go to any one of his houses in the country. This action is tersely recorded in a privy council minute:

> At the court of Whitehall, the 20th of Aprill 1622. Whereas John Pym esquire, was heretofore by his Majestie's command confined to his house here in London, the Lord Keeper of the greate Seal and the Lord Chamberlain did this day signifie that the said Pym, having by his peticion made humble suite to his Majestie for enlargement from that restraynte, that rather in respect of his health being thereby much impaired, his Majestie is thereupon graciously pleased that he may for his health sake repaire to any of his houses in the country, provided that he remayne confyned within a reasonable compasse of the same untill further notice.[66]

Yet though Pym was given permission to leave London, his movements were closely restrained by the government. Documents found in the *Historical Manuscripts Commission* reveal that Pym received a license to attend a meeting concerning the forests of Blackmoor and Pewsame, but that he was not to go beyond fifty miles from home and was to return within fourteen days.[67] These documents are very important and useful, for they give some valuable information about Pym's movements and activities after the close of the Parliament of 1621. He was still a government employee, and his knowledge and talent were regarded as indispensable to the government. Indeed, Pym's parliamentary ''opposition'' never led the crown to seek economic deprivation for him.[68] These documents, moreover, throw some much-needed light upon Pym's relations with Lionel Cranfield. As lord treasurer, Cranfield was in charge of all financial administration and, therefore, was Pym's official superior. It was undoubtedly Cranfield who interceded with the king on Pym's behalf,[69] and perhaps this is the reason that John Pym was silent in the attack upon Cranfield in the Parliament of 1624.

The Parliament of 1621 ended on a terribly sour note; but there would be more Parliaments, that much was sure. Lionel Cranfield was a financial genius, but even he could not make a sterile goose lay golden eggs. Money was needed and Parliament, for all its subordination, was still the best source of revenue. The Parliament of 1621 was, finally, a memorable experience for John Pym. He had served his apprenticeship and had spoken with decisive vigor; he had raised his voice on the issues, matters, and wants of his age, and he had been appointed to many important committees. John Pym was a very busy man during the Parliament of 1621, and he had gained the admiration and respect of his fellow parliamentarians by the soundness of his judgment.

Notes

1. S. R. Gardiner, *History of England from the Accession of James I to the Outbreak of the Civil War, 1603–1642* (London, 1883–84): 219—hereafter cited as Gardiner.
2. *Calendar of State Papers, Domestic, 1619–1623* (James I), pp. 306–8—hereafter cited as *C.S.P.D.; Calendar of State Papers, Venetian, 1621–1623*, p. 167—hereafter cited as *C.S.P.V.*
3. *C.S.P.V. 1621–1623* , p. 172.
4. N. E. McClure, ed., *The Letters of John Chamberlain* (Philadelphia, 1939), 2: 406, 411, 413—hereafter cited as McClure; Gardiner, 4: 232.
5. Wallace Notestein, Francis H. Relf, and Hartley Simpson, eds., *Commons Debates 1621* (New Haven, 1935), 4: 425, 3: 414–19, 5: 400, 6: 193—hereafter cited as CD 1621; *Journals of the House of Lords* (London, 1846), 3: 166–67—hereafter cited as L.J.; T. Tyrwritt, ed., *Proceedings and Debates of the House of Commons, 1604–1629* (Minneapolis, 1940), 2: 185—hereafter cited as P.D.
6. CD 1621, 3: 419–24, 4: 425–28, 2: 435–38, 6: 315–16; P.D. 2: 186–89; L.J., 3: 167–68.
7. CD 1621, 3: 450–54, 4: 437–38, 2: 447–50, 5: 210–12, 402; C.J. 1: 646; P.D., 2: 210–14.
8. Digges, Coke, Perrot, and Phelips.
9. CD 1621, 2: 451, 3: 354–55, 4: 440, 5: 213; C.J. 1: 647; P.D. 2: 215–16.
10. CD 1621, 2: 452, 3: 459, 5: 214, 405, 426; P.D., 2: 217; C.J., 1: 647.
11. CD 1621, 4: 441.
12. CD 1621, 7: 619–20, 3: 459–60, 2: 432, 5: 214–15, 4: 441; C.J., 1: 647; P.D. 2: 217–18.
13. CD 1621, 3: 461–62, 2: 453, 5: 215–16, 405, 6: 200, 322; C.J. 1: 647; P.D., 2: 218–19. In the original manuscript of John Pym's diary, there is a hand drawn in the margin pointing to Pym's speech. CD 1621, 4: 441, n. B.
14. CD 1621, 3: 463–68, 2: 454–57, 4: 443–45, 5: 218–19, 406; P.D. , 2: 221–23; C.J., 1: 648.
15. CD 1621, 2: 459, 3: 473, 4: 446, 5: 220, 6: 204; P.D., 2: 226; C.J., 1: 649.
16. CD 1621, 2: 461, 4: 447, 5: 222, 6: 206; P.D., 2: 228.
17. Pym's diary ends here. CD 1621, 4: 448.
18. Pym is here alluding to King James's policy, which he explained in his opening speech to the Parliament of 1621. See CD 1621, 2: 6, 4: 5–6; P.D. 1: 5–6.

19. CD 1621, 2: 461–64, 5: 222–23, 405, 6: 200, 322; P.D., 2: 228–30; C.J., 1: 650–51.
20. Gardiner, 4: 243.
21. McClure, 2: 412.
22. P.D., 2: 23–41.
23. CD 1621, 2: 466, 6: 329.
24. CD 1621, 2: 467, 5: 225, 409; P.D., 2: 244.
25. C.J., 1: 650.
26. John Rushworth, *Historical Collections of Private Passages of State, 1618–1649* (London, 1721), l: 40–43—hereafter cited as Rushworth; P.D., 2: 261–67; C.J., 1:655; CD 1621, 2:487.
27. CD 1621, 2: 488–92, 6: 220–21, 5: 229–30; P.D., 2: 269–71; C.J., 1: 655–56.
28. CD 1621, 3: 30, 2: 303.
29. CD 1621, 2: 498; C.J., 1: 657; P.D., 2: 274–75.
30. Nicolas listed fourteen. See P.D., 2: 276.
31. CD 1621, 2: 498–99, 6: 223–24; C.J. 1: 657; P.D. 2: 275–76.
32. *Journals of the House of Commons* (London, 1803–63), 1: 657—hereafter cited as C.J.
33. *C.S.P.V. 1621–1623*, p. 199; D. H. Willson, *James VI and I* (New York, 1956), pp. 421–22.
34. Simancas Mss. 2558, Madrid, Gondomar to Infanta Isabella, December 6–16, 1621. Cited from Gardiner, 4: 248–49; Willson, *James VI and I*, pp. 421–22.
35. P.D., 2: 277–78; Rushworth, 1: 43–44; CD 1621, 2: 499, 6: 224, 5: 232.
36. George L. Mosse, *The Struggle for Sovereignty in England: From the Reign of Queen Elizabeth to the Petition of Right* (East Lansing, Mich., 1950), p. 115.
37. P.D. 2: 279; C.J., 1: 658; CD 1621, 2: 500, 5: 232, 6: 224.
38. CD 1621, 2: 500–502, 5: 232; P.D., 2: 278–79; C.J., 1: 658–59.
39. CD 1621, 2: 502; C.J., 1: 659.
40. P.D., 2: 284; CD 1621, 6: 225, 2: 503.
41. CD 1621, 5: 234, 2: 505, 6: 226; C.J., 1: 659.
42. P.D., 2: 297–98; CD 1621, 6: 229.
43. John Forster, *Lives of Eminent British Statesmen* (London, 1831–39), 3:20.
44. See the list of names in CD 1621, 2: 498–99; C.J., 1: 657; P.D., 2: 276.
45. C.J., 1: 661.
46. P.D., 2: 289–93; Rushworth, 1: 44–46.
47. McClure, 2: 414.
48. P.D., 2: 317–27; Rushworth, 1: 46–52; CD 1621, 2: 518, 5: 416, 6: 236.
49. CD 1621, 2: 525–27, 6: 238–39, 5: 239; P.D., 2: 335–37; C.J. 1: 665.
50. *Cabala* (London, 1691), pp. 263–64.
51. CD 1621, 2: 528–30, 5: 240, 6: 240; P.D., 2: 239–41.
52. CD 1621, 6: 243. The "protestation" Pym mentioned was probably the Apology of 1604.
53. CD 1621, 2: 534–36, 6: 244, 425; P.D., 2: 35–52.
54. CD 1621, 6: 337, 244.
55. J. R. Tanner, *English Constitutional Conflicts of the Seventeenth Century, 1603–1689* (Cambridge, England, 1961), p. 49.
56. P.D., 2: 359–60; Rushworth, 1:53; CD 1621, 2: 542, 5: 245.
57. D. H. Willson, *The Privy Councillors in the House of Commons, 1604–1629* (Minneapolis, 1940), pp. 149–50.

58. Godfrey Davies, "The Character of James VI and I," *Huntington Library Quarterly* (1941), V, 33–63.

59. *C.S.P.V., 1621–1623*, p. 199; *C.S.P.D., 1619–1623*, p. 332.

60. Rushworth, 1: 53–54; Thomas Cobbett, ed, *The Parliamentary History of England* (London, 1820), 1: 1362—hereafter cited as *Parl. Hist.*

61. Thomas Tymer, ed., *Foedora* (London, 1735), 17:344–47; *C.S.P.D. 1619–1623*, p. 333; R. F. Williams, ed., *The Court and Times of James I* (London, 1848), 2:256—hereafter cited as *C&T James I*; CD 1621, 6:404.

62. D. H. Willson, *James VI and I* (New York, 1956), p. 423.

63. Simancas Mss., 2558, fol. 7. Gondomar to Infanta Isabella, December 22, 23, 1621. Cited from Gardiner, 4: 226.

64. *Acts of the Privy Council, 1621–1623* (London, 1921), p. 106—hereafter cited as *A.P.C.*; *C.S.P.D., 1619–1623*, p. 333; *C.S.P.V., 1621–1623*, p. 199.

65. *A.P.C., 1621–1623*, pp. 107, 115, 119, 196; *C.S.P.D., 1619–1623*, p. 333; McClure, 2: 418; *C&T James I*, 2: 283.

66. *A.P.C., 1621–1623*, p. 199.

67. *Historical Manuscripts Commission, Fourth Report* (London, 1875), pp. 305–12—hereafter cited as *H.M.C.*

68. G. E. Aylmer, *The King's Servants: The Civil Service of Charles I, 1625–1642* (New York, 1961), pp. 352–53.

69. See *H.M.C., Seventh Report*, p. 257

4. The Parliament of 1624

Two rather frustrating years had elapsed between the close of James I's third Parliament and the opening of his fourth and last one. The times had changed dramatically, for during the interval foreign diplomacy had undergone a historic transformation. Liberated from the bitter criticism of the House of Commons by his rash behavior of December 30, 1621, the king had the unenviable task of effectuating his policy of procuring the restitution of the Palatinate to his son-in-law by Spanish intervention and of guaranteeing this intervention by the marriage of Prince Charles to the Spanish Infanta. The king had to act, for the first factor in the transformation was the ending of the opening stage of the Thirty Years' War. In September 1622, Count Tilly, as the leader of the diverse Roman Catholic League's forces, had captured the capital of the Upper Palatinate. In November, Mannheim and Frankenthal, the last outposts of Protestant resistance in Frederick's lands, fell to the Catholics. On February 25, 1623, Maximilian of Bavaria was officially given the Electorate of the Empire which had formerly belonged to the hapless Frederick, and was made responsible for the government of the Palatinate. King James's daughter and her husband, the "winter king" or "faithless Fritz" as the Catholics mocked him, were overwhelmed with disaster. Having already lost their foolishly adopted homeland of Bohemia, they now lost their hereditary lands of the Palatinate. Henceforth they would be homeless wanderers.[1]

King James's foreign policy, which was determined rather exclusively by the crippled state of his finances, fell back into the familiar pattern. In fairness to the king, it is necessary to point out that he really possessed only two avenues of diplomacy: first, to continue the torturous efforts of diplomacy between Frederick and the Holy Roman Emperor; or, second, to seek the friendship and active assistance of Spain. The first was unfeasible, simply because the emperor had committed himself so fully to Maximilian's ambitions that it was impossible for the latter to surrender his recently won prize of the electorship in the German Diet. The second was equally impossible—although James never fully grasped its impossibility—because Spain was very closely allied to the emperor. Prince Charles, while in Spain, only slowly recognized this interdependent relationship and finally questioned Philip IV's chief minister, Olivares. If the emperor, said the prince, "proves refractory will the king, your master, assist us with arms to reduce him to reasonable terms?" No, replied Olivares. "We have a maxim of state that the King of Spain must never fight against the Emperor." Upon hearing this, Charles replied that "if you hold yourself to that, there is an end of all; for without this you may not rely upon either marriage or friendship."[2]

With hindsight one can readily see that Madrid was a precarious capital in which to seek assistance for the King of England's grand yet illusionary foreign policy. And yet, in actuality poor James could turn only to Spain. There he fully believed that the road to success lay in the marriage alliance, and he worked hard for it in 1622. The marriage would be very costly to England, for in addition to the exclusive control of education for any children of the couple, the terms proposed by the Spanish government included the complete repeal of the English penal laws and the complete freedom of private Catholic worship in England. These terms were far beyond what James had promised or what he could possibly perform. Parliament itself would never have consented to the alliance.

It was under these trying circumstances that Prince Charles and the Duke of Buckingham set out for Madrid in February 1623 to conduct the negotiations in the flesh. Disguised with false beards and under the names of John and Tom Smith, the pair reached the Spanish capital by way of Paris on March 7. The details of their romantic sojourn do not really concern us here; suffice it to say that it failed miserably. Charles was willing to allow the Spaniards all they desired: education of the children, suspension of the penal laws, liberty of Catholic services, and exemption from English law of the Infanta's retinue of Spanish priests. But he lost all his patience when the Spanish refused any assistance to his sister and brother-in-law, and when they refused to allow the Infanta to come to England until a period of probation could reveal the trustworthiness of the English promise of private worship for Catholics. In October, the prince was back in England without his Spanish queen, and the negotiations were, in truth, ended. The rock upon which the Spanish alliance split was undoubtedly the problem of the Palatinate. The prince was willing to yield virtually everything in the interest of a solid marriage alliance, everything except the irretrievable ruin of his sister. He was supported in this policy by James, who wrote to Digby, now Earl of Bristol, that he would not "abandon our honour, nor at the same time give joy to our only son, to give our only daughter a portion in tears."[3]

With the return of the bearded "Smith brothers" from Spain, the direction of England's policy became more and more directed by Charles and Buckingham. Angry at the failure of their journey and outraged by the firm conviction that they had been deliberately duped by the Spaniards, the prince and the duke were now as violently opposed to a Spanish marriage as they had been previously in favor of it. Buckingham in particular was now of this persuasion.[4] Determined to have his way, he was ready to force his policy upon King James—war against Spain in behalf of the Protestant Elector Frederick—and to seek parliamentary support for such a policy. James was horrified. He still clung to his shaken belief that Spain was both an ally and a friend of England. But his mind was so feeble and muddled that he could not resist the vigorous desires of his son and his favorite. The king, wrote the Venetian ambassador, "seems practically lost; he comes to various decisions and inclines to his usual negotiations; he does not care to fall in with the wishes of his son-in-law and the favorite. He now protests, now weeps, but finally gives in."[5] Buckingham now assuming that a war policy would be popular in the country, constantly urged that a Parliament be summoned. James finally gave in and on December 28, 1623, he commanded that writs be issued for the calling of Parliament. James's reign was over and that of the Duke of Buckingham had begun.[6]

Parliament met on February 19, 1624. All the really important members of the previous Parliament were present, including John Pym, who now for the first time represented Tavistock in Devon.[7] There were two notable additions, the lawyer John Selden and Sir John Eliot. Though Eliot possessed scanty parliamentary experience—he had been a member of the Addled Parliament of 1614—he stepped with one stride into the position of both spokesman and champion of the rights of the House of Commons and of the defense of freedom of speech.[8]

James's speech at the opening of this brief Parliament was weak and aimless. He pleaded that he had always striven to rule well and that he dearly deserved the love of his people. He had summoned Parliament, he said, to seek their advice in a great matter. He had hoped to settle peace abroad and at home, but he now fully understood the real pretensions of Spain. There were rumors, he continued, that in recent negotiations with the Spanish he had sacrificed "true religion" to political expediency. This was untrue and the whole tale would be related to Parliament by Prince Charles and the Duke of Buckingham. Stating that, after they had heard it all, he would ask their "good and sound advice," James ended with the hope for a happy conclusion to this Parliament.[9]

On February 24, Buckingham addressed the two Houses,[10] It was a long account of the deliberate duplicity of the Spaniards. He related detailed evidence to demonstrate how the Spanish ministers had never seriously intended to aid with arms the Elector of the Palatinate. He concluded by stating that the Spanish treaties should be "set aside." His majesty, he said,

> were best to trust to his own strength, and to stand upon his own feet. And so his Grace ended with this conclusion, That if the bringing of us into Darkness to Light did deserve any thanks, we owe it, and must wholly ascribe to it, to the Prince, His Highness."

Having been cordially invited to give advice on foreign diplomacy, the two Houses adjourned to their respective halls to take into consideration the much-hated Spanish treaties. On the afternoon of February 27, and in the morning of the 28th, the House of Lords debated the problem. Not a single voice was raised in defense of the Spanish. Indeed, after two days of debate, it was decided that unless the House of Commons should decide otherwise, the king should be asked to break off all negotiations with Spain.[12]

The House of Commons was very unlikely to decide otherwise. The debate was opened on March 1 by Sir Benjamin

Rudyard, who affirmed the complete severance of "both treaties of Match and Palatinate," and issued a clarion call to the Commons to join with the Lords in entreating James to declare both treaties null and void. Sir George Moore agreed with Rudyard, but first desired to settle the marriage alliance. Both Rudyard's and Moore's speeches clearly reflected the ignorance of the members of the House of Commons on foreign affairs, who greatly overrated the overall military strength of Spain in Germany and, conversely, grossly underestimated the strength of the emperor. The Lower House was easily led to believe that a well-aimed blow struck at Spain would have more important results in the Rhine than was likely. Although the condition of the Palatinate was not entirely disregarded, Spain and the intrigues of Gondomar greatly overshadowed it. War with Spain needed no other justification from the parliamentarians than their indignation.[13] And war was exactly what Robert Phelips proposed. Spain, he found, was the "great wheel" that moved and controlled all the states of Europe, and Rome and Spain together were the "twins" who "laughed and weeped" in unison. Phelips ended a long speech by declaring that there was no other choice for England save that of recovering the Palatinate by a diversionary war against Spain.[14] Fleetwood followed Phelips and moved that a petition be delivered to the king stating the Commons' desired an end to the Spanish treaties. Eliot then rose and moved for an immediate declaration of war against Spain.[15]

John Pym followed Eliot, and it is regrettable that we have but meager accounts of his speech. He was thoroughly opposed to a continuation of any treaty with Spain, either the Spanish marriage or the Palatinate. He desired, like the rest of the members of the House of Commons, to send to the king a petition informing him of the Commons' united policy in foreign affairs. Pym concluded his brief speech by moving that the House finish "this business" as quickly as possible by having a conference with the House of Lords.[16] Pym spoke again on the following day. He began by reviving Sir Dudley Digges's motion "to have thanks given to the Lords, for their desire of good correspondence with, and then to desire them to give Thanks to the Prince; and to desire him to give thanks to his Father for calling this Parliament; and to desire him also, that publick Thanks may be given to God by the whole

Kingdom.'' Pym concluded his speech by stating that he believed the road to war was occasioned by numerous pitfalls. The proposed war, he said, was but one step away from the greatest danger that ever threatened England. Therefore, they should not ''relapse'' or shrink from their duty, but rapidly bring this business to a ''conclusion'' by graciously equipping the king for the success of this venture.[17]

From these somewhat sketchy reports it is difficult to construct the diplomatic ideas of John Pym. Perhaps the key to both speeches was his desire to bring ''this business'' to a ''conclusion.'' Pym was probably aware that the members of the Commons were as one in opposition to the Spanish treaties, and that the discussion of such opposition was similar to beating a dead dog. Pym was often exasperated with the House of Commons' built-in inclination to debate an issue to death; he had very little patience with the turtlelike pace of the Commons. Several times throughout the 1620s he would rise and demand an end to the matter.

During the debate on foreign policy, however, a curious exchange took place. Sir Peter Hayman had made a motion, which was eventually carried, that the clerk of the House should not be allowed to enter a man's name to any motion he proposed. John Pym was recorded as being against the motion. He opposed it, he said, because he would ''innovate nothing without good reason,'' and, moreover, many members benefited greatly from the Commons' *Journal*.[18] This belief that nothing should be innovated without sufficient reason was, as we shall see so often, a very important element of John Pym's political philosophy during the 1620s, an element of political philosophy that was essential to his political conservatism.

On March 5, a petition was presented to James by a deputation of both Houses advising the king in no uncertain terms to break off relations with Spain.[19] The king's reply to the petition was a characteristic one, revealing the very great political differences in policy between the crown and Commons. As a ''Peaceable King,'' James said, he was naturally loath to enter into any war. Furthermore, new hopes of restoring the Palatinate had arisen since the commencement of this Parliament. James then elaborated upon the four proposals that Parliament had suggested: that fortifications be adequately repaired, that a strong fleet be fitted out, that Ireland be made secure, and that the Low Countries be effectively supported. But wars cost money and the crown was without funds, and if Parliament, James promised, could gain the funds to support a war, then Parliament itself could appoint its own treasurers to appropriate the money.[20]

James's answer to the petition reveals that the ground which he and Parliament held in common in matters of foreign policy was quite narrow. Indeed, a close examination and comparison of the speeches of the House of Commons with that of James show a radical difference. The Lower House, as in the case of John Pym, was undoubtedly thinking in terms of an Elizabethan policy; they wished to do as much as possible against Spain and as little as possible in Germany. On March 11, in the debates on supply in the House, not a single voice was raised to recommend full-scale war in the Palatinate. In fact, James's demand for supply to pay his debts and for money to wage war in Germany was ignored. The king, on the other hand, was really strongly opposed to war with Spain. His main concern was the restoration of the Palatinate to his son-in-law, and he wanted money not only for this but for his general needs.[21]

On Sunday, March 14, a "humble address" from both Houses containing the stated views of the House of Commons on foreign policy was presented to the king by the Archbishop of Canterbury, who led a delegation from Parliament. James's reply was not what the Commons wanted to receive. The king showed particular rancor at a phrase in the address which condemned the sincerity of Spain. He had come to no conclusion whatsoever, he declared, on the sincerity or insincerity of Spain. Then, adopting a more friendly attitude, James proposed a great European Continental alliance for a war in Germany. To accomplish this goal, the king concluded that he would need at least six subsidies and twelve fifteenths.[22] To the much more militant House of Commons these words were ominous. They apparently meant that there would not be a war after all, or at least not the type of war that the Commons envisioned. The delegation left the king without the usual cry of "God save the King!" Prince Charles showed his annoyance at his father's disavowal of the prince's hopes and aspirations by remaining in sullen silence for the "remainder of the day, whilst the friends of Spain went joyously about with smiling faces."[23]

The report of James's reply to the "humble address" was made to the Commons on March 17 by Sir Robert Heath, the solicitor general. But there was no debate; instead, Friday, March 19, was selected as the day for the discussion of the proposed war and supply. Rudyard once again began the debate. He discussed the various projects which needed financing and urged a speedy vote of a definite sum. Eliot then rose and gave a rousing speech, attacking Spain and asking the House to pass quickly the subsidy bill so that there would be little delay by King James in making known his intentions against Spain. Sir Thomas Edmondes, treasurer of the household and a privy councillor, spoke next and reprimanded Eliot for his oratorical outburst. There was no need, Edmondes declared, because everybody in the House "plainly sees" the problem before it. He believed, strangely enough for a member of the King's privy council, that six subsidies were far too many for the job at hand; he thought that three subsidies, or less than half of what James had asked, were enough for a beginning.[24]

Several other speakers followed,[25] and then the somewhat impatient John Pym reminded the House that they were straying from the true question of their danger, and he feared such a relapse. Let the Commons get back to the propositions of the chancellor of the exchequer, Pym stated; and for the consideration of the English people, let there be a very liberal allowance of time for payment of the subsidy. But above all, he concluded, first let the House settle the general question of necessities, and if the necessities are found to be required, then let the Commons yield fully to the king's demands.[26] One authority[27] then has Pym moving to give six subsidies and twelve fifteenths, twice as much as was finally voted, but exactly the sum that King James had requested.

On the following day the Commons passed the subsidy bill. James was to receive three subsidies and three fifteenths within one year after the king had himself declared that the treaties with Spain had been dissolved. Parliament would control the money, moreover, for the subsidy was to be paid to treasurers who were to be appointed by the House of Commons. Pym, following up his speech of the previous day, stated that he thought it fit to have the first payment in the forthcoming April, the next payment in October, and the third and final payment a year from April.[28] This was carried, [29] and finally on March 23, King James declared that he would end the Spanish negotiations, and the path was cleared for the passage of the subsidy bill.[30]

These were, in brief, John Pym's meager contributions to the debates on foreign policy and the passage of the important subsidy bill. It is obvious from his speeches that Pym, in spite of his questioning of the king's policies in the last Parliament and in spite of the harsh treatment he had received from James for the questioning of those policies, was eager and willing to trust the king with whatever supplies he deemed necessary, provided, however, that the need for such necessities be firmly established, provided that a liberal payment schedule was created, and provided that such supplies were controlled by the House of Commons itself. Indeed, on May 12, Pym rose and reminded the House of the king's promise of parliamentary control of the subsidies, and made a motion, to be entered on the records, to that effect.[31]

John Pym's quiet moderation is clearly shown in his actions during this Parliament of 1624. He supported a king whose policy he did not fully comprehend or accept. Perhaps it was this moderation that helps explain why Pym played a relatively minor role in his second Parliament. He was interested in foreign diplomacy, especially as it affected religion; but perhaps he was more interested in domestic affairs. Yet even this rather tenuous explanation falls of its own weight, for although the other two questions which chiefly engaged Parliament's attention involved domestic problems—monopolies and the impeachment of Lord Treasurer Middlesex—Pym did not play an important part in either of them.

On April 15, Middlesex's impeachment was begun. His chief crime, apparently, was that he had incurred the animosity of both the Duke of Buckingham and Prince Charles. To an economical administrator of the finances of the English nation, Buckingham's lavish expenditures could never be congenial. The lord treasurer, whose financial reforms had enabled King James to exist without parliamentary taxes, looked with displeasure upon the projected war with Spain. Middlesex had placed little faith and value in the popular belief that constant assaults upon the Spanish treasure ships could replace the expenditures for total war. To the lord treasurer the forthcoming war with Spain had but one conclusion: his long years of prudent accounting would be wiped out and a return to deficit spending would result.[32] Furthermore, Buckingham regarded Cranfield as a very real rival to King James's affections.[33] Clarendon wrote that the lord treasurer had gained so much influence with the king that during the duke's absence he not only neglected his duties but also had the courage to dispute the duke's commands. Upon learning of Cranfield's favor with both king and Parliament, therefore, Buckingham quickly plotted his rival's ruin.[34]

King James had been Cranfield's chief supporter. But though he did much to save his lord treasurer, he failed miserably. No clearer proof was really needed to illustrate that James's reign was indeed over. The king, however, was wise enough to comprehend the implications of the impeachment, for he warned both Buckingham and Charles that they would certainly rue the day that they instigated the fall of Middlesex. Said James:

> By God, Stenny, you are a fool, and will shortly repent this folly, and will find that in this fit of popularity you are making a rod with which you shall be scourged yourself. And turning in some anger to the Prince, told him that he would live to have his bellyful of Parliaments, and that, when he should be dead, he would have too much cause to remember how much he had contributed to the weakening of the Crown by this precedent that he was now so fond of.[35]

The second important domestic issue of this brief Parliament was the abolition of monopolies. The Monopoly Act of 1624 has been described as the "greatest victory of the Commons during the reign of James."[36] Indeed, it has been pointed out that it was the first statutory invasion of the crown's prerogative and thus extremely important to the constitutional history of England.[37] But this is deceiving, for the Monopoly Act was framed as a declaratory act, and the true purpose of the act was not to introduce a new law but merely to determine what the common law would allow in its application to letters patent and monopolies. It declared what the law was in general, as the House of Commons had declared what it was in the particular instances raised by the patents they condemned. As a declaratory act, the statute, though it certainly limited the prerogative, cannot accurately be described as an attack upon it. It affected the "prerogative because it gave a statutory definition to the subject's interest in royal grants, and thus set a statutory limit to the area in which the prerogative operated."[38]

Although not entirely what the House of Commons desired, the Statute of Monopolies passed both Houses, and, when it was accepted by King James at the end of the session, it became law. The statute declared void all monopolies except those for new inventions and manufactures, which would be protected for fourteen years.[39]

John Pym's contributions to the passage of the Monopoly Act were almost entirely neglible. On February 25, he spoke, expressing his desire to keep the excess of words used in the last "convencion" from being employed in the present Parliament.[40] The next day Pym rose and moved to have the bill committed. This bill, he said, passed the Commons the last Parliament, but not that of the Lords. He would not speak against it or for it at that moment, but would wait to do that at a committee.[41] Finally, Pym was a member of the committee that conferred with the Lords on April 3 to frame the Act of Monopolies.[42]

On May 29, Parliament was prorogued until November 2, but before that day could arrive there was a second prorogation until February 26, 1625, and before that day arrived there was still a third prorogation. On March 27, 1625, King James I died, and his death automatically brought about the dissolution of the Parliament of 1624.

Fate was indeed unkind to King James. He suffered miserably during his last days, and he has suffered miserably since from the pens of historians far too numerous to count. But there can be no mistaking the significance of the reign of James I, for all the truly great issues which were to produce the conflict of arms between Charles I and Parliament had already been raised under him. The king himself was a good king, good in the sense that he was not a terribly ruthless king, for he had none of Henry VIII's brutality about him. He was moderate and tolerant, wishing always to act rightly. He was far too easily flattered, however, and he knew nothing of the House of Commons or of the sources of its strength or of the effectiveness of its procedure, and he never fathomed the inevitability of its growth to power. Poor James was often under the illusion that it was the mill that made the water flow; he was the mill, Parliament was the water. The contrast between what he conceived to be a king's right and position and what he was willing to do to live up to such pretensions bordered into irresponsibility upon aburdity. To the common law James was a total stranger, and the traditions of constitutional legalism were throughout his reign flouted. He was a deeply learned man, one who possessed the minor cough of poetic expression, but he knew little about running a government. One can forgive King James for ignorance in failing to comprehend the English nation, but one can never pardon such ignorance found in the company of such enormous riches. Grand, peculiar, and many times ridiculous and revolting, he sat upon the English throne wrapped and enraptured in the solitude of his own brilliance. Whatever seemed to him little was great, and whatever was great seemed to him little. James I was a poor, a terribly poor second when compared to the great Elizabeth.

Parliament had come to an end, and for sheer dramatic interest it was far behind that of the Parliament of 1621. The Parliament of 1624 had little of the drama or the historical significance of the Parliament of 1621. But history is often deceiving. Indeed, led by the Prince of Wales, the Parliament of 1624 suddenly appeared to become the "first power of the state." All it lacked was the virtue of self-restraint and leaders who were able to understand the limitations of power.[43] Yet still another aspect of historical importance occurred in this Parliament, for by a curious twist of fortune the court favorite was able to throw all his weight on the side of the House of Commons against the stated policy of the king himself. The Duke of Buckingham, wrote Leopold von Ranke, "may perhaps be set down as the first English minister who, supported by Parliament and by public opinion, induced or compelled the King to adopt a policy on which of his own accord he would not have resolved."[44]

But what of John Pym in this short and sharp Parliament of

1624? It has been illustrated that the chief topics which engaged the attention of the House of Commons were in foreign affairs, the Spanish treaties, the subsidy, and the war, and in domestic affairs, the impeachment of Lionel Cranfield and the abolition of monopolies. On these questions John Pym was often a silent spectator. Was he sleeping when Eliot, Phelips, and Rudyard were orating and when Buckingham and Prince Charles were maneuvering behind the scenes? On the contrary, he was hard at work laying the foundations of his political ascendancy in the 1640s. That Pym was less prominent as a leader of debate in his second Parliament than in his first does not necessarily mean that he was a nonentity. Though the House of Commons was in session only from February 19 through May 29, the records reveal that Pym was a member of more than thirty committees. If one wishes to see the work of John Pym in this Parliament, if one wishes to understand what he was doing, one must read thoroughly the Commons' *Journal*.

Pym was busy in countless and diverse ways. He was enabling Vincent Lowe to sell certain lands; he was helping the creditors of Cope; he was passing considerations of Bennington's estate, and the lands of Aucher, of James, and of Wrath. He was conducting a survey from Little Munden in Hertfordshire to Erith and Plumstead Marshes, which included the lands of Magdalen College, Cambridge. He was speaking of Sea Coals, gold and silver thread, felt makers, legal concealments and fees of the exchequer, and was casting a friendly gaze upon the naturalization of James, Lord Marquis of Hamilton.

He was discovering and repressing, moreover, Roman Catholics, "real as well as legal, especially such as live in any place near to the coast in dangerous places to let in the enemy." He was eliminating simony from colleges and schools; he was actively pursuing a rogue who had somehow crept into the presidency of an Oxford college; he was investigating the orthodoxy of another president at Cambridge and of an obscure Welsh schoolmaster; he was levying a penalty of twelve pence a Sunday to married women who did not attend church to "hear Divine Service"; and he was examining a catalogue of over 100 Catholic books printed within the last two years. Furthermore, he was collecting charges against the Bishop of Norwich, and, above all, he was considering for the committee of religion the book of Richard Montague, which will be examined in the next reign and the next Parliament, when the matter came to a head.[45]

Notes

1. C. V. Wedgwood, *The Thirty Years War* (New York, 1961), pp. 127–28; S. R. Gardiner, *The Thirty Years War, 1618–1648)* (Boston, 1874), p. 58.
2. *Journals of the House of Lords* (London, 1846), 3:226—hereafter cited as L.J.
3. *Cabala* (London, 1691), p. 242; *Calendar of State Papers, Domestic, 1623–1625*, p. 93—hereafter cited as *C.S.P.D.*; see also S. R. Gardiner, ed., *Narrative of the Spanish Marriage Treaty* (Westminster: Camden Society, 1869).
4. M. A. Gibb, *Buckingham* (London, 1935), pp. 138–42.
5. *Calendar of State Papers, Venetian, 1623–1625* (James I), pp. 174, 201, 208–10, 216, 308—hereafter cited as *C.S.P.V.*
6. S. R. Gardiner, *History of England from the Accession of James I to the Outbreak of the Civil War, 1603–1642* (London, 1883–84), 5:160—hereafter cited as Gardiner.
7. *Return of the Names of Every Member Returned to Serve in Each Parliament* (London, 1878), 1:457—hereafter cited as O.R.
8. Harold Hulme, *The Life of Sir John Eliot* (New York, 1957), pp. 42–44.
9. L.J., 3:209–10; John Rushworth, *Historical Collections of Private Passages of State, 1618–1649* (London, 1721), 1:129–31—hereafter cited as Rushworth; Pym. In the preparation of this book extensive use was made of unpublished diaries of the Parliaments of 1624, 1626, and 1618. These are listed in the bibliography. I am using an abbreviation for each diary cited in the text, usually the last name of the author. As the folios in the typescript copies of the original manuscripts are not always given, all folio references have been omitted. References to the diaries can be found from the day cited.
10. Pym revealed a few traces of humor while recording Buckingham's speech. He wrote that the duke gave an extraordinarily long "marracion," and that during this discourse "divers interloquitorie helps of the Prince and the reading of some letters gave Buckingham tymes of breating." Pym.
11. L.J., 3:220–23; S. R. Gardiner, ed., *Notes of the Debates of the House of Lords, 1624, 1626* (Westminster: Camden Society 1879), p. 1; Pym; Nicolas; Erle; Holles.
12. Gardiner, *Lords Debates, 1624, 1626* , pp. 5–13; L.J., 3:234–36.
13. Gardiner, 5:191.
14. *Journals of the House of Commons* (London, 1803–63), 1:675, 722—hereafter cited as C.J.; Pym; Nicolas; Erle; Gurney; Holland; Holles.
15. Nicolas; Pym; Holland; C.J., 1:675, 722.
16. Nicolas; Holland; Holles; Pym.
17. Gurney; Holland; C.J., 1:725.
18. Holles, March 1, 1624.
19. Rushworth, 1:141–42; Nicolas; Pym; Erle; Holland.
20. L.J., 3:250–51; Rushworth, 1:143–44; Nicolas; Pym.

21. Gardiner, 5:193–94; D. H. Willson, *James VI and I* (New York, 1956), pp. 442–44.
22. L.J., 3:265–66; Rushworth 1:136–38.
23. Gardiner, 5:197.
24. C.J., 1:740; Holland; Holles; Harl. 159; Gurney.
25. Pym wrote that there were "many speeches, most being desireous to showe themselves in plausible matter, yet not altogether without varieties of proposicion," while one parliamentarian "was soe transported with an imaginary success of the war as to hope that with an Army, we might pass through Spayne and fetch the Infanta." Pym.
26. Nicolas; Pym; C.J., 1:741.
27. Holles.
28. Nicolas.
29. Ibid.
30. Rushworth, 1:139–40; C.J., 1:750; L.J., 3:279; Nicolas; Pym; Erle; Holland.
31. Pym.
32. R. H. Tawney, *Business and Politics Under James I: Lionel Cranfield as Merchant and Adventurer* (London, 1958), pp. 231–36.
33. Gibb, pp. 159–62; Gardiner, 5:228–29.
34. Edward, Earl of Clarendon, *The History of the Rebellion and Civil Wars in England*, edited by W. D. McCray (Oxford, 1888), 1:42–43—hereafter cited as Clarendon.
35. Ibid., 1:44.
36. F. W. Maitland, *The Constitutional History of England* (Cambridge, England; 1920), p. 261.
37. C. H. McIlwain, *Constitutions Ancient and Modern* (Ithaca, N.Y., 1940), p. 138.
38. E. R. Foster, "The Procedure of the House of Commons against Patents of Monopolies," *Conflicts in Stuart England*, W. A. Aiken and Basil Henning, eds. (New York, 1960), pp. 76–77.
39. A. Luders, T. T. Tomlins, and J. Raithly, eds., *Statutes of the Realm* (London, 1810), 4, part 2, 1212–14.
40. Nicolas; Gurney.
41. Nicolas; C.J., 1:719, 674.
42. C.J., 1:754.
43. Gardiner, 5:235.
44. Leopold von Ranke, *History of England, Principally in the Seventeenth Century* (Oxford, 1875), 2:394.
45. See C.J., 1:672–755; see also the diaries, esvecially Nicolas; Holland; and Holles.

5. The Parliament of 1625

Charles I was in many ways an admirable king. The general feeling in England upon his accession to the throne was one of enthusiasm. Although he carried a shy, reserved, and solemn disposition throughout his life, he was, nevertheless, full of kingly charm. He possessed a high sense of duty and systematically carried out his routine duties. Moreover, he was not only extraordinarily sympathetic to the unfortunate, but deeply religious, extremely loyal to his close friends, and remarkably faithful to his wife, the Roman Catholic Princess of France, Henrietta Maria. Above all, he had a strong personal courage which was vindicated in his tragic end.

Charles I exercised his rule as the absolute king of a free monarchy.[1] On this fact all Englishmen were agreed. But the rule of the king was limited by the rule of the law. In some cases, however, the king was permitted to override the law. To preserve the state—a thoroughly extreme example—he could exercise dictatorial powers that were deeply inherent in English kingship; in fact, it was his kingly duty as governor of the state to do just that.[2] Charles I, quite naturally, never accepted the charge that he was a tyrant; he consistently held that he always acted within the law. He was, nevertheless, a tyrant, for there are many unjust things done according to the law. As Sir John Eliot wrote and maintained throughout his life, the difference between a lawful king and a tyrant is that the good king "will not do what he may."[3] Charles I's claim, therefore, that he acted exclusively within the law did not necessarily mean that he acted correctly, for when his actions approached despotic lordliness, it became justifiable to interpret his designs as the work of a tyrant.[4]

Charles's defects as a ruler far outweighed his merits. His good intentions and utter inefficiency are now a familiar and accepted picture. He was indecisive, narrow, and righteous. He deeply believed in the purity of his opinions and motives, and he was absolutely rigid in all matters of thought. He once confided to William Laud that he could not "defend a bad, or yield to a good cause."[5] It is said that he knew as much law as anyone in England. Perhaps it is true, but he had little conception of what the laws meant to those who lived under them.[6]

There were some who admired him truly; there were still more who feared him greatly; but there were very few indeed who loved him deeply. Charles I did certainly have some estimable traits and these have been described. But he also had two fateful weaknesses. He appears to have acted in the belief that, as a divine-right monarch, he did not need to act with any moral scruples in dealing with those who opposed his will. The way in which Charles gave and broke his promises ultimately convinced his parliamentary opponents, especially John Pym, that he could not be trusted and that he must be removed or greatly limited by acts of Parliament. His second fateful weakness was his inability to select his advisors on any basis except that of personal likes or dislikes. Two persons to whom Charles especially gave his confidence were the Duke of Buckingham and his wife.

Charles was quick to discover that the financial needs of the English crown necessitated the prompt summoning of Parliament. It met on June 18, 1625. Never, wrote Gardiner, "within living memory had there been such competition for seats in the House of Commons. Never had the members chosen attended so numerously on the first day of the session."[7] There was undoubtedly a strong desire to welcome a new king; but there was also a desire to satisfy their curiosity as to the success of the war. This curiosity on the part of the members of Parliament, however, involved some personal risk, for the plague had settled down upon the city of London. On the day that Parliament opened its doors, the mortality rate had reached the staggering total of 165 deaths a week.[8]

Charles's opening speech to the assembled Houses of Parliament was short. The business of Parliament, he said, did not need eloquent explanation to accomplish its ends. He had very little that was new to explain, for the "humble Advice" Parliament had rendered to his father was satisfactory, and he had but the simple task of asking for supplies to carry this advice into execution. He did not fail, however, to remind the House of Commons that the Spanish war had been entered upon by their suggestion:

My Lords and Gentlemen, I hope that you do remember, that you were pleased to employ Me to advise my Father, to break both those Treaties that were then on foot, so that I cannot say that I came into this Business willingly, freely, like a young Man, and consequently rashly; but it was by your Intreaties, your Engagements . . . . And I think none can blame Me for it, knowing the love and fidelity you have borne to your kings; I have likewise some experience of your Affections. I pray you remember that, this being My first Action, and begun by your Advise and Entreaty, what a Great Dishonour it were, both to you and Me, if this Action, so begun, should fail for that assistance you are able to give Me.[9]

From the first day that the Commons met for business, John Pym's activity was very much in evidence. On June 21, William Strode made a motion that there should be a day of fast. Pym then arose and suggested a general, national fast, joining with the House of Lords in petitioning the king for his direction in it. He then moved that a committee be selected to draw up this petition.[10] Pym's motion to join with the Lords to petition the king for a general fast was readily accepted by the Commons, and he was one of nine appointed to this committee.[11] He was, moreover, selected with many others to the committee on privileges.[12]

On June 22, Sir Francis Seymour urged that the House of Commons petition the king to enforce thoroughly the penal laws against the Roman Catholics. [13] John Forster, in his biography of Pym, attributes this speech to Pym.[14] Forster is wrong, for both the Commons' *Journal* and Pym's own diary clearly identify Seymour as the author of the motion. But Pym was this day selected with several others to consider an "Act for punishing divers abuses committed on the Lord's day, called Sunday." [15] On the following day, after the House of Commons had gone into a committee of the whole house to discuss religion and supplies and after Sir John Eliot had made an excellent speech on religion in general, John Pym and Sir Edwin Sandys, at the direction of the House, drew up the petition of religion.[16]

This petition, which was finally completed on June 27, was a declaration of the Commons beseeching Charles I to recognize the great increase of Roman Catholics in England. There was great danger, it declared, in the goals of all Catholics, for they not only aimed at the "complete exterpation of our religion, but also at the possessinge of themselves of the whole power of the State." The petition stated that papists had increased and become a real menace to the nation because of numerous reasons: by the suppression of the penal laws, by the protection they received from many foreign kings, by the freedom which they possessed to worship at foreign ambassadors' chapels in London, by the increasing numbers of alien seminaries which taught children of Catholics, by the licentious printing and publishing of "Popish and seditious" books, and, finally, by the distressed state of Protestantism on the European continent.

The petition then proceeded to suggest several remedies by which Protestantism in England might be strengthened so that it could more effectively combat the increased strength of Catholicism. First, it advocated a better and sterner education for all children in England and a more discriminative selection of schoolmasters. Moreover, it desired that all teachers be well educated in theology so that they could better instruct their students in the principles of the "trew religion." Second, the petition desired more and better discipline in the universities. Third, it wished to have all Protestant preachers restored to kingly favor by the bishops in order that England could better withstand the "multitude of Priests" abounding in the nation. Fourth, it asked that binding restraints be placed on nonresidency, pluralities, and other clerical abuses, therefore helping to eradicate false gods and false religions. Last, it asked that some intelligent plan be established for adequately increasing the income of the poorer clergy.

The petition suggested various methods that could be employed to weaken and thus destroy Roman Catholicism in England. Recusants would be deprived of schools and barred from both foreign seminaries and Queen Henrietta Maria's masses. Catholics were to be disarmed and confined to the country; they were to be prohibited from foreign ambassadors' homes; they were to be denied foreign law jurisdiction and severely punished for their insolence. Moreover, the petition asked King Charles to employ, to their fullest extent, all the existing penal laws, and to banish all Catholic priests and Jesuits by a royal proclamation. The petition, finally, ended by urging the king to subject Ireland to the same laws that applied in England.[17]

The House of Commons' petition of religion was a typical Pym approach to religion—militantly and rigidly anti-Catholic. The peitition, however, did not remain in its original form. The Commons ordered it altered and John Pym along with Nathaniel Rich, Francis Seymour, and Edward Coke were chosen by the House to author these alterations.[18] The petition was then delivered to the king, but it was all in vain and nothing came of it because of the hasty dissolution of Parliament by Charles I.

John Pym was silent throughout the disputed election of Thomas Wentworth. Sir John Eliot, who stood miles apart in temperment and philosophy from the future Earl of Strafford,[19] led the attack against Wentworth.[20] Wentworth was forced to give up his seat in the Commons and return to Yorkshire to contest the vacant seat.[21] He was unanimously elected and returned to Parliament in August at Oxford.[22] Pym didn't play a role in these dreary proceedings, but he recorded in his diary that he believed that Wentworth's defense had been as ''prejudiced to his owne parte as to the other.'' Pym argued that precedent and tradition must always be maintained and that in the case of Pomfret, where a similar situation existed, the election had not been allowed to stand.[23]

The first real struggle in the Parliament of 1625 arose over the question of supply. There was no denying that the needs of the crown were many: money was desperately needed to equip a fleet against Spain, great and expensive assistance had been promised to both the Dutch and Count Mansfeld, and numerous other expenses of the crown were due to a new king.[24] Yet, though the king and his ministers had asked for generous grants, they had offered no precise statement either of their foreign policy or of the amount of money it would require. The House of Commons was wary of granting large sums of money without knowing exactly how the money was to be spent. Sir Robert Phelips reflected the general feeling of the House of Commons—and probably John Pym as well, because Pym recorded only Phelips's speech at great length—when he declared that there is ''noe ingagement; the promises and declarations of the last Parliament were in respect of a warr: wee know yet of noe warr nor of any enemy. Wee have yet noe account of the money which they saye is ready.'' Phelips concluded by suggesting a grant of two subsidies, and this suggestion was passed by the Commons.[25] Such a vote was really difficult for Charles I to accept; in fact, it was really a vote of no confidence in the king and his foreign policy. Charles at first decided to press the Commons for more revenue, but then decided against this policy and reluctantly accepted the two subsidies.[26] But the utterly inadequate supply was clear proof of the House of Commons' unwillingness to vote money to the king until it understood exactly who the enemy was and what policy toward that enemy would be.

On July 5, the issue of tonnage and poundage was first brought forward. Ever since the reign of Henry VI the duties on exports and imports, known under the name tonnage and poundage, had been granted by Parliament for the lifetime of each successive sovereign in the first session of his reign. For the first time this grant met with opposition in the House of Commons, and Robert Phelips was once more the leader of the opposition. He seconded a motion by Walter Erle that the grant be given to Charles for only one year; he also included in his speech, however, a motion that impositions—the great struggle of the Parliament of 1614—be included.[27] Eventually a bill limiting tonnage and poundage to one year was drafted and carried up the House of Lords where it was read once. But the bill was delayed so long in the Lords that it was swept away by the tide of events which brought the session to a rapid close. The bill, of course, never became operative.[28]

Although supply was the chief problem between king and Commons during this brief Parliament, it was not the only one. Religion, too, proved a tremendous difficulty. This was evident even before the debate on tonnage and poundage when Dr. Richard Montague's curious case arose and dominated the attention of the House for several weeks. Richard Montague was the scholarly rector of Stamford Rivers in Essex, a dean of Hereford, and a fellow of Eton. He had discovered in the possession of one of his parishioners a popish pamphlet entitled *The Gagg for the New Gospel*, which was written by a certain Matthew Killison, a Jesuit missionary. Killison had employed the favorite device of Roman Catholics in England by identifying English Anglicanism with European Calvinism.[29] Montague had determinedly set out to destroy what he believed to be these false allegations, and in

1624 he published a quaintly conceived rebuttal called *A Gag for the New Gospel? No. A New Gag for an Old Goose*. In it, Montague, without the slightest qualifications, denied Calvin's doctrine of predestination. He had the bad taste, moreover, to deny that the Roman Catholic pope was a man of sin or that the Roman Catholic Church was the reincarnation of anti-Christ. He believed that Jesus Christ was present in the sacrament of communion, that pictures and images were sometimes useful in developing and maintaining devotion and piety, and that Catholics, although corrupted in their theology and dogmas, were still integrally bound up in the church of Christ.[30]

It was obvious that the opinions of Richard Montague would not pass long without stiff challenges from the House of Commons, and on the complaint of two Ipswich ministers, Yates and Ward, Montague's controversial book came under Parliament's scrutinizing eye. On May 13, 1624, John Pym, in a report to the Commons from the committee for corruption in religion and learning, declared that Montague's book was "full fraught with dangerous opinions of Arminius" and contrary to the Thirty-nine Articles in at least five points.[31] Pym then read the report to the House, and after a brief lapse of time it was resolved that Pym and four others—Dudley Digges, Robert Hatton, Peter Hayman, and James Perrot—should acquaint the House of Lords and especially the Archbishop of Canterbury, Abbott, concerning the contents of Montague's book.[32]

It is probably true that Abbott was not warmly sympathetic with the theological ideas expressed by Montague, but he nevertheless did not really desire the responsibility that had been thrust upon him by the House of Commons.[33] He asked King James what he should do, and the king suggested that the archbishop interrogate Montague. Pym, who was one of the five chosen to interview Abbott, faithfully recorded Abbott's conversation with Montague:

> Mr Montague you profess you hate popery, and noe way incline to Arminianisme; you see what disturbance is grown in the Church and in the Parliament House by the booke by you lately put forth. Bee occassion of no scandall or offence, and therefore this is my advice unto you. Goe home, reviewe over

your booke, it maye bee divers things have slipped you which upon better advice you will reform. If any thing be said to much, take it awaye; if any thing be too little, add unto it; if any thing be obscure, explaine it; but doe not wedd your self to your owne opinion, and remember wee must give an account of our ministrye unto Christ.[34]

Richard Montague accepted none of the conciliatory advice of Archbishop Abbott. Not only did he refuse to review his book, adding or deleting the suggested additions and deletions proffered by Abbott, but he energetically sought to get the King of England wedded to his religious principles. King James, who after reading Montague's book declared that "if that is to be a Papist, so am I a Papist," gave permission to Montague to prepare still another manuscript, and in early 1625, with the steady support of Bishops Buckeridge, Howson, and Laud,[35] he published *Apello Caesarem: A Just Appeale from two Unjust Informers*. Dedicated to Charles I, it was a vindication of his teachings from the charge of Arminianism and popery. "I am none of that Fraternity," he wrote, "no Calvinist, no Lutheran, but a Christian."[36]

The problem was, however, Montague's Christianity was not the brand to which the House of Commons could wholeheartedly subscribe. Quite frankly, Montague's Christianity had the bad odor of Arminianism,[37] and the Commons could not allow those insidious ideas to remain unchallenged. On July 1, as soon as the question of supply had been settled, the House sent a delegation to Abbott to discover what had been accomplished. John Pym was one of those sent and he recorded the archbishop's comments.[38] Abbott explained what had taken place, but soberly reminded the delegation that he could not legally act upon the mere complaint of the House of Commons. He would be glad, he concluded, to give his judgment freely on *Apello Caesarem* when and where "I shalbe orderly directed to it."[39] With the attempt of the Commons to get the support of the Archbishop of Canterbury collapsing, therefore, the House referred the whole subject to a committee.[40]

On July 4, Pym asked the Commons for authority to examine witnesses involved in the publication of Montague's books, and it was granted.[41] On July 7, the committee made its report. John

Forster argued that John Pym was the author of this report.[42] Although he offered no evidence for such a statement and although the Commons' *Journal* and Pym's own diary clearly illustrate that Mr. Recorder reported the proceedings of the committee, Pym was probably the author,[43] for he was the chairman of the committee on religion and the content and language of the report were very similar to the religious speeches of Pym throughout the 1620s. The committee found that Montague's first book, *New Gag for an Old Goose*, contained many theological doctrines contrary to the Thirty-nine Articles established by Parliament, and that on these disputed doctrines, a special conference would be held with the House of Lords. They found Montague's second book, *Apello Caesarem*, "a factious and seditious book, tending manifestly to the Dishonour of our late King, and to the Disturbance of our Church and State." Moreover, Montague had written slightingly of Calvin and Beza while giving enormous credit to the great Jesuit theologian, Cardinal Bellarmine. Furthermore, he had belittled sermons, referring to them as "chewing the cud," and had continually used the phrase "Puritan" to describe those clerics who attacked his theological views—notably Yates and Ward, the very preachers who had first brought the complaint against Montague to the House of Commons.[44] John Pym was especially outraged at Montague's pretensions, methods, and endeavors. He wrote in his diary that Montague had consistently attempted to divide the Stuart kings from their subjects by declaring that there was a "patent prevaylinge faction in the Kingdom etc; and these he calls Puritanes, but doth not defyne a Puritan, and yet he saith a Puritan is worse than a Papist." But, wrote Pym in a revealing sentence, "if Puritans be so bad, it were good wee knew them."[45]

After the report had been read, a debate arose in the House concerning the punishment of Montague. Several members argued that Parliament had legal jurisdiction in the case, while several others contended that many of Montague's theological interpretations were quite popular in England and had never really been condemned by the Established Church. But, as Pym wrote, the greatest "weight both of nombers and reasons" were hostile to Montague,[46] and in the end it was resolved that Montague had committed a contempt against the Commons. John

Pym, along with several other parliamentarians, was ordered to set down in writing the particular charges against Richard Montague.[47]

King Charles came to Montague's defense and promoted him to one of the crown's chaplains-in-ordinary;[48] this appointment was announced to the House on July 9 by Solicitor General Heath. He explained that Charles had taken the cause into consideration and that he desired that the Commons should set Montague free. Sir Nathaniel Rich then rose and made a motion stating that the whole House firmly believed that Montague's books were "seditious" and "seducing" books and deserved a public censure, and that the Commons should not release him but only allow him out on bond.[49] This was done by the House. But, to bring this chapter of the parliamentary trials and tribulations of Richard Montague to a close, on August 2 the sergeant at arms informed the House that Montague was "sick of the Stone." It was then ordered that Montague was to stand committed until he should be discharged by the House.[50] The issue was still in abeyance, however, when Parliament was dissolved. The sequence of the Montague affair and John Pym's further connection with it comes in the second Parliament of Charles I.

In the meantime, the plague had continued to do its dirty deeds; the city of London was especially ravaged and its ravages were reflected in the House of Commons, now reduced to some sixty members from both fear and sickness. On July 11, the two Houses were informed that Parliament would end that very day. The Lower House then proceeded to the Upper House to listen to the royal assent given to the bills which had passed. The lord keeper explained to them that there would be an adjournment and not a prorogation; Parliament would meet again at Oxford on August 1. Furthermore, he stated that they would receive a particular answer to their petition of religion, and that "in the meane tyme, by present execution of the lawes, would make a reall, rather than a verball answere to our contentment, and the contentment of all the Kingdom."[51]

At Oxford, the opposition in the House of Commons to the foreign policy escapades and failures of the Duke of Buckingham, particularly in relation to Spain and French Huguenots, came to a head. The king met the Commons on August 4 and asked them for further help in accomplishing the "great af-fayres" now in operation: "For the great preparations he had made, though they had cost him great sommes of money, yet it were better halfe the shippes should perish in the sea then the fleete should not now goe out." Charles concluded by promising a reply to their petition of religion within two days. Sir John Coke followed Charles and addressed both Houses in behalf of the government. He gave plans for the widespread schemes of war which were in progress, but, unfortunately, did not ask for a specific sum of money to effectuate these plans.[52]

The House of Commons was both puzzled and frustrated.[53] On the following morning Sir Francis Seymour boldly attacked the foreign policy of the Duke of Buckingham. "We were told," he declared, "of a peace in France. Who knowes not that the Kinge is gone against the Protestants? . . . Wee have given three sub-sidyes and three fifteenths to the Q. of Bohemia, for which she is nothinge the better. Nothinge hath been done. Wee know not our enemy. Wee have set upon and consumed our owne people." He went on to explain that Queen Elizabeth had governed by a grave and wise "counsell, and never rewarded any man but for desert," but for the present, he had no confidence in the advisors of the crown. Robert Phelips also attacked Buckingham. In the gov-ernment, he said, there is a desperate lack of good advice, for power had been monopolized. He concluded by asking the Com-mons to "looke into the estate and government and, findinge that which is amiss, make this Parliament the reformer of the Com-monwealthe."[54]

Solicitor General Heath attempted to defend the government's policies by arguing that the Commons was bound to follow the king unless he proposed something to which it was impossible to consent. Alford answered Heath immediately and scored heavily. It was not the Palatinate, he said, but Spain that was in the minds of the parliamentarians, and the House had especially opposed war in Germany. On the following day Rich echoed the temper of the Commons when he proposed five propositions. He desired that the House petition the king to answer their petition on reli-gion, to make known the real enemy, to employ wise counsellors in the conduct of the war, to examine the King's revenue, and to settle the problem of impositions.[55] Edward Clarke, a personal friend of the Duke of Buckingham, rose immediately and passionately defended his patron. "Invectives with bitterness are unseasonable for this time," he declared. But he was stopped at once by a general outburst of indignation from the House—"To the Bar, to the Bar," came the cry from numerous members of the Commons. After the clamor had subsided, Clarke persisted in his attack upon Rich[56] until finally John Pym moved that Clarke be withdrawn, and he was committed to the custody of the sergeant at arms.[57]

On Monday, August 8, Pym delivered his only contribution to the debates of this brief session at Oxford. Sir Miles Fleetwood had just spoken and made a motion proposing three things: that the House of Commons have their petition of religion put into execution, that England declare war on Spain, and that there be a committee selected to give satisfaction to the king. Pym stood and gave his full endorsement to Fleetwood's motion. But before the House selected a committee, he declared, he would have a petition be issued concerning a man named Baker, a "knowne Jesuit" who was set free by occasion of a warrant to the king. He would, moreover, have a "letter written on behalfe of Maria Esmonds to bee carried by some of those that are to attend the conference with the Lords, and to goe away presently; and soe it was ordered."[58]

That same day the Duke of Buckingham met the Commons in Christ Church Hall to deliver a message from the king. Charles, he said, granted freely and fully their petition on religion and the Commons would have their way in the matter of the penal laws. Buckingham then proceeded to justify and defend his foreign policy by pointing to the depression of France, the uprising of the German princes of the Protestant Union, and the vigorous action of both Denmark and Sweden. He denied that he had ever acted without the advice of the council of war and the privy council, and he concluded by asking the Commons to put the sword into the king's hand and, if that were done, they themselves could name the enemy.[59]

John Pym followed Buckingham's long apology with a detailed statement of the crown's debts and engagements. He reported to the House of Commons the speech of the lord treasurer to the House of Lords.[60]

The House of Commons, however, was not convinced of the rightness of government's foreign policy. More and more the discussion was aimed at the Duke of Buckingham. The king's appeal to the Commons to vote a supply at once in return for a royal pledge that Parliament would meet in the coming winter was ignored by the House. Instead, several parliamentarians attacked Buckingham. Sir Francis Seymour finally rose and spoke of that which was on the minds of most members of the Commons. "Let us lay the fault where it is," he declared, "the Duke of Buckingham is trusted, and it must needs be either in him or his agents." The impetuous Phelips was not to be outdone. "It is not fit," he cried, "to repose the safety of the Kingdom upon those that have not parts answerable to their places." A committee was appointed to frame a petition embodying these complaints against the duke. It appeared, though, as if it were all in vain, for the king dissolved his first Parliament the next day in order to save his most trusted advisor, the Duke of Buckingham.[61]

John Pym played a rather significant role in this short and sharp Parliament of 1625. He was deeply involved in the petition of religion and he was the fundamental cog in the machinery of the influential committee of religion. He was very active in committee work and he reported to the House of Commons the important lord treasurer's report on the king's finances. But he was not very active in the attack upon the crown's foreign policy or in the heated assault upon the Duke of Buckingham. He undoubtedly supported both parliamentary positions, for he was violently opposed to war in the Palatinate and consistently advocated war against Spain. He fully agreed, moreover, with the assault upon Buckingham, for, as we shall see in the next chapter, he played an extremely vital role in the impeachment of the duke during the Parliament of 1626.

Notes

1. Corinne C. Weston, "The Theory of Mixed Monarchy Under Charles I and After," *English Historical Review* 75 (1960): 426–33; R. W. K. Hinton, "English Constitutional Theories from Sir John Fortesque to Sir John Eliot," *English Historical Review* 75 (1960): 410–25.
2. R. W. K. Hinton, "Government and Liberty Under James I," *Cambridge Historical*

Journal (1953): 11, 48; Charles H. McIlwain, *Constitutions Ancient and Modern* (Ithaca, N.Y., 1940), chapters 5–6; J. N. Figgis, *The Divine Right of Kings* (Cambridge, England, 1934), pp. 136–40.

3. Sir John Eliot, *De Jure Maisestatis*, edited by B. Grossart (London, 1882), pp. 90–91.

4. R. W. K. Hinton, "Was Charles I a Tyrant?" *Review of Politics* 8 (1956): 69–87.

5. William Laud, *Works*, edited by W. Scott (London, 1847), 3: 146–47.

6. C. V. Wedgwood, *The King's Peace* (New York, 1956), p. 72.

7. S. R. Gardiner, *History of England from the Accession of James I to the Outbreak of the Civil War, 1603–1642* (London, 1883–84), 5:337—hereafter cited as Gardiner.

8. R. F. Williams, ed., *The Court and Times of Charles I* (London, 1848), 1: 32—hereafter cited as *C&T Charles I*.

9. *Journals of the House of Lords* (London, 1846), 3:435–36—hereafter cited as L.J.; S. R. Gardiner, ed., *Debates in the House of Commons in 1625* (Westminster: Camden Society, 1873), p. 1—hereafter cited as CD 1625. This is John Pym's diary, CD 1621, 1:26–61. Sir John Eliot, *An Apology for Socrates and Negotium Posterorum*, edited by A. B. Grossart (London, 1881), 1:44—hereafter cited as *Neg. Post.*

10. *Journals of the House of Commons* (London, 1803–63), 1:799—hereafter cited as C.J.

11. CD 1625, p. 6; C.J., 1: 799.

12. C.J., 1: 799; CD 1625, p. 6.

13. C.J., 1: 800; CD 1625, p. 12; *Neg. Post.*, 1: 60.

14. John Forster, *Lives of Eminent British Statesmen* (London, 1831–39), 3:31–32.

15. C.J., 1: 800.

16. CD 1625, pp. 16, 18, 28; *Neg. Post.*, 1: 74.

17. CD 1625, pp. 18–25.

18. C.J., 1: 803.

19. Harold Hulme, *The Life of Sir John Eliot* (New York, 1957), pp. 74–80; C. V. Wedgwood, *Thomas Wentworth: First Earl of Strafford, 1593–1641* (London, 1961), p. 70.

20. *Neg. Post.*, 1: 95–104.

21. C.J., 1: 804; CD 1625, p. 45.

22. C.J., 1: 812; Wedgwood, *Strafford*, p. 52.

23. CD 1625, p. 45.

24. CD 1625, p. 30; Gardiner, 5: 345.

25. CD 1625, p. 31.

26. The king did not accept the subsidy with "great satisfaction and contentment" as John Eliot contended. See *Neg. Post.*, 1: 92, 105–9; C.J., 1: 802; L.J., 3: 454; CD 1625, p. 41; Gardiner, 5: 348, n. 3.

27. CD 1625, pp. 43–44; C.J., 1: 803.

28. C.J., 1: 805, 807; CD 1625, p. 47; L.J., 3: 463; *Neg. Post.*, 1: 95; Gardiner, 5: 365.

29. Matthew Killison, *The Gagg for the New Gospel*, (n.p., 1623?).

30. Richard Montague, *A Gag for the New Gospel? No. A New Gag for an Old Goose* (London, 1624), pp. 53, 83, 229, 258, 300.

31. C.J., 1: 788, 704.

32. Ibid., p. 788.

33. Gardiner, 5: 350–65.

34. CD 1625, p. 35.
35. Laud, *Works*, 6:244–46; John Rushworth, *Historical Collections of Private Passages of State, 1618–1649* (London, 1721), 1: 176—hereafter cited as Rushworth.
36. Richard Montague, *Apollo Caesarem: A Just Appeale from two Unjust Informers* (London, 1625), p. 35.
37. See Godfrey Davies, "Arminian versus Puritan in England, ca. 1620–40," *Huntington Library Quarterly* 5 (1934): 157–79; W. R. Fryer, "The High Churchmen of the Earlier Seventeenth Century," *Renaissance and Modern Studies* 5 (1961): 106–48; John Rogan, "King James' Bishops," *Durham University Journal* 48 (1956): 93–99.
38. CD 1625, p. 33.
39. CD 1625, pp. 34–35; *Neg. Post.*, 1: 78–79.
40. C.J., 1: 805; CD 1625, p. 35.
41. CD 1625, p. 35; C.J., 1: 802.
42. Forster, *Emminent Lives*, 3: 32.
43. C.J., 1: 805; CD 1625, p. 47.
44. CD 1625, pp. 47–49; C.J., 1: 805.
45. CD 1625, p. 49.
46. Ibid., p. 52.
47. C.J., 1: 806.
48. C.J., 1: 807; CD 1625, p. 62; Rushworth, 1: 174.
49. CD 1625, pp. 62–63.
50. C.J., 1: 809; CD 1625, p. 69.
51. L.J., 3: 464–66; CD 1625, p. 67; C.J., 1: 808–809.
52. L.J., 3: 470–71; CD 1625, p. 73; C.J., 1: 810; *Neg. Post.*, 2: 18–21.
53. *Neg. Post.*, 2: 23.
54. CD 1625, pp. 78–82; *Neg. Post.*, 2: 30–36; C.J., 1: 810.
55. CD 1625, pp. 87–91, 138–39; C.J., 1: 811; *Neg. Post.*, 2: 43–46, 50–51, 53.
56. CD 1625, pp. 91, 139–40; C.J., 1: 811–12; *Neg. Post.*, 2: 51.
57. CD 1625, pp. 139–40.
58. Ibid., p. 141.
59. L.J., 3: 748–84; CD 1625, pp. 94–102; *Neg. Post.*, 2: 56–71.
60. CD 1625, pp. 102–105; *Neg. Post.*, 2: 72–75.
61. CD 1625, pp. 106–108, 118–19; C.J., 1: 813–15; *Neg. Post.*, 2: 94.

6. The Parliament of 1626

Although Charles I had probably saved Buckingham from impeachment by his dissolution of the Parliament of 1625, his problems remained unsolved. Wars are waged with the sole purpose of winning, and while wars involve great financial resources, the English king was thoroughly bankrupt. It was clear that unless some way of replenishing the exchequer arose, Parliament would certainly have to be faced before long. Buckingham believed he knew just such a way to refill the treasury. He believed that with a truly brilliant diplomatic coup and a smashingly splendid naval victory he could both enrich the exchequer and seduce Parliament to the rightness of the king's policy and the competence of his first minister. His plan was simple; there would be a recreation of Drake's wondrous plundering expedition against the Spanish ports. The seaport-fortress of Cadiz would be seized and the Spanish treasure fleet captured and brought back triumphantly to England.

The Cadiz expedition proved to be a study in frustration. From the very beginning it suffered from every possible handicap imaginable. The ships were unseaworthy, the tackle was rotten, and the contractors who supplied the fleet were swindlers who equipped the ships with rotten stores of all kinds. The 15,000 men who were pressed to take part in the adventure were rogues and vagabonds who scarcely knew one end of the musket from the other or had the "wherewithal to cover their nakedness."[1] In their half-starved and half-naked condition, their presence made the local inhabitants of any town through which they walked offer bribes to their commanders to march them farther, in order to avoid demands for "hose, shoes, shirts, and conduct money."[2]

The fleet was commanded by Sir Edward Cecil, the grandson of the great Burghley, who proved brave enough, but unfortunately lacked any experience of the sea. The real trouble lay in the fact that there was no really efficient central administration for the supervision of the troops and their provisions, and consequently the local authorities were in a state of confusion. Buckingham had taken too many duties upon himself and, unwilling-to delegate any of his powers to a competent subordinate, found himself faced by chaos on all sides. Lord Cromwell, who had just recently returned from Holland and involvement in Count Mansfeld's military escapades, suggested some sound and prophetic words of caution to the duke. Writing to Buckingham that he had unwisely taken too much upon himself by having no other confidant than Lord Conway, Cromwell warned against the proposed expedition, arguing that if it succeeded, its success would not be attributed to the duke, but if it failed, its failure would certainly fall to the duke's guidance.[3]

The ill-fated expedition of eighty ships left Plymouth harbor on October 8, 1625. Reduced to the briefest of terms, the tale of the expedition to Cadiz was that of ineffective crews and equipment and incapable leadership, all of which resulted in a humiliating failure. Instead of an immediate attack upon Cadiz, other goals were aimed at until the Spaniards had time to reinforce the garrison, and the treasure ships evaded the English and slipped into ports with their precious cargo intact. By the middle of November the expedition turned homeward.[4]

No more fatal blow for the Duke of Buckingham could have been devised by his bitterest enemy. Nothing was more apt to arouse the smoldering anger of the English people as proof of the incompetence of the favorite and of the inefficiency of the English navy he ruled than such a disaster as the Cadiz expedition. From the king's interpretation, however, the only solution to the disaster and to his foreign policy in general was a summoning of a new Parliament.

The second Parliament of Charles I convened on February 6, 1626. Buckingham had conveniently arranged to rob the "opposition" of much of its thunder by having those individuals who attacked him in the Parliament of 1625 pricked as sheriffs. Since a sheriff was bound to attend to his duties in his own county, it was clear that he could not sit at Westminster.[5] Sir Robert Phelips, Coke, Seymour, Fleetwood, Alford, Sir Guy Palmes, and Sir Thomas Wentworth were those members of Parliament pricked. The inclusion of Wentworth is still a mystery, for King Charles regarded him as an "honest gentleman." Wentworth, however, took it calmly. His father-in-law, the Earl of Clare, wrote to him advising submission, "for we live under a Prerogative Government where Book Law submits under *Lex Lo-quens*, . . . I may conclude it is not good to stand within the Distance of absolute Power."[6]

King Charles's opening speech to the assembled Houses was short and pointed. "My Lords Spiritual and temporal," he said, "and you gentlemen all; of mine own nature I do not love long speeches, and I know I am not very good to speak much. Therefore I mean to show what I shall speak in actions." Sir Thomas Coventry, the new lord keeper, then rose and gave a long speech. He spoke in generalities and gave Parliament no new information about the problems on the European continent, the war with Spain, or the desperate needs of the exchequer. Sir Hineage Finch was then chosen speaker for the Commons and, after he made a long, complimentary speech urging the necessity of war against Spain, the two Houses adjourned.[7]

During the Parliament of 1626 John Pym emerged as an important and influential member of the House of Commons. The records of this Parliament reveal that during the four months that it was in session, Pym was appointed to more than fifty committees. More importantly, however, as chairman, he reported every activity of the influential committee of religion, and was actively involved in the impeachment of the Duke of Buckingham. As never before, Pym was active both behind the scenes and in the debates of the Commons itself. Through hard work and timely debate, Pym was carving for himself a reputation on the honor roll of famous members of Parliament.

On February 10, a motion was made by Pym to allow his servant to have privilege to stay a suit. This privilege, of which no more is heard, was quickly granted.[8] On that same day, after Rudyard had moved that a committee be formed to consider matters of "scandalous ministers," Pym moved for a larger committee. He desired, he said, that the proposed enlarged committee "may also consider of certain other Articles" discussed during the last Parliament, but not included in the petition of religion delivered to the king. He was immediately appointed to this committee.[9] Then with five others, including Rich and Eliot, he was appointed to a committee to examine every Saturday the clerk's entries in the Commons' *Journal*.[10]

It was also during this day that Sir John Eliot, who in the

absence of King Charles's victimized sheriffs catapulted himself into a position of leadership in the House of Commons,[11] gave a veiled attack upon the government of Charles I. Eliot boldly called for an investigation into the failure of the "last fleet." He demanded an inquiry into the "King's estate," an accounting of the Parliament of 1625's subsidies, and an examination of "Miscounseeling" to the king. "Our honour," he said, is destroyed, "our ships are sunk, our men are perished, not by sword, not by an enemy, not by chance, but apparently discerned beforehand out of strong predictions, by those we trust, by that pretended care and thrift that ushers our misfortune."[12] A committee of grievances was appointed by the House to collect evidence for Eliot's charges. Another committee was appointed for religion, and to this committee was referred the curious case of Richard Montague.

On January 26, 1626, Montague's two books had been examined by four bishops—among whom were Andrewes and Laud—who had been asked to investigate the question, and who reported that the books were compatible with the doctrines of the Church of England.[13] King Charles, however, wisely allowed the Parliament of 1626 to pass judgment on the merits of Montague's views. As might be expected, the House of Commons pronounced strongly against the English cleric, and it was John Pym who both wrote and reported the findings of the committee of religion.[14]

It was a typical Pym speech—logical, lucid, and systematically constructed under headings. Pym, accurately reflecting the religious prejudices of the majority in the Commons, accused Montague of espousing doctrines contrary and repugnant to the Thirty-nine Articles of the Established Church. He then proceeded to elaborate, under five headings, the errors of Montague's doctrines. The first error was that the cleric had consistently maintained that the Roman Catholic Church was a "True Church, since it was a Church." The second error was that Montague had insisted that the Catholic religion had firmly established and maintained itself upon the "same foundation of Sacrament and Doctrine, instituted by God." The third accused Montague of believing that the differences between Catholics and Protestants were small and inferior to the doctrine of the brotherhood of all believers. The fourth error was that Montague had written that images were useful for the "instruction of the Ignorant, and excitation of Devotion."

Montague's fifth error was the longest and, in many ways, the most important to Pym. Montague was charged with upholding the special nature of saints. He wrote that saints, like angels, had a special and peculiar patronage, custody, protection, and power over certain persons and countries by God's special deputation, and that it was neither wrong nor irreligious to believe in them. Moreover, he had espoused the doctrine of good works and affirmed that the chosen saints of God here on Earth could depart from a state of grace and fall away from selection. Finally, Pym declared that Montague had succumbed to the pernicious errors of Arminianism, which the late "famous Queen Elizabeth and King James of happy memory, did so piously and delegently labour to suppress." He had attempted to create great factions and divisions in the nation by casting "the odious and scandalous name of Puritans" upon those who conformed to the ceremonies and doctrines of the Church of England. He had given encouragement to popery and seduced many "worthy Divines" in the kingdom. Pym concluded by stating that the House of Commons believed not only that Montague's books should be suppressed and burned, but that he should be punished in such an exemplary manner that it would deter others from attempting so presumptuously to disturb the peace of the Church.[15]

According to Pym, Montague's chief crime lay in giving aid and comfort to the enemy, the Roman Catholic Church. Pym did not accuse Montague of being a Catholic, but he did brand him an Arminian, and to the minds of many militant Protestants such as John Pym, an Arminian was a dangerous "fellow traveler." Montague was dangerous because he advocated the use of images and saints, defended the Roman Catholic Church, and attacked the Puritans. In brief, Montague was attacked not so much because he had broken any laws of the Established Church—they were ambitious enough to encourage numerous varieties of thought—but because he had given encouragement to the growth of Arminianism, and to Pym and numerous other members of the House of Commons, this was as great an evil as Catholicism.

John Pym had established religion as his special province, and he was rapidly becoming the leading member of the Commons when the issue of religion was brought under the scrutinizing gaze of the House. He became a Catholic and Arminian hater of the very first rank. But he was powerless to bring conformity to religion in England because of the opposition of the king. Even though Pym continued his vigorous efforts to bring Montague to punishment by repeating the same grievances in the Parliament of 1628, the hated cleric escaped his vigilant assaults. Before Pym's report could be considered by the House of Lords, the session was brought to a close by the untimely dissolution of Parliament. In July 1628 Charles made Montague Bishop of Chichester, and in January 1629 a special pardon was extended to him, and *Apello Caesarem* was called in so that it might not cause the Church of England further embarrassment.

During the remainder of the session it was upon the Duke of Buckingham that the full attention of the House of Commons was focused. One of the issues which had come to the attention of the committee of grievances, of which Pym was a member,[16] was the reciprocal seizing of ships by England and France. John Eliot in an important speech on February 22 had argued that the seizure of the French ship *St. Peter of Havre de Grace* had precipitated the French seizure of English goods and ships.[17] Eliot, it now appears, was conveniently using the "St. Peter" case as a club with which to beat the Duke of Buckingham, for he was trying to create an unfavorable climate of opinion against the duke in the Commons and in the nation at large. Eliot believed that "the feeling against Buckingham must be developed by relentless denunciations of government policies, by bitter attacks on lesser officials, and by stealthy suggestions that one man was really to blame for all of England's troubles. The *St. Peter* incident, if properly handled, Sir John believed, would most certainly contribute to the downfall of the Duke of Buckingham."[18]

The attack upon Buckingham began on February 24. From the numerous speeches, it is clear that a majority of the members of the Commons was displeased with the policies and actions of the government. The assault began when Wandesford, supported by Eliot and Digges, and demanded an examination of the king's finances by a committee of the Commons. John Pym agreed that a thorough investigation of the crown's estates and revenues was necessary because the recent disgrace of Count Mansfeld's soldiers being thrust into English ships without being sufficiently provisioned was dramatic evidence of incompetently managed government expenditures. Pym was especially worried about the projected image of Parliament to both friend and foe alike, concluding that the members of the House of Commons must free themselves of all imputation and "cleare the wisdom of this state from infamye in such course and ill carridges layde to their charge." [19]

The initial attack upon Buckingham, however, lacked direction, for there appeared to be little leadership or unity of goals in the House of Commons. The duke was on everyone's mind, but nobody attacked him directly. Certain members questioned Buckingham's motives, as Pym did on March 1, when he demanded to know why the English war commissioners had delivered captured French goods to the duke,[20] but nobody forcefully questioned his policies or imputed his patriotism. Instead, the committee of grievances, of which Pym was a member,[21] proceeded to examine the council of war, which had been appointed by King Charles both to manage the affairs of the Palatinate and to appropriate monies for war according to the propositions of James I's last Parliament. There were seven councillors and their examination was undertaken under the terms of the proposals which James I had himself offered to the Parliament of 1624: that the subsidies voted by Parliament should be spent entirely under the direction of treasurers appointed by the House of Commons. These treasurers had taken oaths that only under the direction of the council of war would they appropriate expenditures and, in their turn, the councillors of war had sworn that only for the Commons' propositions would they make order for payment.[22] On March 9, Pym was appointed to a committee of nine to study and analyze the answers of the seven Councillors.[23]

Two days later, on March 11, events took an astonishing turn. Clement Coke, the son of the noted lawyer, surprised the Commons by stating that it was "better to die by an enemy than to suffer at home." [24] And then Dr. Samuel Turner, a member of little stature or influence, astounded the assembled House by an unexpected[25] denunciation of the favorite. Turner declared to his fascinated associates that the cause of all their grievances was the

Duke of Buckingham.[26] The king moved immediately against the two men who had attacked his beloved favorite, demanding satisfaction for what he believed to be seditious actions, and warning the Commons to apply themselves solely to redress of grievances and not to "enquire after grievances." "I must let you know," the king said, "that I will not allow any of my Servants to be questioned amongst you, much less such as are of eminent Place, and near unto me."[27]

The House of Commons, however, refused to back down, and on March 25, Wandesford, reporting for the committee for Evils, Causes and Remedies, listed two evils and ten causes of English grievances.[28] He did not, however, mention Buckingham by name or indeed connect him with the evils. This was done by Sir John Eliot on March 27, when during a debate on supply he delivered a slashing attack upon the domestic and foreign policies of the Duke of Buckingham, demanding the duke's impeachment and citing the rule of Hubert de Burgh in the reign of Henry III and that of the Earl of Suffolk in the reign of Richard II as precedents for such a policy by the Commons.[29]

Charles wasted little time in answering the Commons' actions, warning the members of Parliament that Parliaments were completely in the crown's power for their summoning, sitting, and dissolution, and that if the activities of the Lower House were good, they would continue to sit, if evil they would be dissolved. "And remember," he concluded, "that if in this time instead of mending your errors, by delay you persist in your Errors, you make them greater and irreconcileable."[30] The king's speech was a fighting one; he had thrown the gauntlet at the feet of the Commons; he had told the House to leave Buckingham alone and to get on with their proper business or face a speedy dissolution. The next day, March 30, the Commons was summoned to hear Buckingham's explanation of his past policies and actions. In a long speech the Duke related the whole story of the Cadiz expedition, the immense labors with which he had endeavored to carry out the war policy of Parliament, and the many projects he had promoted and which had been carried out only by large-scale contributions from his own pocket.[31]

The House of Commons, not mending "their Errors," ignored Buckingham's defense of his policies and proceeded to prepare a remonstrance to the king which would vindicate the Commons' right to attack ministers of the crown. On April 1, after Pym had completed his report of the meeting with the House of Lords concerning Buckingham's speech, the Commons went into a committee of the whole house to debate the remonstrance. To draft this document, a subcommittee of twelve, including John Pym, was named.[32] On the third Pym reported from the subcommittee that the remonstrance was not quite finished[33]; finally on April 4, the remonstrance was approved by the House of Commons. It demanded, as a privilege of Parliament, the right to discuss all matters concerning the commonwealth, the right to proceed on any matter which was presented to the Commons, the right to "question and complain of all persons, of what degree soever, found grievous to the Commonwealth, in abusing the power and trust committed to them by their sovereign."[34] Although they had written a thoroughly revolutionary doctrine,[35] it is doubtful that the members of the House of Commons were aware that they were engaged in revolution, for they presented the remonstrance to Charles and then adjourned for the Easter holidays.

The Easter holidays did not weaken the desire or the determination of the members of the House of Commons to attack Buckingham. On April 18, the House approved a committee to consider the "great Business now in hand," the impeachment of the duke. A select committee of twelve, including John Pym,[36] was appointed to "consider and examine, of any new matter, to be propounded unto them, concerning the Duke of Buckingham." The Commons then proceeded to pass the eight resolutions against the duke that made up the charges of impeachment. King Charles, recognizing his inability to block the Commons' actions without a dissolution of Parliament, reluctantly conceded to the inquiry of the policies of Buckingham.

On May 3, Pym reported to the House from the committee of twelve for the framing of a petition.[37] Digges then informed the Commons that the charges against the duke would be divided among eight managers. The eight, one of whom was Pym, were naturally selected from the select committee of twelve. Each of the managers was allowed two assistants, and Pym selected Rich and Browne.[38]

During the debate on the subsidy bill which followed, Pym, showed that although he desired to see the king's chief minister impeached, he was still deeply committed to Charles I and his policies. Like many other members of the "country"[39] faction in the House of Commons, Pym, believed that the king and indeed the very concept of English kingship was essentially good. Pym held that the crown was neither evil nor harmful, that it was only the king's ministers who were bad, and that if the incompetent counsel were removed from the crown, the king would rule perfectly. It took the personal rule of Charles I to convince Pym that the king must be bound to the law and that the law must be interpreted by Parliament. After some effusive comments on the character and rule of Charles I, Pym asked the House to have the time in the collection of the supply be proportionally divided, since the Commons had proportionally divided the total sum to be paid for important occasions. He moved that the subsidy should be paid within one year for two specific reasons: first, because the English subjects must above all serve the executive, the crown; second, because the money was desperately needed by Charles over and above his extraordinary expenses.[40]

The House of Commons completed its preparations for the impeachment of the Duke of Buckingham before the House of Lords by May 6. Digges, as spokesman for the select committee of twelve, read the articles of impeachment and assigned them to the individual managers. Digges would begin the proceedings with an introduction, while Eliot was assigned the task of summarizing and concluding the articles of impeachment. John Pym was given articles nine and ten, which dealt with the sale of titles of honor and the sale of places of judicature.[41]

On May 9, a long debate took place in the Commons concerning whether the House of Lords should commit the Duke of Buckingham to the Tower. The discussion had become quite heated when a certain Diatt thoroughly angered numerous members of the House by vigorously defending the policies and actions of the duke. Pym was especially angered. We see, he declared, that Buckingham still exercised a great deal of influence upon some men and that these men dared to speak in his defense in a most arrogant manner. He moved that Diatt be summoned to the bar, admonished, and then suspended from the House. This was ordered by the Commons, and the Commons then voted for the imprisonment of the duke.[42] On May 11, Rich carried the Commons' demand for the imprisonment of the duke to the Lords. The Upper House replied that they would consider the message and give the Commons an answer shortly.[43] The answer never came. Pym was right; Buckingham exerted much influence over many men, especially in the House of Lords.

The stage was thus decorated to enact the great drama, and on May 8, the eight managers, together with their sixteen assistants, appeared in the Painted Chamber to read and explain the charges of impeachment. Buckingham was present, and he was openly contemptuous of what he believed a pitiful attempt to bring him down. The duke laughed and jeered in the faces of the managers as they presented their case, so infuriating Glanville that the parliamentarian declared he could illustrate to Buckingham ''when a man of greater blood than your Lordship, as high in place and power, and as deep in the favour of the King as you, hath been hanged for as small a crime as the least of these articles contain.''[44]

Digges opened the proceedings, attributing to Buckingham all the calamities which had befallen the nation. He concluded by stating that the ''Laws of England teach us, that Kings cannot command ill or unlawfull things, when even they speak, though by Letters Patents, or their Seals. If the things be evil, these Letters Patents are void; and whatsoever ill events succeeds, the execution of such commands must answer for them.''[45] No one rose to question this rather curious doctrine of parliamentary sovereignty,[46] so there followed the articles of impeachment. The first three articles were read and analyzed by Herbert, who discussed the dangers to the state from the numerous offices held by one man, the purchase of the Cinque ports from Zorch, and the purchase of the Admiralty from Nottingham. John Selden appeared next with articles four and five. He spoke of the Duke's failure to guard the Channel and of Buckingham's order to seize the French ship *St. Peter of Havre de Grace*. To Glanville were entrusted articles six, seven, and eight, which included the East India Company and the ships loaned to France to serve against the French Protestants at La Rochelle.[47] Then, because it was growing late and hot, the trial was closed for the day.

John Pym began the proceedings on the morning of May 10 and disposed of articles nine and ten. As was his custom, Pym began on a humble note, stating that, although he knew he would speak to his own disadvantage, he would labor to speak with little disadvantage to the issues. He realized he had no learning or ornaments to decorate his oration, but that deficiency was essentially irrelevant, for he desired only to show the charges against the duke plainly: "For all that I aim at, is, that I may lose nothing of the cause. And, therefore, my Lords, I shall apply myself with as much convenient brevity, as one that knows that your Lordship's time is much more precious than my words." Pym then proceeded to read the articles, claiming that Buckingham's selling of places of honor was so notorious and apparent that it needed no proof that these honors had been sold. Instead, he would show that, because of these consequences, the duke had committed a great insult against the state and that this offense had produced grievous dishonor to the commonwealth. "And I will conclude," he declared, "in strengthening the whole by some precedents of former times, that Parliaments have proceeded in that course, in which your Lordships are like to proceed."

Buckingham's sale of honors, Pym stated, was an offense against the state because, as the sworn servant and chief minister and advisor of Charles I, he should have put the king's honor and service before his own pride. It was not enough to say that the duke's greatness and position put him above suspicion and responsibility, for it is the rule of all states that vice must be surpressed and virtue encouraged by corresponding punishments and rewards, and it is the duty and right of the court of Parliament to insist upon prosecuting those individuals who were able to avoid punishments by evading the common-law courts. Whoever advised the king to bestow honors, moreover, bound himself to choose excellent and virtuous men, because they must act meritoriously in the service of the crown and state and must transmit to their successors a vigorous example and stately reputation.

Pym interpreted honor as a sublime and spiritual matter, transcendent in that it could not possibly be purchased. It was divine, he believed, because the Bible stated that kings were gods, and that those men who served and honored kings must resemble the very powers that had endowed them with offices and duties. Because honor was "such a Divine thing," said Pym, "it must not then be bowght with so base a price as money." Honor was a public policy, a reward for public achievements, and the sale of honors by the Duke of Buckingham was, therefore, an unnatural offense against the laws of nature. Pym then proceeded to elaborate on the various ways the sale of honors contributed to the grievous state of affairs in the nation, claiming that it was a prodigious scandal to the English commonwealth, that it denied to the crown the deserving services of able and competent men, that it destroyed the dignity of the English crown by cheapening honors in the eyes of all men, and that it made men more greedy for "lucre" and gain than for virtue, because all men knew that they could obtain titles of honor according to the "heaviness of purse, and not for the weightiness of their merit."

There were no precedents in this charge against Buckingham, Pym said, because it was unlike any other precedent. But Pym believed the impeachment was most certainly a "veryfit time" to make a precedent of this "great Duke," who had raised himself to such dazzling heights and who believed he did not shine bright enough unless he darkened all other honors by making them contemptuous and common, this man who not only sold honors but compelled many unwilling men to purchase titles. It was a strange matter indeed, reflected Pym, that this "noble man" who was the principal patron and supporter of Arminian and popish factions in England and who espoused the doctrine of free will, should not allow freedom in "moral things. And that he should compel one to take Honour and Grace from a King whether he will or no; what is that, but to add Inhumanity and Oppression to Injury and Incivility?"

Pym then proceeded to explain that the fact that the common law forced some men, because of the size of their land holdings, to become knights did not detract from the infamous charges against Buckingham, for it was the function and wisdom of this curious law to employ able and competent men for the good of the state. But any man, for personal gain, who forced other men to accept honors was not to be "countenanced" either in this nation or in any other. It would be a dangerous precedent, Pym believed, to allow such a practice to go unpunished, for what would then keep the duke from selling another man's land at whatever price he deemed fit or of marrying another man's children as it pleased him? The House of Commons, Pym concluded, believed the consequences of these actions to be disastrous, and they "conceive that it is of so great a consequence, that if it not be stopped, it may come in time to make way for a dangerous subversion, and demonstrates a Great Tyranny of a subject, under a most wise, most gracious, and most moderate King."

After effusively elaborating upon the benevolent rule of Charles I, Pym proceeded to the second article under his command, stating that the sale of places of judicature was a grievous disgrace to the state. He took his opening stand on clause forty of Magna Charta, "nulli vendemus, nulli negabimus justitiam,"[48] and then enumerated the numerous evils that automatically followed the sale of places of judicature or any other place of great trust. Pym claimed that all good men would eventually be driven from office by incompetent men able to purchase a judicial sinecure, and that all judges who purchased their positions would naturally increase the number of cases to reimburse themselves for the money used to buy their positions. He argued that ambitious men would not devote themselves to the scholarship necessary for advancement, but would concern themselves solely with "scraping together enough money to purchase places." The richest men, Pym believed, those who had the "best purse but the worse cause," would always prevail over the more deserving applicants, and that these men would attempt both to maximize their annual value and to sell again for more than they had, and Buckingham, as the broker-in-chief, would be bound to support them in this bribery. In brief, Pym was demonstrating how the buying and selling of places of judicature was like a giant auction, with the rich always victorious over the competent and well intentioned.

The selling and buying of offices of trust, Pym declared, had been condemned by both Christians and "Moral Pagans." Even the popes, "a generation full of corruption," had condemned the sale of honors and places of trust, for by the bull *Pius Quintus*, Catholics had laid the penalty of confiscation of goods upon anyone who purchased an office. And Aristotle wrote that no merchant should take any place in a government for at least ten years after his retirement from business, because the most successful merchant was always he who gained the most and all merchants would naturally advance themselves for their own profit.

Pym concluded his long speech condemning the actions of the Duke of Buckingham by citing several precedents to illustrate that both the seller and receiver of any sold office had committed crimes against the laws of England. "And certainly with your Lordships favor," he stated, "it is more just and probable, that they that profess themselves to be Patriots, and shew by their actions, that they aim at their own lucre, and labour to hinder the distributing of justice; it is more just and proper, that those Men should return again to the Publick Treasury of the King and the Kingdom, what they have by their unsatisfied lucre gotten." Pym closed his speech by stating that he humbly left himself to the judgments of the House of Lords and prayed that this "great man," the Duke of Buckingham, would be justly censured.[49]

John Pym had done his homework well. He had delivered a logical and devastating attack upon the sale of honors and places of judicature. He had chosen the wisest plan of attack, for by assaulting the evils condoned and espoused by the duke and not the duke directly, he was in a sense prosecuting Buckingham in abstentia. Pym created a strong impression against the duke and left his judgment to the jury, the House of Lords. He probably simplified and exaggerated the charges, but he was dealing with a difficult case and up against a powerful and dangerous enemy.[50]

Sherland followed Pym with articles eleven and twelve, which dealt with Buckingham's procuring of titles and pensions for his relatives and his obtaining and embezzling the king's lands and revenues. The conclusion was left to Sir John Eliot, who summarized the House of Commons' indictment of the evil deeds and disastrous conduct of Buckingham. After elaborating on the power and practices of the hated duke, Eliot attacked the personality of the favorite, comparing him to a "Beast," "Canker," and "Moth." Then moved by the force of his own emotions and oratorical fervor, Eliot uttered some tart and ill-advised words,[51] comparing the duke to "Sejanus who is this described by Tacitus, *Audax sui obtegens in Alios Criminator iuxtra adulator et superbus.*"[52]

The reaction of Charles I to the Commons' impeachment of Buckingham was immediate and sharp, for the king interpreted the attack upon the duke as an assault upon himself.[53] On the next day, May 11, addressing the Lords in behalf of the duke, the king defended his minister and vowed to punish some parliamentarians for their "insolent speeches."[54] Charles was especially angered by Eliot's speech, stating that if the duke "be Sejanus, I must be Tiberius."[55] On that same morning while the Commons was in debate, Eliot and Digges were summoned to the door, "and by a warrant from his Majestie carried to the Tower."[56] The members of the Commons were shocked at the arrest of their colleagues and the House was thrown into an uproar. Member after member rose from his seat and shouts of "Rise! Rise! Rise!" were sounded on all sides of the House. John Pym did his best to quiet the tumult by advising patience and wisdom,[57] but it was all in vain and the Commons adjourned in confusion and consternation.

The next day Sir Dudley Carleton, the vice-chamberlain, addressed a silently assembled House of Commons. He began by commending Pym's remarks to the House on the preceding day to do "things wisely and temperately and not tumularity." He then warned the Commons that they should "move not his Majesty by trenching upon his prerogatives lest you bring him out of love of Parliaments." Carleton concluded by stating that Eliot and Digges were arrested because they had implicated the Duke in the "death of his late Majestie, whereas the House of Commons had only charged the Duke with presumption."[58]

During the next few days the Commons spent most of its time debating and analyzing the reasons for the arrest of Sir Dudley Digges—Eliot was forgotten for the moment. The really crucial matter was that Digges had not spoken the words of which he had been accused. On May 13, Pym rose and asked every member of the Commons who was present at the impeachment of the Duke of Buckingham before the House of Lords to make a solemn protestation before God that Digges had never spoken these words and to enter such a protestation in the clerk's book. He demanded, moreover, that the Commons make a determined effort to acquaint the House of Lords and the king of this "greatest treason that cann be against the King."[59] Digges was examined by the Lords, acquitted of any crime in his speech, and returned to the Commons on May 16. On the following day Pym came to the defense of Eliot and the privileges of the House of Commons. Sir John Eliot's arrest, Pym declared, was neither just to Eliot nor just to the liberties of the House of Commons, and it was "our duty" to clear his name and hear his defense. The king's actions, Pym concluded, were dangerous precedents, and the Commons must do everything that "shall be most fitting."[60] Eliot was examined by the Lords, and after his papers had been searched, was finally released on May 19. On the next day Pym moved that Eliot be summoned to the House; this was ordered and Eliot resumed his seat.[61]

One of the results of the arrest of Digges and Eliot was the Commons' preparation of a remonstrance on the violations of its parliamentary privileges. The remonstrance was assigned to a subcommittee, and John Pym was one of its members. On May 22, Pym moved in a committee of the whole house that the remonstrance be laid aside and that the Commons proceed instead with a bill of rights to confirm their privileges.[62] Pym here, of course, foreshadowed the actions of the Parliament of 1628. His motion was sidetracked, however, and it was not until June 3 that the Commons definitely moved to substitute a bill for the remonstrance; then the hasty dissolution of Parliament destroyed the bill. Pym's views on the problem were clearly recorded, nevertheless, and they are essential for a firm understanding of his political philosophy throughout the 1620s. There were rules of law and rules of wisdom, he said, and sometimes they were compatible and sometimes incompatible. There were some privileges that individually belonged to each member of Parliament and some that belonged to the House of Commons as a whole; but if anyone assaulted either, he attacked both, because they were indivisible, inseparable, one. As the Commons had defended "our" privileges, he said, so must "we" defend the privileges of each particular member of Parliament. The privileges of the House of Commons, he concluded, were "ours" simply by reason of "our sitting here"; they were, in fact, inherent in the institution of the House of Commons itself.[63]

In June a final attack was made upon the Duke of Buckingham after the Cambridge University, under the careful prodding of King Charles,[64] selected Buckingham as its new chancellor. The

House of Commons was outraged, for their declared enemy had received honors and rewards instead of prison and punishment. On June 5, Pym rose and declared that it was a known fact that a member of the House of Lords had gone to Cambridge to solicit support for the duke's chancellorship, and that many men at the university, such as "Dr. Cosens and Mr. Mason," were Arminians who openly inclined to the theological opinions of Dr. Richard Montague.[65] On the following day Pym reported to the House from a select committee for the framing of an explanatory letter to the university concerning the election of Buckingham as chancellor. Here the chancellor of the exchequer informed the Commons that they had no right to examine the duke's election, for if there were some error in the "form" of the election, the king would attend to the matter.[66] John Pym remained unimpressed and unconvinced with the king's advice, for on the next day, June 7, he remarked that it was a grave public disgrace for the governing body of the university to be committed to a man accused of great crimes in Parliament. Pym declared that the election of Buckingham as chancellor of Cambridge University was both an affront to Parliament and a contemptuous reproach to the House of Commons. He concluded his speech by stating that the matter clearly fell under the jurisdiction of the Commons, and he therefore moved for a petition to give satisfaction to the Commons for these grievous insults and crimes.[67]

Nothing came of Pym's petition, however, for King Charles moved to end the attack upon the favorite. On June 9, the king informed the House to pass the subsidy bill. The Commons, having failed to prove Buckingham guilty before the Lords or the king, decided to issue a declaration against the duke—a really pivotal move—and therefore using public opinion to force Charles to dismiss his minister. On June 13, during a debate on the declaration, Pym, accurately reflecting the beliefs of the majority in the Commons, vigorously defended the actions and policies of the "country" faction from an attack by Sir Clement Throckmorton, who had argued that the Commons had no jurisdiction over the favorite. Pym declared that the House of Commons had jurisdiction over the policies of the duke because the members of the House sat as lawmakers, as councillors, and as judges and because this declaration was in reality the Commons' advice to the crown.[68]

On the following day, Wednesday, June 14, the House of Commons passed the declaration of grievances against Buckingham, demanding the exclusion of the duke from all aspects of the king's government.[69] When the king was informed of the Commons' actions, he declared that they would not sit a "minute longer,"[70] and on June 15 he dissolved his second Parliament.

King Charles dissolved Parliament, but he was not yet through with some of the members of the House of Commons. On June 17, Heath wrote a letter to the members of the select committee of twelve, of which Pym was a member, requesting them not to leave London until he had a brief conference with them. When the twelve parliamentarians met Heath they were informed that the king had decided to bring the Duke of Buckingham before the Court of Star Chamber and that the committee of twelve was required to supply proof of their accusations against the Duke. After privately consulting with each other and after obviously seeing through the king's subterfuge, the committee of twelve, with Eliot as its spokesman, wrote to Heath informing him that the charges of the house of Commons against Buckingham were the business of the House of Commons only, "done by Command of the House of Commons and by their direction."[71]

What then could the king do? To prove Buckingham's innocence to the nation at large, Charles ordered the Star Chamber to undertake the trial of the duke. Several witnesses were examined, but the case never came to a judicial hearing in that court. Two years later, on June 16, 1628, King Charles wiped the slate clean for his beloved friend by having the charges against Buckingham taken from the court's files.[72]

Notes

1. *Calendar of State Papers, Domestic, 1625–1626* (Charles I), p. 177—hereafter cited as *C.S.P.D.*
2. George Roberts, ed., *The Diary of Walter Yonge, M.P.* (Westminster: Camden Society, 1882), p. 82.
3. *Cabala* (London, 1691), p. 377.
4. See Charles Dalton, *Life and Times of Sir Edward Cecil, Viscount Wimbledon* (London, 1885), 2: 83–241.
5. See Harold Hulme, "The Sheriff as a Member of the House of Commons from Elizabeth to Cromwell, "*Journal of Modern History* (1929): 361–77.
6. William Knowler, ed., *The Earl of Strafforde's Letters and Dispatches* (London, 1739), 1: 15.

7. *Journal of the House of Lords* (London, 1846), 3:492–93—hereafter cited as L.J.; John Rushworth, *Historical Collections of Private Passages of State, 1618–1649* (London, 1721, 1:202–6—hereafter cited as Rushworth; Thomas Cobbett, ed., *The Parliamentary History of England* (London, 1820), 2:38–43—hereafter cited as *Parl. Hist.*

8. *Journals of the House of Commons* (London, 1803–63), 1:817—hereafter cited as C.J.

9. C.J., 1: 817; *Parl. Hist.*, 2: 46.

10. Whitelocke. In the prevaration of this book extensive use was made of unpublished diaries of the Parliaments of 1624, 1626, and 1628. These are listed in the bibliography. I am using an abbreviation for each diary cited in the text, usually the last name of the author. As the folios in the typescript copies of the original manuscripts are not always given, all folio references have been omitted. References to the diaries can be found from the day cited: Rich; C.J., 1:818.

11. Harold Hulme, "The Leadership of Sir John Eliot in the Parliament of 1616," *Journal of Modern History* 4 (1932): 361–86.

12. Sir John Eliot, *An Apology for Socrates and Negotium Posterorum*, edited by A. B. Grossart, (London, 1881), 1:148–56—hereafter cited as *Neg. Post*; Whitelocke; Rich; C.J., 1: 817.

13. William Laud, *Works*, edited by W. Scott (London, 1847), 6: 246; H. R. Trevor-Roper, *Archbishop Laud* (London, 1940), p. 77.

14. In *Debates in the House of Commons in 1625*, edited by S. R. Gardiner (Westminster: Camden Society, 1873), pp. 178–86—hereafter cited as CD 1625—there are several pages of notes on Pym's report dated April 17, 1626.

15. Rushworth, 1: 209–12; Whitelocke, April 17, 1626; Rich, April 17, 1626.

16. C.J., 1: 818; Whitelocke, February 10, 1626.

17. Whitelocke; Rich; C.J., 1: 823.

18. Harold Hulme, *The Life of Sir John Eliot* (New York, 1957), pp. 109–10.

19. Whitelocke; Rich.

20. Whitelocke; Rich.

21. C.J., 1: 818; Whitelocke, February 10, 1626.

22. Rushworth, 1: 213; C.J., 1: 833.

23. C.J., 1: 834.

24. Rich; Rushworth, 1: 218; C.J., 1: 836.

25. S. R. Gardiner does not believe that the "county" faction was behind Turner's speech; indeed, Pym had just declared that he did not think that this day was a "fit time" to discuss this "business." See S. R. Gardiner, *History of England from the Accession of James I to the Outbreak of the Civil War, 1603–1642* (London, 1883–84), 6:77—hereafter cited as Gardiner; Whitelock; Rich.

26. Rushworth, 1: 217; Whitelocke; Rich.

27. Rushworth, 1: 218; Whitelocke; C.J., 1: 835–36.

28. C.J., 1: 841–42. "Evils—1. Upon question, the Diminution of the Kingdom in Strength and Honour, a general Evil, which we suffer under. 2. Upon question, the Stoppage of Trade, at home and abroad, is another general Evil which we suffer under. Causes:—1. Upon question, the increase of papists, and countenancy of them, a cause of the Evils, under which we suffer. 2. Upon question, the not sufficiently

Guarding of the Narrow Seas, sitence the Dissolution of the Treaties with Spayne, a cause. 3. Upon question, the plurality of Offices in One man's hands; another cause. 4. Upon question, Sales of Honors in general, another cause. 5. Upon question, the conferring of Honours upon such, for Maintenance of whom the King's Revenue exhausted, another cause. 6. Upon question, the Intercepting and unnecessary Exhausting and Misemployment of the King's revenue, a cause. 7. Upon question, the putting to sale of Offices and Places of Judicature, a cause. 8. Upon question, the Delivery of our ships to the French, which were employed against Rochell, a cause. 9. Upon question, the Impositions upon commodities, native and foreign, without the consent of Parliament, a cause. 10. Upon question, the question concerning the Misemployment of the three subsidies and three fifteenths or the Employing of it to the four Ends Mentioned in the [Act] to be respited for further consideration.''

29. Rushworth, 1: 220–21; Whitelocke; Rich.
30. Rushworth, 1: 221.
31. Rushworth, 1: 225–31; Whitelocke.
32. C.J., 1: 843.
33. C.J., 1: 843; Whitelocke.
34. Rushworth, 1: 243–45; C.J., 1: 843–44.
35. Gardiner, 6: 99.
36. C.J., 1: 847; Whitelocke. The eleven other members were Wandesford, Whitby, Eliot, Herbert, Hobby, Digges, Selden, Sherland, Erle, Glanville, and Lake.
37. Whitelocke.
38. C.J., 1: 854; Grosvenor. The seven other managers were Eliot, Digges, Herbert, Whitby, Erle, Selden, and Wandesford. Eventually Glanville took Erle's place and Sherland Whitby's.
39. The term ''country'' suggested that the ''men whom it designated should be regarded as persons of public spirit, unmoved by private interests, untainted by Court influence and corruption, representing the highest good of their local communities and the reaction in whose interests they, and only they, acted.'' Perez Zagorin, ''The Court and Country: A Note on Terminology in the Earlier Seventeenth Century,'' *English Historical Review* 77 (1962): 308–309.
40. Grosvenor.
41. Grosvenor; Whitelocke.
42. Grosvenor; C.J., 1: 857.
43. L.J., 3: 628; C.J., 1: 858–59.
44. R. F. Williams, ed., *The Court and Times of Charles the First* (London, 1848), 1:102–3—hereafter cited as *C&T Charles I*.
45. Rushworth, 1: 302–6; L.J., 3: 595–96.
46. Gardiner, 6: 99.
47. Rushworth, 1: 306–34; L.J., 3: 596–608.
48. Wrongly cited by Pym as clause twenty-nine. William Stubbs, *Selected Charters and Other Illustrations of English Constitutional History*, revised by H. W. C. Davis (Oxford, 1921), pp. 297, 338, 343, 350.
49. Rushworth, 1: 335–39; L.J., 3: 610–12.
50. G. E. Aylmer, *The King's Servants: The Civil Service of Charles I, 1625–1642* (London, 1961), p. 230.

51. Hulme, *John Eliot*, pp. 137–38; Gardiner, 6:103–4.
52. Rushworth, 1: 353–56; L.J., 3: 617–24.
53. Gardiner, 6: 107.
54. Rushworth, 1: 357; L.J., 3: 592.
55. *C&T Charles I*, 1: 101.
56. Grosvenor.
57. Grosvenor; *C&T Charles I*, 1: 103.
58. Grosvenor; Whitelocke; Rich; Rushworth, 1: 358–60.
59. Whitelocke; Grosvenor.
60. Grosvenor.
61. Whitelocke; Grosvenor.
62. Whitelocke; Grosvenor.
63. Grosvenor; Whitelocke.
64. *C&T Charles I*, 1: 107.
65. Grosvenor; Whitelocke.
66. Grosvenor.
67. Whitelocke; Grosvenor.
68. Whitelocke.
69. Rushworth, 1: 400–406; C.J., 1: 871; Whitelocke.
70. *C&T Charles I*, 1: 111–12; L.J., 3: 682; Rushworth, 1: 406.
71. Sir John Eliot, *The Letter Book of Sir John Eliot*, edited by A. B. Grossart (London, 1882), pp. 6–11.
72. Rushworth, 1: 413, 626–27.

7. The Parliament of 1628

Between the dissolution of the second Parliament of Charles I and the summoning of his third lay a period of two long years. Abroad and at home it was a truly momentous period. The fortunes of the hapless Elector of the Palatinate had sunk lower and lower, and the cause which he had so recklessly sponsored had been utterly destroyed. Before the Parliament of 1626 had been dissolved, that mysterious and enigmatic adventurer Wallenstein had completely routed Count Mansfeld at the bridge of Dessau. A few months later the able Count Tilly had put the Danish king, Christian IV, to flight at the battle of Lutter, and before the year was out Count Mansfeld was dead. By 1627, Wallenstein had driven the Danes out of Germany and occupied the Duchies of Schleswig, Holstein, and Jutland.

Defeat was not limited to the failure of the war in Germany, for England's relations with France, having deteriorated dismally, finally culminated in a declaration of war. Several events had combined to reverse the policy of the Anglo-French alliance which had been based upon the marriage of Charles with the sister of the French king, Henrietta Maria. Fundamentally the marriage at first proved rather irksome to Charles, for the queen was wayward, ill-humored, and obstinate. Charles firmly believed that the queen's actions were inspired and applauded by her French attendants,[1] and in August 1626 he had them expelled. Louis XIII was resentful, for he believed that England's actions were an insult to his sister and to France, and a breach of the marriage alliance. Still another cause of the breach was the almost constant friction between ships of the two countries. In September 1626 the English captured three French merchant ships on the suspicion that they carried Spanish goods. French opinion of Englishmen naturally deteriorated and the authorities issued a decree for the total sequestration of English property. A climax was reached in November 1626, when some 200 English ships laden with wine from Bordeaux were seized by the French.[2]

These actions led to English reprisals and on December 3, 1626, an order-in-council was issued for the seizure of all French ships found in English waters. In March 1627 Pennington, the commander of the English fleet, was ordered to attack French merchants wherever they were found. Such an order was a virtual state of war, and Buckingham, filled with genuine enthusiasm for immediate war, began to make plans for a daring expedition for the relief of the beseiged Huguenot stronghold at La Rochelle. The duke and the king believed that the assault upon La Rochelle would be followed by a full-scale rising of the Protestants in France and a nation-splitting civil war. Charles was especially anxious for war. He had not yet abandoned his desire to recover the Palatinate or, indeed, concealed from himself the hindrances that a costly war with France would be to the accomplishment of that design; but he was so thoroughly committed to a war against France that whatever the odds, whatever the consequences might be, he convinced himself that he could not act otherwise.[3] And yet, as throughout his reign, he was desperately in need of money, and it was this desperate need for money that gave rise to the most outstanding domestic event of these two years, the famous "forced loan."

King Charles's attempt to rule without parliamentary subsidies depended entirely upon his ability to finance his government. Since he was not granted any subsidies or tonnage and poundage during the Parliament of 1626, it was obvious that he would need income of a nonparliamentary nature. Various methods were employed. First, under heavy governmental pressure, the city of London reluctantly agreed to lend the king £ 20,000.[4] Second, Charles continued to levy tonnage and poundage as though it had been granted to him by Parliament.[5] Finally, Charles hit upon the idea that a "free loan" should be given by the English people to their king for the defense of the realm. These desperate and piecemeal measures, however, proved inadequate as sources of income for the crown. By September 1626, Charles had painfully discovered that his "free loan" or benevolence was producing not nearly enough money to keep the government solvent. He thus eagerly accepted the advice of Sir Allen Apsley, who suggested that the subsidies that Parliament had failed to vote in 1626 be raised by means of a general "forced loan." The total amount to be collected was fixed at five subsidies, and all taxpayers were to be forced to pay.[6]

In the immediate counties surrounding London, the loan was generally paid; but in the more distant counties there was much greater resistance. Many men simply refused to submit, declaring that the king was taxing them without the consent of Parliament. The Five Knights Case became the single most important event of the whole issue. But many individuals, prominent members of Parliament, such as John Hampden, Sir John Eliot, and Sir Thomas Wentworth, suffered a prison term for failing to pay the loan.[7] The name of John Pym does not appear among those who refused to pay the loan. It is possible that Pym believed that it was not the duty or function of a member of Parliament to oppose the will of the king outside the institution of Parliament. But whatever the reason, this fact is conveniently omitted by John Forster in his life of Pym. Forster claimed, instead, that after the dissolution of the Parliament of 1626, Pym was "thrown into prison and only again released on his return to the third Parliament for Tavistock."[8] This claim is wrong, for neither Pym nor any other member suffered imprisonment for speeches in the Commons after the dissolution of the Parliament of 1626.

In the meantime Buckingham set sail, in June 1627, for France. Although the duke showed himself to be brave, energetic, and resourceful, the enterprise, like the Cadiz expedition, proved to be a failure. Buckingham's plan was not complex: he was determined to occupy the small adjacent island of Rhe, which would give the English a strong base against the French and enable privateers to wreak havoc on French shipping. Unfortunately, the French had strongly fortified St. Martin, the chief town of Rhe, and various attempts to capture the island became a sorry tale of three months' disasters. In October the expedition returned home. Over 4,000 men were lost, Rhe had not been captured, and La Rochelle had not been relieved. Buckingham had once again failed and England was ablaze with humiliation and indignation. One Englishman described the failure of the Rhe expedition as the "greatest and shamefullest overthrow the English have received since we lost Normany."[9] Denzil Holles wrote a fiery letter to his brother-in-law, Sir Thomas Wentworth, blaming the duke for the indecision and confusion of the affair and stating that the only clear aspect of the whole situation was that England had never been so dishonored.[10]

The king's policies and postures seemed disastrous. The forced loan, which had been fairly successful—more than seventy-five percent had been collected of the sum originally expected—had not relieved the desperate financial problems of the government. What was really needed was peace. But even though the French war was opposed by many privy councillors and was universally disliked in England, peace was the last thing that either Charles or Buckingham desired, for they were determined to humiliate the French. Such sentiments and desires necessitated enormous resources, and the militant views of the king and the duke resulted in but one conclusion: although Charles couldn't get along with Parliament, he couldn't get along without it, and Parliament must be summoned. Buckingham, heedlessly or arrogantly blind to the feeling of the country at large, pleaded with the king to summon Parliament. Charles, vividly remembering the bitter sting of his last Parliament, was at first stubbornly opposed to such a policy. But eventually the earnest pleadings of the duke and other courtiers had their effect, and on January 28, 1628, Charles issued writs for the summoning of a new Parliament.[11]

Before the Parliament of 1626 opened, it is claimed that John Pym attended a rather curious meeting. John Forster in his biography of Sir John Eliot wrote that four days before King Charles met his third Parliament, some

> leaders of the Commons met at Sir Robert Cotton's house. The number cannot now be stated; but from a memorandum among Eliot's papers it is certain that among others they comprised himself, Sir Thomas Wentworth and his brother-in-law Mr. Denzil Holles, Sir Robert Phelips, Mr. Pym, Mr. Edward Kryton, Mr. Selden, and Sir Edward Coke; and that their conference turned mainly on the question whether the impeachment of Buckingham should be revived.[12]

Eliot, passionately committed to an attack upon Buckingham, was overruled by the majority, who desired instead to subordinate all grievances to the protection of English liberties which had been violated during the last two years. S. R. Gardiner accepted the existence of such a meeting but offered no other source for it than Forster.[13] A more recent and more thorough examination of the Eliot papers has revealed that no such memorandum exists. Indeed, although it is quite certain that King Charles had been assured by the "country" leaders that they would not attack Buckingham,[14] it is the opinion of the newest biographer of Eliot that the meeting at Cotton's house was more likely the creation of the imaginative mind of John Forster.[15] It is important to note that Forster, in his life of Pym, stated that a somewhat similar meeting took place just before the Parliament of 1621, although those whom he identifies in 1621 are not identical with those who met in 1628.[16]

During this Parliament, as in similar Parliaments throughout the 1620s, John Pym served on a rather large number of committees. On the first day that Parliament met for business, March 20, Pym was appointed to no fewer than four: the committee of privileges, the committee to consider a disputed election in Cornwall, the committee to draw up a petition to the king concerning a general fast throughout the kingdom, and the powerful committee of religion.[17] It is a prominent committeeman that Pym's leadership is most striking, for although he spoke often in this Parliament and spoke well, the real leader of the House of Commons during the Parliament of 1628 was Sir Thomas Wentworth.[18]

During the first three days of the week beginning on Monday, March 24, the House of Commons spent most of its time organizing its attack against the illegal actions of Charles I. On Tuesday March 25, Pym spoke for the first time. Secretary John Coke had just read a message from the king informing the House that the time was growing short and that the pressing necessities of the Crown demanded the speedy passage of the subsidy bill. Pym would have none of it. The members of the House of Commons, he said, all agreed in giving aid and deeply desired to give it, but they could not act out of fear or threat. The nation and the Commons, he declared, had not yet received satisfaction for their present grievances or yet "been thoroughly tempered." Let the debate continue, he concluded, and it will appear whether "we are befitting to do what is required of this House."[19]

That same day, during a debate on illegal imprisonments, Pym spoke again. While they were discussing the matter of imprisonments without due cause, he began, he wished to relate to the

Commons what a "plain" and undeniable right all Englishmen enjoy. That right, he said, was liberty under the law, for even though William the Conqueror had succeeded in conquering England, he never succeeded in conquering the law, because the rule of law was the fundamental and inherent rule of all nations. Pym concluded by asking the many lawyers in the House to explain their interpretations and to cite records and precedents to prove this point.[20] This was done and for the next several days in a committee of the whole house the lawyers, the Cokes and Seldens, dominated the highly technical debates. It was not until April 1 that the House of Commons was able to pass three resolutions against the crown: against imprisonment without showing cause, against denial of *habeas corpus*, and against refusal to allow bail to a person unlawfully imprisoned.[21]

That same Tuesday, April 1, the king sent a message to the Commons urging the members to hasten supply. On the next day the debate on the subsidy bill began. Exactly one week before, on March 26, the crown, in the person of Secretary Coke, had presented fourteen propositions which the government needed to finance, and it was these fourteen points which the Commons discussed on April 2. The debate in which many members participated was long and futile. There was an ominous undercurrent throughout the speeches, although never clearly expressed, that the king could not expect much aid from the Commons until he changed some ministers and redressed grievances. Pym spoke only briefly. He spoke, he said, only to keep the debate from becoming a forum of "guesses and estimations," especially for the "deficits" in the crown's finances, for these may be due to the mishandling of the king's revenues. He concluded by stating that, when the debate came to the discussion of the handling of the debt, "I shall give my opinion."[22]

On the next day, April 3, Secretary Coke read to the assembled House a letter from the king. It was a most conciliatory message, for Charles expressed profound concern for the safeguarding of English liberties, and stated that he not only agreed with the Commons in guaranteeing these liberties, but assured the House that he would join with them to redress their grievances either by way of a bill or a petition. Most of the leaders of the "country" faction, including Eliot, Holles, and Phelips, expressed satisfaction with the king's letter.[23] On Friday, April 4, Pym expressed similar satisfaction. He rose to speak, he said, to "take hold of that gracious message" from the king so that it may be considered and recorded. He would now, he declared, presently retire to the committee chamber and there record it or else "bee showed to his Majesty himselfe."[24]

Pym repeated his satisfaction with the king's message in a long speech later that day, and it was a typical Pym speech, full of impatience at the time wasted on words and not actions. In every great matter, he began, dispatch was far better than discourse. They had great incentive to give, he declared, for they knew the dangers their adversaries planned and, therefore, must give heartily to supply expedition after expedition. The king, he continued, had showed himself to be more a man than a king, and in his manhood he had become a greater king. Let them forget the particulars which surrounded the passage of supply, for a "man in a journey is hindered by asking too many questions." Pym firmly believed that England's peril was as great as it could possibly be, and that those men who complained of this peril and did nothing to alleviate it merely encouraged the enemy. Let them give, he said, and give speedily, for their "wants" were general and they must not sit still while their enemies moved closer to victory. Actions were far more precious than words; the king had taken their desires and grievances to his heart and now should take their gratitude as well. He concluded, however, by asking that all "fifteenths" be omitted from the subsidy bill because "those veynes have bled too much already."[25]

Pym spoke, however briefly, still a third time on this day, when he declared himself in favor of giving five subsidies to the king. The king led them, he said, "the King goes before us, therefore five subsidies."[26] Most of the leaders of the House of Commons, including Sir Edward Coke, Sir Dudley Digges, and Wentworth, were also recorded as supporting five subsidies. Sir John Eliot, however, opposed this position because he feared that such a policy without redress of grievances was both unwise and dangerous.[27] But Eliot's opposition fell on deaf ears, and at last they determined to grant the crown five subsidies. Before the House adjourned for the day, however, Wentworth moved that the Commons pass a resolution that this "gift is upon assurance that the King will settle the fundamental rights of the subject."[28]

During the first three days of the new week which began on

Monday, April 7, these "fundamental rights of the subject" kept the House of Commons active. The members were particularly interested in the billeting of troops and the commissions for martial law. On Tuesday the Commons passed a resolution against all billeting of troops and then provided a subcommittee to prepare a petition to the king on this problem.[29] But there appeared to be very little organization or planned activity on the part of the members and very little agreement on how the House should present their grievances to the king. This problem was quite apparent to John Pym, for on the next day, April 9, during the debate, he rose and asked the House to put all these violations into the hands of a select committee so that some semblance of order could be achieved. After order was achieved, he would move for a petition to the king, and after that a parliamentary law.[30] Wentworth followed Pym and moved for a similar procedure, a petition and then a law.[31] But no decision was reached.

That same day the House decided to adjourn on Thursday morning for the Easter holidays and not to reconvene until the following Thursday.[32] But on April 10, the day selected for adjournment, the speaker read a message from the king suggesting that the Commons stay in session over Easter just as the House of Lords was doing. Eliot and Sir Francis Seymour expressed open dissatisfaction with the king's message. But Sir Edward Coke and John Pym took it all in stride. Coke said he would follow the king's desires, while Pym assented by asking if they couldn't "accept a mocion from his Majestie as willingly as we doe from a member of this House?"[33]

On the following day Sir Edward Coke staggered many members of the House by suggesting the voting of the five subsidies.[34] Sir John Eliot was, with good reason, dumbfounded. He opposed such a move, he declared in a long speech, because if supply were passed, the redress of grievances would come less freely. Pym, however, supported Coke. Why did they grudge the king a day, he asked, when they had spent a whole week upon themselves? "This I thinke will satisfy any subject that desires to know what service wee perform. All our libertyes are in question both with our friends and enemies. I desire wee may goe on cheerfully and speedily."[35] The debate continued with many members participating. Finally Wentworth rose and moved that grievances and supply should go hand in hand, and upon the motion of Sir Nathaniel Rich it was resolved that the subsidies would be paid within one year from the day they were voted.[36]

During the next two weeks following Easter the House of Commons, under the fiery leadership of Eliot, Digges, Wentworth, and Rich, was deeply involved in debating and investigating the illegal acts of the government and laying the foundations for the Petition of Right. John Pym, extraordinarily active with his chairmanship of the committee of religion in preparing the charges against Dr. Roger Maynwaring, spoke only twice, first on April 19, when he introduced a bill entitled "An Act Concerninge Appropriations and Vicaridges." It demanded an increase in the annual stipends for vicars and curates to create a "better" and "fitter" clergy.[37] Pym's second contribution to the Commons' debates occurred on April 24, when he declared that there were some liberties of the subject that had not yet been settled. "Let the House," he said, "proceed to this Business."[38]

During the week of April 21, the Commons had two conferences with the House of Lords. The first was held on the twenty-third; the second, with thirty-six members of the Lower House including John Pym, was held on the twenty-fifth. The Lords attempted to undermine the Commons' goals. In place of the resolutions of the House of Commons on the fundamental liberties of the subject, the Lords proposed five "propositions" that were essentially opposed to what the Lords interpreted as the Commons' "pinching" of the royal prerogative.[39] On Saturday, April 26, the Commons immediately adjourned themselves into a committee of the whole house to discuss the Lords' propositions. Many members spoke and almost all were opposed to the Lords' five propositions. Generally speaking, propositions four and five, especially the latter, which concerned the royal authority "intrinsical" to the king's sovereignty, were particularly difficult for the members to accept. Pym declared that all five were difficult to reconcile to the traditional liberties of the subject, and he moved for a committee to frame several amendments to make those propositions more palatable to the Commons' taste. Pym found the fifth proposition especially obnoxious. He would relinquish it outright and would "never desire to see it become law." But, like Sir Dudley Digges, Pym believed that some of the Lords' propositions, perhaps the first three, might be combined with the Commons' resolutions.[40] Digges also proposed a petition of right, but as the discussion neared a close, Wentworth rose and stated that he believed that a printed bill would be more effective than a petition, which would be lost among the parliamentary rolls.[41] No decision was reached, however, and the House adjourned until Monday, April 28.

On the day, the Commons joined the Lords to listen to the policy of the king from the mouth of Lord Keeper Coventry. He stated that Charles, in order to hasten matters, had decided to guarantee the rights of all subjects, to maintain "all his Subjects in the just Freedom of their Persons and Safety of their Estates," and to govern "according to the Laws and Statutes of this Realm." Coventry concluded by assuring the assembled members of Parliament that they would find "as much security in his Majestie's Royal Word and Promise as in the strength of any Law you can make," and henceforth would never "have cause to complain."[42] The king undoubtedly believed that this conciliatory message would end the nonsense in the Lower House and stimulate the passage of the desperately needed promised subsidies. But the Commons replied by creating a select committee to draw up a bill concerning the liberties of Englishmen, based upon the resolutions passed during the current session of Parliament.[43]

On Tuesday, April 29, the select committee, working with remarkable speed, reported to the House. Sir Edward Coke made the report and introduced the bill. A long debate followed, with most of the discussion over the stating of the cause of imprisonment. A small minority of members did not want the cause of imprisonment stated at all, while still others wanted it only declared on return of the writ of *habeas corpus*. The great majority, however, desired the expressing of the cause at the same time a man was arrested. John Pym sided with the majority. This matter was so terribly great, he said, because it involved the safety of the king and the kingdom. Although he would not differ on the way the majority decided, he would like to see all "fruitless" resolutions omitted. There were two matters under consideration, he declared, which involved the liberties of the English nation. The first was the prevention of injustice. Imprisonment without just cause was against the law of the land, and no king, no council, and no judge, either by God's law or by man's law, could imprison any man without cause. The second was related to the first. If any man were imprisoned without due cause, Pym said, then that man must be released, for it is "the law of the land and the law must be followed." [44]

The House of Commons was unable to reach a decision on the proposed bill of rights, however, and during the remainder of the week, the members discussed and debated the charges against the government. The crown was, of course, not blind to the actions of the Commons, and hardly a day passed without some message from the king. On May 2 Secretary Coke read a letter to the House from Charles advising them to keep themselves "within the Bounds and Laws of our forefathers, without restraining them, or inlarging them by new Explanations, Interpretations, Expositions or Additions in any sort." [45] On Monday, May 5, the king informed the Commons that he would accept a parliamentary bill confirming Magna Charta and six other statutes, but would not accept a bill with "explanations" that would "hazard an encroachment" upon his prerogatives. [46] An impasse had been reached. Charles would allow the Commons only a bill which he sanctioned; the House of Commons wanted all the old laws not only confirmed by a bill, but also fully and adequately explained so that no future king or even the present king in the future could ignore these laws.

On Tuesday morning, May 6, the House of Commons immediately adjourned itself into a committee of the whole house. [47] In a long and heated debate, numerous and memorable opinions were expressed. On the one side were the "courtiers," led by Sir John Coke, who stood firm for trusting the word of the king. On the other side were the more radical members of the "country," led by William Coryton and Edward Littleton, who demanded exactly what King Charles had forbidden, a parliamentary bill confirming all the old laws with additional "explanations." Pym had decided views. The king's word and promise, he said, did not add any strength at all to his coronation oath. Pym declared that he himself did not believe that the king had desired to make the crown the master of the law during the numerous violations of the law since the last Parliament, but he firmly maintained that the king's promise to uphold the laws of the land did not give relief at all to English liberties. Only when the king publicly explained that there would be no more violations, concluded John Pym, or when certain gentlemen whom he trusted were among the privy councillors distributing "justice" to soldiers, then and only then would he "gladly rely or trust to the satisfaction of his Majestie and myne owne conscience."[48]

Secretary Coke rose immediately and reprimanded Pym for what he believed to be audacious remarks. He prayed, said Coke, that they have only interpretations in these matters and not unworthy "stigmas" or "negatives" upon the king's honor. But Pym, refusing to back down, reaffirmed his previous speech. He repeated that he did not believe that Charles's word added anything in substance or matter to his coronation oath. Surely, said Pym, it would be ideal if they needed only the king's word to guarantee liberty under the law, but that situation was possible only if the king understood the law. By binding the king to the law of the land, Pym declared, the House of Commons had a better "ty" on the Crown.[49]

John Pym followed up his assault upon the government by warmly supporting Sir Nathaniel Rich, who cleverly devised a scheme which seemingly embraced the best of both sides, "courtier" and "country." Rich proposed that a vote determine whether the satisfaction already promised by Charles was adequate. If the answer were in the affirmative, then the king should be requested to explain the law and to declare certain practices illegal, so that Parliament would understand just what the king meant when he asked the members to accept his promise to rule according to the traditional laws of the kingdom.[50] In short, Pym, and Rich were obliquely advocating just what Charles had expressly forbidden the House of Commons to do: they were following Littleton and Coryton and seeking a parliamentary bill with "explanations."

With such a variety of proposals, it appeared impossible for the House of Commons to come to any decision. But then Sir Edward Coke rose and moved that the Commons join with the House of Lords in presenting their four resolutions in the form of a petition of right. A petition was not only proper parliamentary procedure, he said, but also not a bill, which had been prohibited by the king.[51] Coke's proposal was not new; Sir Dudley Digges, supported by John Pym, had advocated a petition of right on April 23.[52] But the Digges-Pym proposal was issued during the period when the king had not yet prohibited a parliamentary bill with explanations. What made Coke's proposition so terribly significant was that he had supplied a method of compromise which would solve the dilemma faced by the Commons.[53]

Coke's proposal, however, was not immediately accepted by the House. Sir John Eliot, who spoke next, ignored it entirely and returned to the Rich-Pym proposal. Eventually, however, the significance of Coke's plan penetrated the minds of the members. The Rich-Pym-Eliot proposal was ignored and member after member rose to give his support to a petition of right. Seymour, Glanville, Hoby, and the radical Littleton supported Coke's proposal. Even Pym was converted. He agreed to proceed by way of petition, he said, only if the substance of the petition contained the full substance of the Commons' grievances and not merely the substance of their resolutions.[54] John Pym apparently desired a working and binding petition, a petition with some power to it, not just a diversionary sop.

Coke's proposition soon reached steamroller proportions. Wentworth, Phelips, Rich, and Eliot all fell in line and, finally, a resolution was passed which contained three articles of the Petition of Right. The House of Commons protested against forced loans, against arbitrary imprisonment, and against compulsory billeting of troops. On the next day, the subject of the illegality of martial law came under a long and quite technical discussion,[55] and it was not until May 8 that this abuse was incorporated into the famous petition.[56] The Petition of Right had been passed by the House of Commons, but its acceptance by the House of Lords and the king took many weeks of negotiations.

During the next several days the House of Commons marked time by discussing religion and the subsidy bill. On May 9, Pym made a very long and detailed report on the somewhat obnoxious actions of a certain Richard Burgesse, Vicar of Whitney in Oxfordshire, who had written and used a rather scandalous catechism. Pym was especially angered at Burgesse's activities, for he concluded his report with his own "humble" opinion on the punishment of the vicar. He desired, Pym said, that a petition be delivered to King Charles asking him to imprison Burgesse immediately in the Tower.[57]

The king delayed his prorogation of Parliament, and during the next three weeks the House of Commons, the House of Lords, and the crown were busily engaged in negotiations over the Petition of Right. The Lords showed some reluctance to agree to the wording of the petition. But eventually a compromise was reached when the Commons accepted some minor alterations, and on May 26, the Lords accepted the Petition of Right as presented to them by the Lower House. On Wednesday, May 28, the king addressed both Houses and informed the members that he would consider the petition. The House of Commons had a trump card in the five subsidies, and they would not play it until the king agreed to accept the petition. The next move was up to the crown.

Throughout this long period of great agitation, John Pym was silent except for two times he spoke on rather superficial matters. The first was on May 24, when he moved that the House give a reading of the Petition of Right on the following Monday.[58] The second was on May 27, when he declared that it was necessary for the Commons to have the petition presented as a petition in cooperation with the Lords, or to intercede with the king to put a stronger wording upon it.[59] Pym was undoubtedly busy with his committee of religion gathering evidence for his denunciation of Dr. Roger Maynwaring.

On Monday, June 2, the king, in the person of the lord keeper, addressed the two Houses. After the Petition of Right had been read, the lord keeper declared that Charles desired that all justice be done according to the traditional laws of the land .[60] The men of the House of Commons were extremely disappointed, for no mention was made by the king of the Petition of Right. Charles's answer was in reality worthless, and on the following day Sir John Eliot, after a long silence in the Commons, gave a rousing attack upon the government for its failure in foreign policy and for its failure to destroy Roman Catholics at home. Sir Humphrey May, however, interrupted Eliot and declared that, if Eliot continued with his attack, he would leave the House. May was greeted with cries of "Be gone! Be gone!" But May stayed to hear Eliot out and Eliot did not disappoint him, for the parliamentarian proceeded with a subtle attack upon the Duke of Buckingham, carefully pointing out the failures of the Rhe and Cadiz expeditions caused by the "ignorance and corruption of our ministers." Eliot concluded his fiery speech with a call for a reformation of all these disorders, adding that the first step in such a reformation must be the preparation of a remonstrance to the king.[61]

Eliot was naturally reprimanded by various courtiers in the Commons, but the idea of a remonstrance gained widespread support. No decision, however, was reached that day. On the following day the House, expecting to continue the debate on the proposed remonstrance, was jolted into silence by a message from the king. He was satisfied, Charles declared, with his answer to the Petition of Right and had no intention of altering it and, because he planned to end the session on June 11, there was not any time for the discussion of new grievances.[62]

On the following day, June 5, the Commons convened at seven o'clock, determined to discuss the remonstrance. But before they could proceed to the new grievances, the speaker read to them still another message from the king. Charles reminded the Commons that the day for prorogation had been set, that he had no intention of changing it, and that because there was little time left, he desired that the House "enter not into or proceed with any new business, which may spend greater time, or which may lay any Scandal or Aspersion upon the State, government, or Ministers thereof."[63]

The members of the Commons were staggered and cries of anguish filled the House. The king had forcefully challenged the parliamentary privilege of freedom of speech. Phelips could hardly be heard or understood, for his speech was interspersed with outbursts of weeping. Eliot began to speak but was stopped by the speaker, who, believing that Eliot was about to attack Buckingham, declared that "there is a command laid upon me that I must command you not to proceed."[64] Insult had been added to injury, for the king had not only prohibited freedom of speech but had imposed the prohibition that very day. Tears and wails flowed even more freely until finally an eerie silence dominated the House, and the sad parliamentarians gloomily set comtemplating the fate of their sacred privileges.

Sir Nathaniel Rich broke the silence. Unless the members of the House of Commons spoke now, he declared, they would never be able to speak again. He moved that the Commons assemble with the Lords and explain to them that the liberties of the nation had been violated and the king had been endangered. John Pym agreed with Rich. He could be happy, he said, only when the nation is happy. He supported fully the motion propounded by Rich and moved that a committee be appointed to resolve some general heads of a resolution dealing with the "violations of the liberties and of the dangers to the Kingdome."[65]

Heated discussion followed. After the House had adjourned into a committee of the whole house, the aged Coke rose and denounced Buckingham as the "grievance of grievances." Valentine, Coryton, Sherland, and several other parliamentarians followed Coke and also attacked the favorite. Then, just before the motion "that the Duke of Buckingham shall be instanced to be chief and principal cause of all these evils and enemy to the state" was about to be read, Speaker Finch reappeared in the Commons from his personal conference with the king and informed the House that Charles requested the Commons to adjourn immediately. This was done and the members left the House emotionally spent.[66]

When the Commons met on Friday, June 6, the speaker explained that the king had no intention of prohibiting freedom of speech, for Charles's only intention was to avoid any scandals upon his ministers who had acted in his name. This conciliatory message put the House in a more amiable spirit. A long debate followed in which Pym played a prominent and influential role. The question before the House was whether the Commons should seek another answer from the king on the Petition of Right or whether they should proceed with the proposed remonstrance. John Pym moved that, since the time was short, the House should proceed with the remonstrance and forget for the moment the king's answer to the petition, because it would consume too much of the precious time that remained to the session.[67] This motion was accepted by the House, and the Commons proceeded to discuss the remonstrance to the committee of the whole house.

During the debate that day on the remonstrance, or declaration as it was now called, Pym spoke twice, and both times revealed his religious preoccupation. In the first speech, he said that there were two grievances to be investigated. One concerned the distressing state of Ireland, which, although united to England and subject to the same laws, was audaciously tolerant of Roman Catholics; indeed, declared Pym, the army was commanded only by Catholics. The other grievance concerned the king's finances. Pym moved that the House make a head of the resolution and "inquire after" how the "King's money had been employed." [68] In his second speech, Pym attacked and condemned the Countess of Buckingham for "countenance" of Catholics in England. "More goe to her home," said Pym, "than to Church." [69]

Although many grievous topics had come under the scrutinizing eyes of the men of the Commons—the billeting of Irish troops in England and the decay of trade and shipping—no decision was reached that evening. The House continued the debate, however, the next day. A proposed excise tax was under attack when a message arrived from the Lords informing the Commons that the peers desired a conference with the Lower House concerning the king's answer to the Petition of Right. At that conference the Lords and the Commons agreed to seek a clear and satisfactory answer to the petition. The king's assent was now almost assured, and when the Commons returned to their own house, a committee, of which Pym was a member, was selected to write the preamble to the subsidy bill. [70]

On Saturday afternoon, June 7, King Charles met the assembled Houses and after the Petition of Right was read, he gave his royal endorsement of the famous document. The Petition of Right was now a matter of record and, according to the interpretation given it by both Houses of Parliament, it was the right of Parliament acting in the capacity of the High Court of Parliament "to declare what the law was." [71] It was not a statute, however, and it did not lay down any wide constitutional principles that judges could regard as binding. The great gain of the House of Commons, the great significance of the Petition of Right, was that the Commons had placed on record the king's acceptance of that statement that according to these laws certain definite acts were illegal. The Petition of Right, in brief, was exactly what its name implied: "the recognition of a claim that every subject of the Crown had been wronged in certain specific matters, and that, in the future, in those matters, the law would be observed." [72]

When the Commons reassembled on Monday, June 9, a congenial atmosphere prevailed. The only issues that remained were the subsidy and the declaration. Arrangements were made to pass the subsidy bill, and the rest of the day was spent discussing the various heads of the declaration. Pym spoke only briefly, and that was merely a reiteration of his speech on June 6, when he attacked toleration of Roman Catholics in Ireland. He was here, however, more specific, for he declared that there were at least 40,000 priests in Ireland, "divers friars to preach," and a "Popish Bishop" in every diocese. In Ireland, Pym said, every bishop was out to "make desolate" all Protestants by excommunicating all Catholics who did not boycott Protestant merchants. Pym concluded by stating that this "countenancing of Popery" could not be maintained.[73]

While these memorable political events were taking place, the question of religion was once more raising itself in acute form and, as in the last Parliament, it was to John Pym that the Commons turned as their leader. In late April, the dismal Montague case reared its disruptive head once more. Pym reportd to the House from the committee of religion the "diverse complaints" in "divers Parliaments" against the hated Montague. The whole complicated affair was dug up, hashed over, and then put back into storage. In his report, however, Pym was very careful to point out that because Montague was now a chaplain-in-convocation, he must be treated in a most friendly manner.[74]

It was really Dr. Roger Maynwaring, vicar of St. Giles-in-the-Fields, London, and chaplain-in-ordinary in Charles I, who provoked the most vehement outburst on the part of the House of Commons during the Parliament of 1628.[75] In July 1627, Maynwaring had preached two sermons to Charles asserting in the strongest language possible the absolute duty of all Englishmen to obey the king or suffer eternal damnation as the ordinance of God demanded. Charles, Maynwaring declared, represented the rule of justice as opposed to those men who had refused to pay the forced loan of 1627. The cleric also struck out at those members of Parliament who, instead of upholding the king's designs, sought to satisfy their own "private humours, passions or purposes" by dilatory debate.[76]

These were, in brief, the political and religious arguments of Dr. Roger Maynwaring which King Charles wished to see published for the enjoyment and instruction of his subjects. Archbishop Laud, wisely foreseeing the antagonism such tenets would arouse, remonstrated with the king against the licensing of the sermons. There were certain remarks in the sermons, Laud declared, "which would be very distasteful to the people." [77] But his protest was in vain, for Charles was resolute and he ordered Montaigne, Bishop of London, to license the sermons. [78]

It was clear that once Parliament convened, the House of Commons would attack the doctrines of a man who argued that the authority of Parliament was not necessary for the raising of taxes and subsidies, and throughout the month of March several parliamentarians, notably Sir Robert Phelips, protested against the absolutist tendencies of Maynwaring's sermons. It was, however, John Pym who, as chairman of the committee of religion, emerged as the champion of the Commons' cause. [79]

On June 2, the House issued a declaration against Maynwaring:

> Whereas by the Laws and Statutes of this Realm the free Subjects of England do undoubtedly inherit this Right and Liberty not to be compelled to contribute any Tax, Tallage, Aid, or to make any Loans not set or imposed by common consent, by Act of Parliament.... Nevertheless the said Roger Manwaring in contempt, contrary to the Laws of this Realm hath lately preached in his Majestyes presence two several sermons.... Both which sermons he hath since published inprint in a Book entituled Religion and Allegiance, and with a wicked and malicious intention to seduce and misguide the Conscience of the Kings most excellent Majesty, touching the observation of the Laws and Customs of this Kingdom and of the Rights and Liberties of the Subjects. [80]

On June 9, John Pym carried up to the House of Lords the charges which had gradually been collected against the cleric. As he did with constant regularity, Pym began with an exposition of basic principles and then proceeded to vindicate those principles by citing the case under review as an illustration of the violations of those principles. Pym's speech was a summary of the political creed of the "country" leaders in the House of Commons. Through the mouth of John Pym, the members of the House of Commons rationalized and justified their Petition of Right. [81]

Pym read the charges and appealed to the assembled Lords to

remember the king's answer to the Petition of Right in which Charles professed himself bound in conscience to preserve those liberties of the subject which Maynwaring had lectured the king to ignore. He then proceeded to state the position of the House of Commons against the accused cleric. The best form of government, Pym began, "is that which doth actuate and dispose every part and member of a state to the Common Good; and as those parts give strength and ornament to the whole, so they receive from it again strength and protection in their several stations and degrees." If this harmonious relationship were broken, he continued, the entire social structure and body politic of the state would immediately disintegrate and the result would be chaos. Instead of harmony and mutual interdependence, instead of interrelated and interchangeable support, there would be one side seeking to uphold the old and established government and the other side seeking to introduce a new form of government, and in their struggle and war they would miserably devour each other. The history of the world, Pym declared, was full of calamities of states that refused to recognize such honored principles. "It is true," said Pym, "that time must needs bring some alterations, and every alteration is a step and degree toward a dissolution; those things only are eternal which are constant and uniform." It has been observed by the very greatest of writers, he said, that those states which had been the strongest, the most durable, and the most lasting, were those nations that had reformed themselves according to their "first Institution and Ordinance." And by these means the wisest nations had remedied and repaired the evils and the ordinary and natural defects of time that grew upon their governments.

The "first Institution and Ordinance" of the laws of England, Pym declared, were the "plain footsteps of those laws in the government of the Saxons." They were so vigorous and dynamic, Pym said, that they had outlived the Norman conquest; indeed, they had limited and tied William the Conqueror to the law. It was true, Pym stated, that those laws had often been broken; but they had also been reaffirmed numerous occasions by charters of English kings and by acts of Parliament. And the petitions of the English people upon which those kingly charters and parliamentary acts had been requested, Pym believed, were never based upon any desire for new laws, but were, as in the Petition of Right, merely petitions of right demanding the respect of old and established laws.

It may appear to some men, Pym said, that there was a contradiction in the interpretation that the liberty and freedom of the subject was not only "convenient" and profitable to the people, but most honorable and most necessary to the king. But the contradiction disappeared, Pym declared, when one understood that, if these liberties were dissolved, there would be no more industry, no more justice, and no more courage. And what man, Pym asked, would endanger himself for "that which is not his own?" If all these liberties were withdrawn, there would be no means for Englishmen to support their sovereign. The permanent income of the king, Pym declared, the wardships, "treasure-trove, Felons' goods" and tonnage and poundage, had been so "alienated, anticipated, overcharged with annuities and assignments" that no revenue was left for the very pressing needs of the crown except the voluntary and free gift of the subjects in Parliament. The hearts of the people and their bounty in Parliament, Pym said, was the only permanent revenue of the king which could never be "alienated, anticipated, or otherwise charged and incumbered."

John Pym then moved to the actual charges against Maynwaring, accusing the cleric of attempting to misguide and seduce the conscience of the king, of scandalizing, impeaching, and subverting the "good laws" and government of the kingdom and the authority of Parliament, of alienating the "Royal Heart" of King Charles from his gracious people, and of causing jealousies, seditions, and divisions within the nation. The cleric, Pym charged, had informed the king that Parliaments were not necessary for the raising of taxes, that the slow proceedings of the House of Commons were not effective enough to supply the urgent necessities of the state, that all Parliaments were apt to produce several impediments to the just designs of kings and give rise to numerous occasions for displeasure and discontent, that King Charles was the master of the law, and that anyone who refuted the king's proclamations would suffer eternal damnation.

Pym denied these claims by stating that Parliament was the greatest and highest representation of the commonwealth. If there were no Parliaments, Pym declared, there would be no orderly government; if Parliaments were abolished, mischief and disorders would increase daily and grievances would multiply without any possibility or opportunity to reform and redress them. Could there be any greater means or readier way, Pym asked, to destroy that precious harmony between the king and his subjects or to create chaos and revolution within the state than to rule without Parliament?

Pym accused Maynwaring of abusing his position, of disgracing the Protestant ministry, and of seeking preferential promotions. Maynwaring, said Pym, claimed to be a preacher of God's word and yet he endeavored to employ that rule of justice and goodness for violence and oppression. He claimed to be a messenger of peace, but had attempted to sow the seeds of strife and dissension not only among private citizens but also between the king and Commons. He claimed to be a "Spiritual Father," but, like the evil father in the Bible, he had given his children stones instead of bread, scorpions instead of meat. Maynwaring claimed to be a minister of the Church of England, but, according to Pym, he was like a Jesuit who labored for the destruction of England, for the Jesuit dissolved the oath of allegiance taken by all Englishmen and Maynwaring dissolved the oath of protection and justice taken by the king.

Maynwaring defended his theory of divine-right monarchy by citing several speeches of James I before Parliament and by appealing to the authority of several "Fryers and Jesuits," especially Francisco Suarez. To John Pym this was no defense at all, for "in these times we are to distinguish betwixt the State of Kings in their first original, and between the state of settled Kings and Monarchs that do at this time govern in Civil Kingdoms." Every just king in a peaceful kingdom, Pym declared, was bound to observe and obey the pact made to his people by the laws of the land. All kings must bind themselves to the limits of their own laws, and all men who persuaded their king to do the contrary were "Vipers and Pests" against the crown and commonwealth.

John Pym concluded his long speech by citing several precedents to uphold the opinion of the House of Commons that Maynwaring had committed grievous offenses against the king and the country. He then summarized the charges against the accused and informed the lords that the Lower House desired

8. The Parliamentary Session of 1629

Between the Parliament of 1628 and the parliamentary session of 1629, several events of truly critical importance took place. The first was related to the renewed attempt to relieve the desperately beseiged Huguenot stronghold at La Rochelle. Buckingham had attempted just such an expedition between June and November 1627, when he had sailed to the Isle of Rhe. In May 1628 another force of some fifty ships had been sent to the starving city under the command of the duke's brother-in-law, the Earl of Denbigh. It failed miserably; the mere sight of the well-fortified defense erected by the French had sent Denbigh scurrying home without making the slightest effort either to storm or to evade the fortifications. As soon as Parliament had been prorogued, therefore, Buckingham began preparations for yet another expedition, and it was for the supervising of the supplying of the fleet that the duke had gone to Portsmouth.[1]

Death intervened, however, and saved Buckingham from further disappointments and embarrassments. Buckingham had been, in reality, a rather nimble fugitive from the law of averages; a man as hated as he could not forever escape the bitter sting of an assassin's dagger. On August 23, 1628, John Felton, a disgruntled naval lieutenant, who believed he was executing the general will and desires of Englishmen,[2] struck down the despised duke. King Charles was overwhelmed by the death of his dear and intimate friend and openly wept at the passing of this enigmatic man, whom he now called his "martyr."[3] But England, and especially London, greeted the news with unabashed jubilation. It is said that men went about with smiling faces and that toasts were drunk to the health of the assassin. "God bless thee, little David," cried one woman to Felton as he passed through Kingston-upon-Thames on his way to the Tower, while others cried out with a general voice, "Lord comfort thee! The Lord be merciful unto thee!"[4]

The most important question was now who would take the esteemed place of Buckingham. No one, of course, ever really replaced Buckingham in King Charles's affections or in the inti-

macy of his political confidence. Nevertheless, the second significant event of the recess was that the king had discovered an
important new advisor and it was none other than Sir Thomas
Wentworth. The various reasons for the "apostasy" of Wentworth do not concern us here, for there have been and there
probably always will be numerous opinions concerning his diverse motives. But as a summation of those very motives, one
may readily accept the balanced judgment of the best and most
recent biographer of the Earl of Strafford, who believed that there
was no sense of betrayal in his actions. A practical man, Wentworth judged men and events by their usefulness toward efficient
government and his own advancement, and because he saw that
government by both the crown and Parliament was not working,
he believed that the crown must govern until a correct harmony
between them could be achieved, for the crown was the supreme
authority in power.[5]

Among Wentworth's colleagues in the last session of Parliament, the news of his defection to the king undoubtedly provoked
reactions of surprise, bitterness, and cynicism. Denzil Holles
looked upon his brother-in-law with indignant contempt.[6] Years
later, while in prison, Sir John Eliot wrote that Wentworth's
"covetousness and ambition were both violent, as were his ways
to serve them . . . and those affections raised him to so much
pride and choler as any opposition did transport him."[7] And it
would be written that John Pym, perhaps the most able of all his
colleagues in Parliament, had unhesitatingly declared to Wentworth that he was "going to be undone; and remember also that,
though you leave us now, I will never leave you while your head
is upon your shoulders."[8] This is most assuredly wonderful
drama, for the great parliamentary leader had declared a poeti-
cally prophetic, indeed, fatalistic challenge to the future political
advisor of Charles I. With this declaration in mind, we may hold
our breath as the blade of the axe falls upon the poor, defenseless
head of the Earl of Strafford. But we need not hold it for long, for
this remark is more appropriate to theaters or novels than to the
political life of John Pym. This declaration is most decidedly
poor history. It just does not seem possible for Pym to have
uttered such a statement, for those words were the words of a
revolutionary, and Pym was certainly no revolutionary in 1628.

There was simply no logical reason for John Pym to declare anything so extreme, and the quote looks more and more like a melodramatic tale constructed after the event.

When Parliament finally assembled on Tuesday, January 20, King Charles, confident of his good success with this Parliament,[9] did not even deign to address the Houses on his present program or future plans. The House of Commons, however, as soon as they proceeded to business on the next day, indicated that they looked upon the events of the past months with an entirely different interpretation. John Selden immediately moved for a committee to be appointed to examaine the various "innovations" that had been imposed against the Petition of Right upon the liberties of Englishmen by the crown since the end of the last session of Parliament. John Pym followed Selden and moved that all debate on the subject be deferred until the following week because there were so very many members absent. Eliot agreed with Pym, but argued that it was perhaps "good to prepare things." He desired, he declared, that a select committee be chosen to investigate how the "Liberties of the Kingdom be invaded."[10] This select committee was accepted by the Commons, and Pym, Eliot, Rich, Selden, and four others were chosen as members.[11] Yet this special committee, which had such a promising birth, died rather ignominiously; by the end of January the entire issue of the investigation of the liberties of the subjects in relation to the Petition of Right was discarded. It was put into cold storage so that other issues could be given greater exposure.

During this short and explosive session the members of the House of Commons were mainly concerned with the discussion of religion and tonnage and poundage. On January 26, Francis Rous, Pym's stepbrother, introduced the delicate subject of religion into the debates. He made a rousing speech in which he issued a clarion to all members of Parliament to stand firm against the encroachments of Catholicism, that "confused mass of errors, casting down Kings before Popes, the precepts of God before the traditions of men, living and reasonable men before dead and senseless stocks and stones," and against the encroachments of Arminianism, that confused error "that maketh the grace of God lackey it after the will of man, that maketh the sheep to keep the shepard, that maketh mortal seed of an immortal God."[12]

After several speakers had thoroughly denounced both papists and Arminians, the whole subject of religion was referred to a special committee. As in every other committee of religion during the reign of Charles I, the chairman was John Pym.[13]

On the next day Pym, obviously involved in some fundamental spadework for his committee, reported to the House that he wished to examine the remonstrance presented to the king during the last Parliament so that he might see exactly what was written on it concerning religion. Informed by the clerk that the Lord Privy Seal had the remonstrance by order of the king, Pym decided that the committee of religion would not proceed in any other matter concerning religion until the "House were aquainted therewith."[14]

That same day, however, Pym delivered a long speech elaborating his views on Arminianism, Catholicism, and the English constitution. In a truly brilliant address, Pym assailed the corruptions and hindrances in the Church of England. There were two principal religious diseases, he argued, the one old, the other new; the old was popery, the new was Arminianism. Roman Catholicism had grown enormously in recent years, he said, for several reasons: the recusancy laws were not enforced, the Catholics were being given "countenance" and employment, and superstitious rites and ceremonies had been brought into England and allowed to grow. What most Englishmen desired, Pym asserted, was a return to the wonderful purity of religion that characterized the reign of Edward VI in both the articles set forth in 1552 and the catechism of Edward VI, in both the writings and teachings of Peter Martyr, Martin Bucer, and John Wycliffe, and by the "constant profession sealed by the blood of so many martyrs as Cranmer and Ridley." What Englishmen craved, Pym delcared, was a return to the purity of practice exemplified in the Elizabethan Thirty-nine Articles and in the Stuart Lambeth Articles. What Englishmen wanted to know, Pym said, was why, how, and when Catholics and Arminians had been advanced in positions of power, and what manner of preachers and preaching had been directed to Charles I.

John Pym then proceeded to advise the House of Commons to reserve to itself the right of preserving the "purity" of the Established Church, for it was the "only body" which could successfully deal with the "mischiefs" of Catholicism and Arminianism. Only Parliament could adequately meet those dangers, and it was the duty of Parliament in general, and of each Christian in particular, to use every possible means to redress those evils. Pym believed that Parliament must become the watchdog of the English Church, and that whoever argued that it was neither the right nor the function of Parliament to judge matters of faith and religion was ignorant of established and fundamental truths, for Parliaments had confirmed the acts of general councils, whose conclusions on matters of faith were not accepted or received until they had been authorized by Parliament. Moreover, Parliaments had enacted laws for trials of heretics by jury, and had punished the Earl of Essex for "countenance" of heretics. But above all, Pym believed that Parliament possessed the right simply because there was no other institution which could "meet with this mischief but the court of Parliament. The Convocation cannot because it is but a provincial Synod, only of the jurisdiction of Canterbury, and the power thereof is not adequate to the whole Kingdom; and the Convocation of York may perhaps not agree with Canterbury. The High Commission cannot, for it hath its authority derived from Parliaments, and the derivative cannot prejudice the original, the judgment of the King and of the three estates of the Whole Kingdom." [15]

Pym's speech is highly significant, for he clearly saw the intimate relationship of all the various questions by which the Stuart rule had been agitated. He argued that the true path to safety lay exclusively in the combined supremacy of the crown in Parliament, and of the harmony of these two institutions. All other institutions—ecclesiastical, judicial, military—must work in accordance with those rules and policies established by the king and Parliament together. At the same time, Pym clearly pleaded for parliamentary control of religion. By arguing that the House of Commons should become the guardian of purity within the Established Church, Pym rejected the exclusive sovereignty of the king, the high commission, and the convocation of the clergy in ecclesiastical matters. Pym wished to control and purify the English Church in accordance with the ideals and aspirations of Parliament. John Pym's state in matters of religion was to be composed not of the king and clergy, but of the king and the

House of Commons, possibly even the House of Commons alone.

It was finally resolved that the committee of religion would have precedence over all other committees, and that it "should be taken into consideration by a committee of the whole house which would meet the next day." But it was not until two days later, on January 29, that the Commons transformed itself into a committee of the whole house for religion. Pym was in the chair, and after some introductory remarks by Rudyard and Harley, Sir Eliot rose and gave the most important speech of the day, attacking the king's declaration on religion which was published early in December 1628.[16] In this declaration King Charles maintained that the Thirty-nine Articles possessed the fundamental word of God and ordered his subjects "to continue in the uniform possession thereof." Eliot agreed that the king was the supreme head of the English Church, but argued that any religious differences arising from "external policies," "injunctions," "canons," and "other constitutions" would be decided solely by the clergy in convocation. It was this part of the king's declaration that Eliot interpreted as a danger to religion. True religion, he declared, was indeed found in the Thirty-nine Articles, but differences might arise over the ambiguous meaning of some of the articles, and those clerics in power would then have the golden opportunity of expressing their own views, with the result that Catholicism and Arminianism would be both introduced and strengthened. "Witness the men [Neile and Laud] complained of," he said, "and you know what power they have. Witness the man nominated, Mr. Montague. I reverence the order, I honour not the man; others may be named as bad." Eliot concluded that the sole remedy lay with the House of Commons, and that Parliament must be given the power to determine who violated the Thirty-nine Articles.[17]

Eliot's speech was revolutionary, and John Pym had expressed similar sentiments two days before. But speeches are one thing and actions are another, and the members of the House of Commons shrank from the uncongenial path upon which they had been invited to stroll by Pym and Eliot. The committee of religion, even with John Pym at its head, in effect rejected Pym's and Eliot's proposals. A resolution was passed and approved by the Commons upholding the Thirty-nine Articles of the Established Church. Pym read to the House the frame of the Declaration:

> That we the Commons, assembled in Parliament, do claim, profess and avow, for truth, that Sense of the Articles of Religion, which were established in Parliament, in the 13th Year of the Reign of Elizabeth which, by the publick Act of the Church of England, and by the general and current Expositions of the writers of our Church, hath been delivered unto us; and we reject the Sense of Jesuits, Arminians and of all other, wherein they differ from it.[18]

During the rest of the session religion was quite prominent in the debates of the House of Commons.[19] Led by Eliot, Phelips, and Pym, the House incessantly attacked, and attacked furiously, those individual prelates who were suspected of being lenient on Arminianism. First Laud and then Neile and then Montague came under the biting and stinging assault of the Commons. Neile in particular was singled out for a most damaging attack. Montague's confirmation as Bishop of Chicester was thoroughly examined and questioned. John Pym, who seems to have selected Montague as his special whipping boy, made a full report to the House of all the proceedings against Montague from the last Parliament of James I. The royal pardons for Montague, John Cosin, and Roger Maynwaring were ordered investigated. The House of Commons, moreover, went into violent rages against Roman Catholics. Jesuits had been arrested and then released; of those brought to trial, two were acquitted. Why, asked numerous members of the Commons, were papists allowed to walk audaciously on the streets of London?[20]

It is ironic that the prolonged attack on Roman Catholics and Arminians throughout this session produced little more than a harmless resolution.[21] This resolution, called Heads and Articles, repeated the grievances of the Commons made in debate. In very great detail the articles gave evidence of the rather alarming growth of "Popish, Arminian, and superstitious opinions and practices." Catholicism and Arminianism were spreading rapidly in Europe and in England, it stated, because "those persons who have published and maintained such Popish, Arminian, and superstitious opinions and practices, and who are known to be unsound in Religion, are countenanced, favoured and preferred,'' while the more orthodox were ''discountenanced and hindered'' by Bishops Laud and Neile. The articles declared that bold and unwarranted new ceremonies had been introduced and practiced: altars were erected and candlesticks had been placed on them; women were required to use veils; congregations had been compelled to stand at the chanting of the *Gloria Patri*; pictures, lights, and images had been brought into the churches; prayers were said to the East and churchgoers had crossed themselves *"ad omnem motum et gestum."* To the list of these complaints was added a list of "ten remedies." The penal laws were to be fully and effectively executed, compulsory uniformity was to be enforced, and severe punishments were to be inflicted upon those individuals who published or taught anything contrary to the orthodox religion. Moreover, bishoprics and other ecclesiastical preferments were to be conferred soley upon the most pious, the most learned, the most orthodox of men. But perhaps the single most important remedy advanced by the Heads and Articles was the demand that "Parliament be considered of, for providing competent means to maintain a godly and able minister in every parish of their Kingdom." The House of Commons, in brief, desired to construct a network of preachers throughout the nation. This vanguard of puritanical conformity would be controlled and guided by parliamentary supervision.[22] These remedies, of course, would have brought forth a quiet, but thoroughly effective religious and political revolution in Stuart England.

It is clear that John Pym was the principal author of these Heads and Articles. He was, first of all, chairman of the committee of religion and deeply involved and extremely interested in the debates on religion and in the framing of all religious declarations and resolutions. The declaration, moreover, was written in the style and language of John Pym. "Heads and Articles," "remedies propounded," "Catholicism and Arminianism countenanced," and many other phrases and stylistic habits of this document were the very words, the very declarations of John Pym. The articles, furthermore, may be fairly compared with the Grand Remonstrance of the Long Parliament. That document, too, was a summing up of debates, a summary, as it so happens, by a committee headed, as the committee of 1629, by John Pym. Both the Heads and Articles and the Grand Remonstrance were written to justify the case of the House of Commons to the English people. Indeed, a careful reading of the two together reveals that especially along the issue of religion there were some very great similarities.[23]

While these emotional and delicate debates on religion were proceeding, a similar set of emotional and delicate debates were taking place on the problem of tonnage and poundage. No sooner had Parliament opened its door for business than this issue was the subject of heated discussions. On Tuesday, January 22, John Rolle, a merchant and member of Parliament, informed the Commons that "his goods were seized by the customers for refusing to pay the customs by them demanded, although he told them, what was adjudged to be due by law he would pay." Phelips and Eliot immediately took up the defense of the privileges of the House of Commons. "Great and weighty grievances," declared the fiery Phelips; "cast your eyes which way you please, and you shall see violations on all sides. Look on the liberty of the subject, look on the privilege of this House; let any man say if ever he read or saw the like violations by inferior ministers that overdo their commands. They knew the party to be a parliament man; nay, they said, if all the Parliament were in you, this we would do and justify." To Sir John Eliot there were three essential points: the right of John Rolle, the right of individual Englishmen, and the rights and privileges of the House of Commons. To him and others—but not necessarily to John Pym—the last was the most important.[24] A committee was eventually selected to investigate and report on the incident, and John Pym was named to this committee of twenty.[25]

The Commons, however, was faced with a difficult constitutional problem, for in spite of the many impassioned arguments for the privileges of the House, no infringement on the privileges of the Commons could really be proved. When the Lower House enthusiastically accepted the case of John Rolle, they were on legal ground that was entirely insecure. A member of Parliament's right to freedom from arrest while Parliament was in session was a well-established and recognized privilege. But Rolle had not been arrested and there was certainly no clearly defined precedent to prove that the privilege of freedom from arrest was applicable to the member's goods as well.[26] Rolle's merchandise, moreover, had been seized on October 30, 1628, more than four months after the close of one session of Parliament and more than two months before the opening of another. King Charles, however, apparently believed that it would be unwise to allow the debates to continue without some words from himself. On January 24, he summoned Parliament to Whitehall and attempted to placate the Commons with a speech in which he declared that he had no intention of levying tonnage and poundage by his hereditary prerogative:

> For it ever was and still is my intention in my speech at the ending of the last Session concerning this point was not to challenge Tonnage and Poundage as a right, but *de bene esse*; showing you the necessity, not the right by which I was to take it until you had granted it to me; assuring myself according to your general professions, that you wanted time not will to give it to me.[27]

The king's speech created a most favorable impression within the House of Commons. "This speech," wrote Sir Francis Nethersole to the king's sister, Queen Elizabeth, "has given great satisfaction."[28] The Commons, nevertheless, refused to consider passing a tonnage and poundage bill introduced by Sir John Coke on January 26 until the liberties of the House were secured. The Commons again refused to pass the bill two days later; indeed, the House presented a declaration to the king objecting to the manner of presenting the bill in the name of King Charles by one of his own ministers.[29] In the meantime, debates on religion chiefly occupied the House of Commons for several days.

Tonnage and poundage was again brought to the attention of the Commons on February 10, when John Rolle informed the House that "since his last complaint of the breach of Liberties of this House, his warehouse hath been locked up by one Massey a pursuivant; and that yesterday he was called forth from the Committee in the Exchequer Chamber; but that since he received a letter from Mr. Attorney that it was a mistake."[30] The tempers of many parliamentarians were greatly aroused. Phelips declared that the members of the House of Commons were "made the subjects of scorn and contempt," while Eliot, committing the "error of identifying the liberties of the Kingdom with those of the Commons,"[31] argued that the privileges of the House had been violated.[32]

The House of Commons sent Acton, Sheriff of London, to the Tower for giving unsatisfactory answers to the seizure of John Rolle's merchandise. And on February 19, the custom officers[33] were summoned to the bar of the Commons to answer for their actions:

> Mr. Dawes, a customer was called to the Bar and was asked by what authority he took Mr. Rolles goods. He said by virtue of a warrant sent from his Majesty, and being asked if Mr. Rolles demanded privilege, he said he knew Mr. Rolles was a Parliament man, and had privilege for his person, but not for his goods as he conceived. And he said he did not inform the Lords of the Council that Mr. Rolles demanded privilege of Parliament.[34]

Richard Carmarthen, another customs official, gave similar evidence.

Sir John Eliot intervened and declared that "we see it is not only for the interest of the goods of a member of this House, but also for the interest of this House; if we let this go, we shall not be able to sit here." Eliot, in brief, wanted the actions of these men to be interpreted solely as a violation of the privileges of the House of Commons, and not from the broader view of the rights of all Englishmen. Eliot urged the Commons to discuss the question of whether the customs officials were delinquents or not. "Here are two degrees, or steps," he said, "to come to our conclusion: the first whether we conceive these parties to be delinquents or no, and to have violated our privileges, whether one or both; and if they be delinquents, what punishments they shall meet."[35]

John Pym then rose and presented a remarkably different interpretation of these very important constitutional matters. This was neither the time nor the manner, he argued, to debate the issue, for the House of Commons must first decide the principal issue and then settle each individual incident. The liberties of the kingdom have been broken, moreover, and these liberties are far superior to the liberties of the House of Commons, for above everything else, public liberty must be determined and guaranteed. The liberties of this House, declared Pym, are inferior to "the liberties of the Kingdom," and to determine the privileges of Parliament before those of the nation is "but a meane matter." The major goal for the House of Commons in this issue, Pym, believed, was to establish the fundamental liberties of the subjects, "and to take off the Commission and Records and orders which are now against us." The way to accomplish this goal and to "sweeten the business with the King and to rectify ourselves," Pym concluded, was to settle these matters first, and then and only then proceed to the vindication of parliamentary privileges.[36]

Pym's speech reveals a masterful tactician playing a wise and moderate policy. Eliot's espousal of the violation of the privileges of the House of Commons was, according to Pym, a petty question when compared with the individual rights of all Englishmen and should be recognized as such and kept in the background, while the great cause of the liberties of Englishmen should be recognized and brought into the foreground. Pym firmly believed that the main business, indeed perhaps the only business that really mattered, was the firm establishment of the rights of Englishmen; when these were guaranteed, then the Commons should seek the establishment of their parliamentary privileges. No other incident more clearly illustrates the somber contrast between the political qualities of John Eliot and John Pym. Eliot was most assuredly a great leader for parliamentary freedoms, but John Pym was a more able national statesman.

John Selden, however, did not agree with Pym's interpretation. In the past, he argued, if an issue involving parliamentary privilege had been raised, all other business was laid aside until the Commons had settled the problem to their satisfaction. Eliot then rose and struck back at Pym. He would never "undervalue" or deprecate the privileges of the House of Commons, he said, for the liberties of Parliament are not inferior to the liberties of the nation. Indeed, Eliot maintained that the liberties of the Commons were the very basis of the liberties of the whole kingdom, for if the Commons were not there to debate their privileges, there would be no freedom in the nation.[37]

Eliot had scored a point, for there was certainly an element of truth in his speech—the House of Commons was undoubtedly the major institutional roadblock to Stuart absolutism. But the policy proposed by John Pym was not left entirely without support. Dudley Digges and Francis Seymour accepted it warmly, and Sir Humphrey May, chancellor of the Duchy of Lancaster, not only supported Pym's interpretation but raised the terrible ire of Eliot by suggesting that the king's sovereignty was being questioned. Eliot countered by clothing himself in the robes of privilege and declaring that the essential question was "whether an act done or pretence of the King's command to be a breach of the priveledges be a delinquencey or noe; he hath heard that the King cannot command a thing which tends to the breach of parliament privilege."[38]

Despite the wise counsel of Pym and its warm support from Digges, Seymour, and May, the House of Commons enthusiastically followed the lead of Sir John Eliot. It was resolved

> That this House shal now take into consideracion the violacion of this House by Mr. Dawes and Carmarthen. Resolved that this business of Dawes and Carmarthen shalbe debated now of att a Grand committee: Mr. Herbert in Chayre.[39]

Sir John Eliot, by force of his eloquence and the vigor of his beliefs, had won the majority of the House of Commons to his side. Pym, whose much broader proposal had been rejected, would try still another approach, and when this too failed, he would relapse into silence.

On the next day, Sir John Wolstenholm, the third customs official, appeared before the Commons to answer for his part in the case of John Rolle. His answers were substantially the same as those of Dawes and Carmarthen. The debate in the committee of the whole house involved all three officials. Two questions were outstanding: the first, whether the three men had acted in their own behalf in order to make money, or whether they had acted in the name of the king; the second, whether John Rolle had claimed privilege of Parliament when his goods were seized.

Pym, who obviously was deeply concerned with the problem as it related to Charles's sovereignty, moved that the lease be read showing that the customs officials acted as officers of the king under the "Kings command: as officers to the Exchequer: injunctious of that Court." [40] A little later in the debate Pym spoke again. He remembered, he declared, that on the affadavit in the exchequer, it indicated that "Wohstenholme, Dawes, and Carmarthen did not take the said goods for any interest of their owne or pretense of interest of their own but only for the King's use; it may be that there is some covenant or condicion in the lease that the profit of tonnage etc. is to be collected only for the King, and afterwards is to be distributed among the Farmers to reimburse the money they have advanced; and that they seized the same as officers not as Farmers." [41] Pym apparently wanted the Commons to recognize and understand the true significance of the problems at hand—that to persist in an attack upon the custom officials would inevitably result in a direct challenge to the king's sovereignty. It was Humphrey May who first grasped the significance of the problem, but it was John Pym who took up its defense. The question of the customers' responsibility was the question of King Charles's sovereignty, and that was the heart of the matter. If it were decided against the king, a "complete revolution would have been affected in the relations between the King and his subjects, as those relations had been understood by four generations of Englishmen." [42] John Pym wished simply to get back to what he considered the far more important issue—the individual rights of individual Englishmen. It was not only the broadest and wisest position, but, more significantly, it did not directly challenge the king's prerogative as did the policy of Sir John Eliot.

After a rather long and legalistic debate on the privileges of a member of Parliament, the Commons passed a resolution declaring that members of Parliament should have privilege for their goods as well as for their persons. [43] But did this privilege mean against the king? This, of course, was the very essence of the problem. As Dudley Digges, who supported Pym's position, rightly pointed out, it was virtually impossible to avoid involving the interests of the king in the Commons' claim. The distinction between the customs officials as private individuals and as royal officials was so terribly delicate that it would fall apart with just a little reasoning or debate. If you give John Rolle privilege, reasoned Digges, "to whom will you direct your warrant: at length it will tend to examine the King's interest. Where the Kings officer leaves there the Farmer begins: and nothing yet done by the Farmer."[44] Diggs and Pym had exposed the dilemma of the House of Commons.

King Charles now came galloping into this battle of words, mind, and wit. On Monday, February 23, Sir John Coke, speaking in "plain" English, informed the House that

> his Majesty commanded me to tell you, that it concerns him in an high degree of justice and honour; that truth cannot be concealed, which is that they [Customers] did was either by his own direct order and command, or by order of the council-board, himself being present and assisting, and therefore he will not have it divided from his act.[45]

It was now clear that the House of Commons could not proceed without challenging the king, and they could not do that without revolution. So the House adjourned until February 25. On the 25th the House met, only to be informed that King Charles desired an adjournment for a week. The Commons could only obey and wait for March 2, the day Parliament would reassemble.

The memorable events of March 2 have been described countless times.[46] The excitement, the drama, and the significance of these events not only make good reading, but they are vitally important to English constitutional history. The king was determined to put an end to the House of Commons' questioning of his prerogatives and to their interference in ecclesiastical matters. Charles shared his father's belief that no bishops resulted in no king, and he therefore ordered the speaker to adjourn the House. "Noe noe," came the cry from the Commons on all sides. When the speaker attempted to leave the chair, two members, one of whom was Denzil Holles, restrained him until three resolutions were read and passed by acclamation of the Commons. The resolutions declared that whoever introduced Catholic or Arminian innovations in religion should be considered a capital enemy of the king and kingdom, that whoever advised the taking and levying of tonnage and poundage without parliamentary consent should also be considered a capital enemy, and that whoever paid tonnage and poundage, under those conditions, was also deemed a traitor to the liberties of the English nation. The House of Commons then voted its own adjournment.[47] Sir John Eliot, the leader of the events of March 2, and his radical friends, even though they were not conscious of their revolutionary behavior,[48] had given to the world more than a declaration of their intentions; they had provided a classic demonstration of impetuosity which left no doubt that to achieve their aims, they were quite willing to follow a course that was in every facet revolutionary.[49]

March 2, 1629, was an especially important day in the constitutional history of England; it was in many ways a watershed. It was interpreted by many as a sad day for England. Sir Simond D'Ewes wrote that March 2 was the "most gloomy, sad and dismal day for England that happened in five hundred years last past."[50] It became an even sadder day for John Eliot, for he died in the Tower for his contributions to the events of March 2. We do not know, however, whether it was a sad day for John Pym. Undoubtedly he did not wish to see the dissolution of Parliament, for he maintained throughout the 1620s that Parliament had much work to do throughout the nation; but he also, undoubtedly, did not desire to see a reenactment of the events of that day. John Pym did not play an active role in the drama of March 2. Perhaps it was because he was not there, but there is really no way of discovering this factor, and it would be far better to assume that he was present than that he was not. Perhaps he was silent because he was angry that his more moderate proposals had been overborne by John Eliot's eloquent and electrifying remedies. But this would be the reason of a petty and grasping individual, and John Pym was neither petty nor grasping. It seems probable, instead, that Pym was a silent spectator to the events of March 2 simply because he had ceased to identify himself with the revolutionary and audacious actions of John Eliot and he had ceased to cooperate with them in the House of Commons.

King Charles dissolved Parliament a week later. If Charles had had his way, he would never have summoned another Parliament. He ruled for eleven long years without parliamentary support, and only a Scottish war forced him to call another Parliament. And when he summoned that Parliament in the summer of 1640, it was John Pym who led the House of Commons in opposition to the crown. Pym, with nine years of parliamentary experience and eleven years of witnessing what he believed to be Stuart tyranny, had finally concluded that the King of England must be limited by the law and that the law must be interpreted by the king and Parliament together. The king in Parliament was John Pym's basic philosophy and he promoted a revolution and waged a civil war to achieve it.

Notes

1. *Calendar of State Papers, Domestic, 1628–1629* (Charles I), p. 247—hereafter cited as *C.S.P.D.*

2. Edward, Earl of Clarendon, *The History of the Rebellion and Civil Wars in England*, edited by W. D. McCray (Oxford, 1888), 1:54–56; R. F. Williams, eds., *The Court and Times of Charles the First* (London, 1848), 1:386–88—hereafter cited as *C&T Charles I*.

3. *C&T Charles I*, 1: 396; Clarendon, 1: 62.

4. *C.S.P.D., 1628–1629*, p. 268; *C&T Charles I*, 1: 394–96.

5. C. V. Wedgwood, *Thomas Wentworth: First Earl of Strafford, 1593–1641* (London, 1961), pp. 70–71.

6. Arthur Collins, ed., *Historical Collections of the Noble Families of Cavandise, Holles . . .* (London, 1752), p. 95.

7. Sir John Eliot, *An Apology for Socrates and Negotium Posterorum*, edited by A. B. Grossart (London, 1881), 1:118—hereafter cited as *Neg. Post.*

8. James Welwood, *Memoirs of the Most Material Transactions in England for the Last Hundred Years to 1688* (London, 1700), 6: 47.

9. John Rushworth, *Historical Collections of Private Passages of State, 1618–1649* (London, 1721), 1:643—hereafter cited as Rushworth; S. R. Gardiner, *History of England from the Accession of James I to the Outbreak of the Civil War, 1603–1642* (London, 1883–84), 7:30.

10. Wallace Notestein and Francis H. Relf, eds., *Commons Debates for 1629* (Minneapolis, 1921), pp. 4–5—hereafter cited as CD 1629; Thomas Fuller, *Ephemerus Parliamentaria* (London, 1654), p. 235—hereafter cited as *Eph. Parl.*

11. *Journals of the House of Commons* (London, 1803–63), 1:920—hereafter cited as C.J.

12. CD 1629, pp. 12–14, 109; Rushworth, 1: 645–46.

13. CD 1629, pp. 64, 119, 121, 128, 130, 138, 144, 191, 204, 207, 213.

14. Ibid., p. 111.

15. Ibid., pp. 20–21; Rushworth, 1: 647; Thomas Cobbett, ed., *The Parliamentary History of England* (London, 1820), 2:446–47—hereafter cited as *Parl. Hist.*

16. S. R. Gardiner, ed., *The Constitutional Documents of the Puritan Revolution, 1625–1660* (Oxford, 1951), pp. 75–76.

17. CD 1629, pp. 24–28, 116–17; *Eph. Parl.*, p. 243.

18. C.J., 1: 924; Rushworth, 1: 649–50.

19. The "True Relation" manuscript in CD 1629, pp. 65–69, credits Pym with a long speech on religion. Actually it was Richard Grosvenor who authored the speech. See Edward Hughes, "A Durham Manuscript of the Commons Debates of 1629," *English Historical Review* 74 (1959): 672–73.

20. CD 1629, pp. 36–39, 64–72, 122–23, 144–46, 152–54, 215–20; C.J., 1: 926.

21. Martin J. Havran, "Parliament and Catholicism in England, 1626–1629," *Catholic Historical Review* 44 (1958): 273–89, argues that most members of Parliament knew that Catholicism was too weak to seriously threaten the Established Church, and that the main reason an inordinate amount of time was spent exposing and attacking Catholics and Arminians was because this device could be used as an effective means of forestalling the granting of subsidies and, therefore, a convenient method of attacking the "absolute monarchy" of Charles I.

22. CD 1629, pp. 96–101.

23. Ibid., p. 101, n.a.

24. Ibid., pp. 7–8; Rushworth, 1: 643–44.

25. C.J., 1: 921.

26. John Hatsell, *Precedents of Proceedings in the House of Commons* (London, 1785), 1: 67–99.

27. CD 1629, pp. 10–11; Rushworth, 1: 644–45.

28. *C.S.P.D., 1628–1629*, p. 456.

29. CD 1629, pp. 12, 23, 29–30, 108–10; Rushworth, 1: 651–52.

30. CD 1629, p. 55; Rushworth, 1: 653: C.J., 1: 928.

31. Harold Hulme, *The Life of Sir John Eliot* (New York, 1957), p. 291.

32. CD 1629, pp. 55, 135–36, 186, 190.

33. Sir John Wolstenholm, Abraham Dawes, Richard Carmarthen, Michael Measy, John Beaupell, and Bryan Rogers. C.J., 1: 921.

34. CD 1629, pp. 84, 155–56, 221–22.

35. Ibid., pp. 85, 156, 222–23; *Eph. Parl.*, p. 263.

36. CD 1629, pp. 156–57, 222–23.

37. Ibid., pp. 223, 157.

38. Ibid., pp. 157–58, 224.

39. Ibid., pp. 158, 224; *Eph. Parl.*, p. 263.

40. CD 1629, p. 227.

41. Ibid., p. 160.

42. Gardiner, 7: 63.

43. CD 1629, pp. 93, 166, 234; *Eph. Parl.*, p. 267.

44. CD 1629, p. 232.

45. Ibid., pp. 94, 167–68, 236–37; Rushworth, 1: 659.

46. See I. H. C. Fraser, "The Agitation in the Commons, 2 March, 1629, and the Interrogation of the Leaders of the Anti-Court Group," *Bulletin of the Institute of Historical Research* 30 (1957): 86–95.

47. CD 1629, pp. 264–67; *Eph. Parl.*, p. 267.

48. Vernon L. Snow, "The Concept of Revolution in Seventeenth Century England," *The Historical Journal* 5 (1962): 167–74.

49. I. H. C. Fraser, "The Agitation of the Commons, 2 March, 1629, and the Interroga-

tion of the Leaders of the Anti-Court Group,'' *Bulletin of the Institute of Historical Research* (1957), p. 95.
50. James O. Halliwell, ed., *Autobiography and Correspondence of Sir Simond D'Ewes* (London, 1845), 1: 402.

9. The Early Parliamentary Career of John Pym

I

Election to the House of Commons was worn as a badge of honor in the seventeenth century; to be a member of Parliament was a demonstration of political, economic, and social power in a world thoroughly obsessed with powerful men. Some Englishmen made Parliament their hobby, and there was always a hard core of veteran members in the Commons in every session of Parliament throughout the reigns of the first two Stuart kings. They were, generally speaking, remarkable men. They were the elite of the country, and eventually every man with a claim to fame or a flash of brilliance beat his path there. They were well off, well trained, and well educated. Indeed, almost all the members of Parliament were educated in the universities or the Inns of Court, and the overwhelming success of these branches of learning bred trouble for the Stuarts. When one contrasts, for instance, the mediocrity of the privy councillors of the first two Stuarts[1] with the abilities of men such as Sir Edwin Sandys, Sir John Eliot, John Selden, and John Pym, the consequences of this conjunction of circumstances can begin to be fully appreciated.[2]

It has been argued that, despite the fact the members of the House of Commons were improving each year, despite the fact that they were the intellectual and political leaders of the nation, despite the fact that the quality of the executive had declined geometrically with the accession of the Stuart kings; despite it all, the fact remains that there was a decline in the idea of parliamentary government during the reigns of James I and Charles I. The thesis runs as follows: Parliament governs by parliamentary acts and when the number of acts of Parliament increases over a period of time, one may speak of rise of parliamentary government, and when it decreases, of decline. Under the early Stuarts, taking into consideration the length of their reigns, parliamentary government declined, because in the reign of James I fewer acts

166

were passed than under Henry VIII, Edward VI, or Queen Mary, and fewer still were passed in the reign of Charles I.[3]

This thesis, like most statistical essays, is rather appealing and seductive. But it would be rather foolish to believe that the power of Parliament of the early Stuarts was not so strong or widely developed as the sparse Parliaments of the early Tudors. The Tudor monarchs were quite adept at using their Parliaments to carry out many of the changes they wished to make; the history of the early Stuart Parliaments is that of the brilliant efforts of numerous members of the House of Commons to carry out changes they wished their king to make. It is certainly true that, compared with twentieth-century Parliaments, the Stuarts Parliaments were remarkably weak. But enormous strides had been made since Sir Thomas More had sat as Speaker of the House of Commons in the Parliaments of Henry VIII. The House of Commons had on numerous occasions dramatically asserted its power of independence and it had won several important privileges. It had established itself as a court of record, painfully developed its procedure, revived its practice of impeachment, and greatly enlarged the scope of its debates. The House of Commons had grown mightily and was winning the "initiative" from the feebleness of the crown's representatives in the House.[4] The members of the House of Commons in the Parliaments of the 1620s were far more conscious of their position and far more knowledgeable of their power than their predecessors. They were failures in only one important respect—and the Personal Rule of Charles I was an illustration of the failure—they did nothing to assure their continual existence. But under the leadership of John Pym in the early 1640s, they solved that problem as well.

II

John Pym was a perfect illustration of the member of Parliament in the 1620s. Well educated and well trained, intelligent and capable, he wore his election to the House of Commons as a badge of honor; indeed, after 1620, Parliament became the avocation to which he devoted his life.

Pym fills an ample space in English history, but it is really difficult to form a vivid conception of him. His personality was harsh and he seemed to have a very melancholy disposition. Reserved and simple in tastes and character, Pym had very little nonsense about him. He was really all business, and if he never laughed or smiled, he did, at least on several occasions, come very close to doing just that. On February 5, 1621, he wrote that a certain Sergeant Davis undertook to debate the subject "with more length of speeche than the howse had patience to heare." On February 12 of that same Parliament, he wrote that "most of the daie was consumed in this debate, newe proposicions producing newe exceptions, and every man being more fortunate in overthroweing anothers opinion than fortifying his owne." On November 17, in the same Parliament of 1621, Pym wrote that the chancellor of the exchequer spoke with more "elegance than I will undertake to describe."[5] On February 24, 1624, Pym described Buckingham's explanation of the marriage negotiations with Spain in tones of genial sarcasm. The whole speech, he wrote, was "sprinkled with some glances of taxation upon the Earl of Bristol and of insinuation of his own merit," and that during the discourse "divers interloquitorie helps of the Prince and the reading of some letters, and dispatches gave him tymes of breathing."[6]

John Pym was not consistent in his action and speeches during the Parliaments of the 1620s, but that is hardly a remarkable observation, for what man has ever been truly consistent? Historians are sometimes remarkably naïve. They find it difficult to understand why great men of the past have changed their interpretations and shifted their allegiances when they themselves are constantly and often dramatically changing their interpretations and shifting their allegiances. They find it difficult to accept the fundamental fact that great men are only human beings bound to the human condition and environment, John Pym was subject to the same fears, the same crises, and the same doubts that almost all great men have inevitably faced. It is no derogation of character or criticism of intelligence to state that Pym's views changed as the conditions in which he expressed these views changed. In the Parliament of 1621 Pym systematically challenged the religious and foreign policies of James I, and he was rewarded for his efforts with imprisonment by the crown.[7] In the succeeding Parliament of 1624 Pym, despite the rather harsh treatment he had received from the king in 1621, faithfully supported the crown in all its desires.[8] In the Parliament of 1628, during the debates on the proposed bill of rights, John Pym, after King Charles I had proclaimed that he would galdly join with the Commons in redressing grievances, staggered some of the more adamant members of the House by declaring that he desired to vote on the subsidy bill even before the king had in fact redressed those very grievances.[9] Less than a month later, after Charles had stubbornly refused to allow the Commons to frame a bill of rights with "explanations" guaranteeing the fundamental liberties of the kingdom, Pym boldly challenged the "word" of the king and demanded parliamentary acts to "ty" the crown to the law.[10]

Pym was, however, remarkably consistent in his religious activities throughout the 1620s. Indeed, his most persistent allegiance, his most tenacious interpretations during the Parliaments of the 1620s are found in his religious policies. "The greatest liberty of our kingdom," Pym once said, "is religion,"[11] and this he placed above everything else in his life. It was the very bread that fed his body, the very spirit that infused his soul and mind. Religion for Pym was the "immediate hand of God,"[12] and he reverently wore his faith on his sleeve as a badge of humility. Religion was for him an ornament in prosperity and a refuge in adversity; but, like most men whose lives are dominated by religious considerations, Pym's religious views were not only his contentment but also his despair.

John Pym suffered from papalphobia. He possessed an imperious and unyielding spirit against popery and a steadfast hatred of all things Catholic. He was wise enough, however, to understand that not all men think alike, that not all men interpet or analyze the Bible or any other religious work in the same way, and that truth is assuredly not so narrow a virtue as to be confined to any one man, party, or ideology. In the Parliament of 1628 Pym declared that, although he himself deeply revered *The Book of Common Prayer*, he thought it "strange" that many men failed to realize that not everyone fully accepted that book. He thought it "strange" that many men failed to understand that it was almost impossible not to be contrary to particular "clauses" of that religious work.[13] In the Parliament of 1621 Pym had stated that he would never have any man "suffer for his conscience."

Heresies and religious errors, he argued, which arise only from different interpretations and lack of understanding, must never be changed by force; they must be righted and persuaded by logic and reason. The English laws against Catholics, he proclaimed, were not designed to restrain the conscience of Catholics; they were not created to persecute an alien religion or to attack a faith that desired to win souls for its God. Instead, they were created solely to keep papists from doing harm to Protestants; they were created to limit the "wealth" of Catholics from doing "that which they think and believe they ought to do"; they were created above all to restrain the Catholic powers from practicing "against us." [14]

In a memorable and influential address before the House of Commons on November 28, 1621, however, Pym persuasively argued that Roman Catholicism could never be tolerated. It must be restricted and limited fron committing crimes just as mad men are restrained and limited from committing outrages. King James, Pym cautiously said, was utterly deceived in his religious policies. The king, Pym declared, wrongly assumed that his clemency, his leniency, his piety, his justice, and his friendship with English Catholics and foreign Catholic powers would win their "hearts" and goodwill and therefore procure his own safety. But the king was deluded, Pym reasoned, if he thought any safety could be gained by this connivance, for though he might win their favors, he could never win their hearts. Having gained favor at court, the Catholics would "expect toleration, after toleration. They will look for equality, after equality for supremacy, and having supremacy they will seek the subversion of that religion which is contrary to theirs." Friendship, Pym lectured the English king, required a mutual respect and a mutual giving and receiving; but the English monarch had given far more to the Catholics than he had received from them. Foreign Catholic ambassadors, for example, had been able to prevail in England to the disadvantage of the Protestant religion, but the English ambassadors in Catholic states had enjoyed no such liberties. Do not kings, Pym asked, desire that all their subjects be wholly dependent upon them; but are not papists first and foremost dependent upon the pope? And must not monarchs demand that they themselves be the most popular personages of their realm; but must not papists revere above and before all others the pope? Catholicism, Pym maintained, was far too "swollen" with its own glory to be either suffered or tolerated. Roman Catholicism, by its very desire to seek control over everything, destroyed any possibility of friendship with English Protestantism.[15]

Pym was remarkably consistent in his anti-Catholicism throughout the 1620s. In the Parliaments of 1625 and 1628 and in the parliamentary session of 1629 he labored in the Commons to remind the members of the dreadful increase of Catholics in England and Ireland, and of the crown's failure to enforce effectively the penal laws.[16] He found this growth a dangerous symptom of a disease that must be destroyed lest it bring about the decay and fall of the English Protestantism he loved so dearly. He firmly maintained that Roman Catholicism was an uncompromising religion whose members were never "idle" and who would admit "no mean." And it was this incompatibility of Catholicism with any other religion, Pym believed, that had set Europe and all of Christendom aflame in the Thirty Years' War. The sparks from the flames, Pym believed, had been blown abroad by the "Pope's breath," who had written letters to the King of France commending him for his persecution of the Huguenots, an act which the pope equated with St. Louis's crusade against the Saracens. The pope, furthermore, was ardently enjoining Louis XIII to spread his policy across the Channel and to clean out that "nest of heresies," England. Unfortunately, Pym lamented, the crown's failure to enforce the recusancy laws would make all Protestants in England like dry tinder to those sparks. How was it possible, Pym asked, for England to grant religious, political, and social toleration to English Catholics, who owed spiritual allegiance to the pope, whose stated policy was the destruction of Protestant England? According to Pym, England could not afford such a luxury.[17] Catholics in England must be hounded, controlled, and imprisoned because they seriously threatened the constitution of the nation and the security of the commonwealth. They must be destroyed because they aimed not only at the "complete exterpation of our religion, but also at the possessinge of themselves of the whole power of the State."[18]

Pym's anti-Catholicism was clearly a most militant doctrine.

He firmly believed that Protestantism was at war against Roman Catholicism and that it was a total war. Abroad, England, the leader of Protestantism in Europe, according to Pym, was in a death struggle with the forces of the Catholics. At home, where England was combatting the devilish agents of the pope, Pym was a Catholic-hunter extraordinary. Numerous times throughout the 1620s Pym, often in the middle of debates on entirely different topics, would rise and request a petition for the capture of some English Catholic or "knowne Jesuit" who was free to spread his wretched doctrines.[19] He would demand the immediate imprisonment of some hapless Anglican cleric who had employed a "scandalous" Catholic catechism.[20] He would seek parliamentary support for the censuring of the Countess of Buckingham for her "countenance" of Catholics. "More goe to her home," Pym said, "than to Church."[21] Pym's solution to the English Catholic "problem" was simple: the full and effective execution of the recusancy laws and the total and brutal suppression of English papists. Catholics would be deprived of schools, deprived of arms, and forbidden to attend foreign seminaries. They would be denied entrance to foreign ambassadors' chapels and confined to the country. Above all, every Jesuit and every priest would be banished immediately and all Catholics would be "punished severely for their insolence."[22]

Every intellectual product, of course, can be judged intelligently only from the point of view of the age and the people from which it was produced. No man's knowledge can really go beyond his own experience. How can men reason but from what they know? John Pym knew only that the papists intended to destroy his Protestantism, and he reacted to this knowledge by creating a policy designed to destroy Catholicism. Of course, it made little difference to the English Catholics whether they suffered and died for a religious or for a civil crime; they suffered and died, nevertheless. Indeed, Pym's anti-Catholicism had the rather delicate odor of an old pair of socks; his papist policy was merely religious persecution subtly perfumed. To accept the fact of Pym's belief that religious persecution was of itself an evil thing is difficult when one considers that by his definition Catholics were suspect and warranted persecution simply because they were Catholics. But let us at least recognize the fact that

Pym's espousal of theoretical religious freedom was a relatively moderate and tolerant policy in an extremely immoderate and intolerant age.

John Pym was a preeminent anti-Catholic, but he was no less a prominent opponent of Arminianism. There are two principal religious evils in England, Pym said in the parliamentary session of 1629, the one old, the other new; the old was Catholicism, the new Arminianism.[23] As chairman of the powerful committee of religion in the Parliaments of 1625, 1626, and 1628, John Pym was in a powerful position. But he was absolutely powerless to bring about his desired conformity of religious practice in England because of the opposition of the crown, and this, too, was Pym's despair. This impotence, however, neither silenced him nor kept him from attacking those English clerics whom he considered indoctrinated "full fraught with dangerous opinions of Arminius."[24] He savagely attacked Richard Montague in the Parliaments of 1625, 1626, and 1628 because the Anglican bishop had had the exceedingly bad taste to deny that the Roman Catholic pope was an evil, sinful man and that the Roman Catholic Church was the contemporary reincarnation of anti-Christ.[25] In the Parliament of 1628 he bitterly assaulted the divine-right theories of Dr. Roger Maynwaring because Maynwaring had not only censured the House of Commons, but had also rationalized and justified his censure by appealing to the authority of the great Spanish jurist, Francisco Suarez, and other "Fryers and Jesuits."[26] In the Parliament of 1626 he angrily challenged the decision of Cambridge University to confer upon the Duke if Buckingham the chancellorship of the university, not only because the action was a direct affront to the House of Commons, which was at that very moment impeaching the duke, but also because many of the men at the university, "like Dr. Cosens and Mr. Mason," were Arminians who "openly inclined to the opinions of Montague."[27]

Pym attacked Arminianism because it tolerated Catholics, it expressed doctrines contrary to the Thirty-nine Articles of the Established Church, and it fully accepted many papist beliefs and practices: the doctrines of good works and of the special nature of saints, and the use of altars, images, and pictures. He severely assailed many Arminian clerics because they were giving special encouragement to the English Catholics by publicly stating that the Roman Catholic Church was a "true church since it was a church," that papists did not err in matters of faith, and that the Roman Church had firmly established itself upon the "same foundation of Sacrament and Doctrine instituted by God."[28] John Pym despised these Arminian clergymen because they refused to recognize what John Pym clearly perceived: that Catholicism and Protestantism were in an ideological and physical death struggle. Indeed, these clerics, according to Pym, were in a sense pursuing the wretched and undermining policy of coexistence; they were minimizing the differences between Catholics and Protestants and preaching the doctrine of the brotherhood of all Christians. To a dedicated and militant anti-Catholic such as John Pym, such ideas were not only heretical but downright subversive; the Arminians not only gave aid and comfort to the enemy, they were, in fact, "fellow travelers" who were "soft" on Catholicism.

Pym remained throughout his life a member in good standing of the Established Church. He did, however, deeply sympathize with the program of the English Puritans and with their desire to protect that Church from popish encroachments. In his maiden speech in the House of Commons he vigorously defended the honor and reputation of a fellow member against the charges of Puritanism.[29] In the Parliament of 1625 he wrote that it would be a very good thing indeed for England to know more Puritans.[30] He sympathized with the Puritans if for no other reason than that he sincerely resented the steady intrusion of Anglican churchmen such as Laud, Andrewes, Montague, and Maynwaring into politics and government. He constantly raised his voice in the Parliaments of the 1620s against the romanizing romance of these Anglican clerics, and he consistently demanded to know why and how these clergymen were being put into positions of power. But he was no rigid religious fanatic seeking to establish a millennium. Actually he was little inclined to theocracy of any kind, Puritan or Anglican. The godly utopia of Geneva never appealed to him. In 1629 he eagerly advocated the political regulation of religion by espousing parliamentary laws to select, train, and guide all Protestant preachers. Only this remedy, he declared, could successfully deal with the twin "mischiefs" of Catholicism and Arminianism.[31] This was not any exclusively anticlerical sentiment, for John Pym was anticlerical only when the clerics were Arminians.

What John Pym desired, what he deeply believed all good English Protestants desired, was a return to the purity of religion that characterized the reign of Edward VI in both the writings and teachings of Peter Martyr, Martin Bucer, and John Wycliff, and in the "constant profession sealed by the blood of so many martyrs as Cranmer and Ridley." What England craved, he believed, was a return to the purity of religion as exemplified in the Elizabethan Thirty-nine Articles.[32] To establish this purified and thoroughly Protestant religion in the Church of England, John Pym, in the Parliament of 1625, advocated better and "properly educated" schoolmasters who could instruct their students in the principles of the "trew religion."[33] In the parliamentary session of 1629 Pym devised a more ambitious and more definite scheme. The laws against the Roman Catholics in England were to be fully and effectively executed, compulsory uniformity was to be enforced, and severe punishments were to be inflicted upon those who published or taught anything contrary to orthodox religion. Bishoprics and other ecclesiastical preferments, moreover, were to be conferred solely upon the most pious, the most learned, the most orthodox of men; and—most significantly— Parliament was to be "considered of, for providing competent means to maintain a godly and able minister in every parish of this Kingdom."[34] This vanguard of puritanical uniformity would naturally be supervised and governed by the House of Commons. These remedies proposed by John Pym throughout the Parliaments of the 1620s, as any observer can readily observe, would have brought forth a quiet but thoroughly effective religious and political revolution in Stuart England. And John Pym advocated these policies solely to combat the Arminian nonsense of the higher Anglican clergy and the great "multitude" of Roman Catholic priests who toiled in England. Pym's religious policies in the Parliaments of the 1620s were really quite clear; he was a most faithful son of the Protestant Reformation who desired to uphold conformity in religion tempered by indulgence to many Puritans more rigid than himself. His object was clear; he desired a strong, militantly Protestant England led not by preachers but by religious, upright, and God-fearing men.

III

In politics, like most politicians, John Pym desired good government. In 1626 he declared that the "ill government here at home may be putt in amongst the evils" that plagued England.[35] Pym gladly joined in the impeachment of Buckingham not because the duke had committed treason by assaulting the king's person or by physically attacking the crown's government—indeed, nothing could be farther from Pym's mind. He attacked Buckingham, as he would attack the Earl of Strafford, simply because the duke in his political capacity had undermined the nation, the laws, the government, and the crown by exposing the nation, the laws, and the government, which essentially constituted the greatness of the crown, to disasters, to humiliations, and to corruptions. He attacked Buckingham because he honestly believed that the duke was an incompetent and even evil advisor. Pym maintained that Buckingham put his own ambition, his own interest before those of the crown and that he therefore desecrated the king's honor and destroyed the trust that the state had confided upon him. According to Pym, service to the English commonwealth was a noble virtue. It is the wisdom of the state and of the state's laws, he said in the Parliament of 1626, to employ wise and able men for the greater good of the nation. Pym believed, however, that Buckingham was neither wise nor able. The duke was irresponsible, for he put himself before the welfare of the state, he was contemptuous of Parliament, he created a great tyranny, and he oppressed the laws to his own benefit.[36] The House of Commons, Pym claimed, sat as lawmakers, as counsellors, and as judges, and the impeachment of the Duke of Buckingham was the Commons' method of advising and counselling the English crown.[37]

The best form of government, said Pym, is that state which creates, represents and, in fact, exists for the common good of every member of the commonwealth. Government, he argued, is an interdependent and interrelated contract between the government and the governed. If the harmonious bond that united them were broken or destroyed, chaos, confusion, and anarchy would result. It was not only "convenient" and "profitable" but absolutely necessary for all governments to seek harmony and to maintain the fundamental laws and freedoms of the land, simply because it makes a state strong and powerful. Pym believed that a free state was a prosperous state, and that a prosperous state was a strong state. In a free and prosperous state, subjects naturally support their government with both money and allegiance, for it is to their advantage to do so. Pym believed, moreover, that government was an organic growth with a very life and personality of its own, and that the strongest, most durable, and most lasting governments of the world were those nations which reformed themselves, reconditioned themselves to the natural and "ordinary" defects and evils of time. The basic elements of all governments, the fundamental foundations of all states, he maintained, were the rule of law. In the case of England, this law was found in the might and gravity of judicial tradition and customs which were established upon Anglo-Saxon law.[38]

John Pym was a faithful supporter of the English crown during the 1620s. He fully realized that the crown was the "greatest hope of the prosperitie and reformacion of the Kingdom"; he fully realized that the English king was the "prime mover from whence all prosperitye of this and other affairs of Parliament must be derived."[39] Pym believed, however, that the nation could never tolerate the illegal or despotic actions of the crown, or that the king could act outside the state as if he were separated from it. He believed that the king must act as the leader of the English state. Every just king, Pym said, is bound to observe and obey the contract made to his subjects by the laws of the land.[40]

John Pym was fully aware of the power, the rights, the duties, and the privileges of Parliament. In the Parliament of 1626 Pym declared that the House of Commons sat as lawmakers, as counsellors, and as judges.[41] In the Parliament of 1628 he declared that the Commons did not sit in Parliament merely as judges for "strict" or "book" law, but as "law makers as well as law interpreters."[42] Indeed, during the impeachment of Buckingham, Pym declared that it was the duty of Parliament to initiate proceedings against any man when the charges against that man were ambiguous or were not clearly defined in the established law of the land.[43] Members of Parliament, he argued, as the representatives of the nation, had a clear and fundamental right to interpret and determine the law. The privileges of Parliament, he believed, moreover, were neither the favors of English kings nor scraps of goodwill that a patronizing crown fed to a humble and starving institution. They were the basic and essential liberties and birthrights of all Englishmen; they were the fundamental privileges and freedoms of Parliament. In the Parliament of 1621, after King James had denied almost all parliamentary privileges by asserting his right to punish any man's speeches in or out of Parliament, Pym declared that a letter from the king could not take away from the House of Commons their liberties, because the Commons' privileges were founded upon the liberties and privileges of the nation itself. The king, moreover, had challenged their liberties, and if the ''speakinge in the defence of our privileges should offend, yet he would speak in the defence thereof.''[44] In the Parliament of 1626, after the arrest of Digges and Eliot for their role in the impeachment of Buckingham, Pym stated that there were some privileges of Parliament that belonged individually to each member of Parliament and some that belonged to the House as a whole. If anyone attacked either of these privileges, Pym said, he attacked both, for they could not be separated from each other but were indivisible, inseparable, one. As we have defended the privileges of the House of Commons as an institution, he declared, so must we defend the privileges of each particular member of that House. The privileges of the Commons, he boldly declared, were ''ours'' solely because of ''our'' sitting here. They were, in fact, inherent in the House of Commons itself.[45]

Pym was not blind to the problems of the House of Commons throughout the 1620s. He constantly labored for a united House and he consistently implored his fellow parliamentarians not to run into disunity or to relapse in their duties.[46] But most of all John Pym despised the turtlelike pace of the Commons, the inclination of the parliamentarians to debate and discuss issues to death, and the faculty of the House to become bogged down in trivial matters. Numerous times throughout the 1620s he rose and pleaded with the members of the Commons to quicken their pace and speedily conclude their business. He expressed this sentiment best of all in the Parliament of 1628, when, during a long and often fruitless debate on supply, he rose and declared that a ''man in a journey is hindered by asking too many questions.'' Actions, he said, were far better than words, for in every important matter ''dispatch is better than discourse.''[47]

John Pym was impatient with the slow pace of the House of Commons, but he was never especially eager for radical change. That which is honorable and good of itself, he said in the Parliament of 1628, is honorable and good for all time.[48] His policies and postures were in fact overwhelmingly conservative. In the Parliament of 1624 he stated that he would never innovate anything without good reason,[49] and in every crisis in a nation, he declared in the Parliament of 1626, there were only three grounds for action: law, precedent, and reason.[50] Pym was most certainly not a reformer or idealist in the sense that he was impatient for change or that he desired to improve his world in his own way and in his own image. Indeed, Pym's position throughout the 1620s was essentially conservative, and the House of Commons acting, or better reacting, in the institution of Parliament was the greatest conservative force in the land. Parliament was the fundamental guardian, the last bastion of the English law and the English Protestant religion against the unlawful acts of the king, against the incompetence of Buckingham, and against the romanizing tendencies of Montague and Maynwaring.

Pym was loyal to the crown throughout the 1620s, but he was never afraid to oppose its actions in Parliament or to criticize publically its policies. Pym believed, in fact, that it was his parliamentary duty to do just that. Parliaments, Pym, said in the Parliament of 1621, were the "greate watch of the Kingdom to find oute all faults."[51] As Pym understood it, Parliament was summoned not only to supply the king with monies or to vote or propose laws. It was called above all to maintain the laws of the kingdom and to guarantee that those laws were executed in accordance with the interpretation of the House of Commons and not merely in accordance with the interpretation of the king and his judges. Parliaments, Pym said in the Parliament of 1628, were the greatest and highest representations of the nation. If there were no Parliaments, Pym believed, English grievances would multiply daily without any possible means or laws to redress them. Is there a readier means, Pym, inquisitively asked, to bring about disharmony between king and subjects, to bring about revolutionary anarchy, or to create disorder in the land, than to govern without Parliament?[52]

John Pym believed that the numerous petitions sponsored by the House of Commons were neither new nor revolutionary de-

vices; they were actually conservative devices, seeking to preserve the established law. The petitions upon which Parliament
requested charters and acts, Pym said in the Parliament of 1628,
were merely petitions of right demanding the respect of old and
established freedoms and birthrights of all Englishmen. And the
Petition of Right, Pym said, was an illustration of this political
philosophy, for it did not ask for changes in the law but desired
only to keep the crown from changing that law—the petition was
not advocating new laws, but only seeking a guarantee from the
king that he would observe established laws.[53]

John Pym, moreover, demanded parliamentary supremacy in
religion throughout the 1620s simply because Parliament was the
most conservative force in the nation to assure religious conformity. Only Parliament, Pym said in the session of 1629, could
meet the two dangers of Roman Catholicism and Arminianism in
England. Pym believed that Parliament, and especially the House
of Commons, must become the official watchdog of the English
Church and must reserve to itself the right to preserve the purity
of the Established Church. And Pym believed that whoever challenged the right of Parliament to judge matters of faith and religion was ignorant of the English constitution. Parliaments, Pym
said, had confirmed the acts of general councils of the Church,
whose decisions were not binding upon England until they had
been authorized by Parliament. The institution of Parliament,
moreover, had enacted laws for trials of heretics by jury. Above
all, however, Pym declared that Parliament possessed the right to
legislate religious conformity simply because it was the only
institution capable of dealing with the problem:

> The Convocation cannot because it is but a provincial
> Synod, only of the jurisdiction of Canterbury and the power
> thereof is not adequate to the whole Kingdom . . . . The High
> Commission cannot, for it hath its authority derived from Par-
> liaments, and the derivative cannot prejudice the original, the
> judgment of Parliament being the judgment of the King and of
> the three estates of the whole Kingdom.[54]

John Pym quite clearly understood the close parallels between
all the various problems that dominated England during the early
seventeenth century. He firmly believed that all men, all institu-

tions, whether ecclesiastical, political, or judicial, must work in harmony and in accordance with those rules and policies established by the king and Parliament together. As he maintained in his first Parliament, the House of Commons made inquiries, the House of Lords passed judgment, and the king executed the direction of the will of Parliament.[55]

IV

John Pym was an important and influential member of the House of Commons throughout the 1620s. He was in the thick of debate against the foreign policies of James I. He was consistently in the forefront in the discussion of the impeachment of the Duke of Buckingham, in the attack upon Catholicism and Arminianism, and in the struggle for the Petition of Right. But his influence in the House of Commons in the 1620s had a very special quality to it, for it was both moderate and responsible. Pym was, in fact, a truly great national statesman who consistently put the welfare and glory of the nation before that of the crown, Parliament, or himself. As Pym succinctly put it in the Parliament of 1628, "I can be neither happy nor miserable but in the misery and happiness of the Kingdom."[56] On December 18, 1621, the very day the members of the Commons were ferociously defending their privileges by framing the Great Protestation, Pym revealed his admirable sentiments by declaring that the nation must come first, and that Parliament must get back to its more important duty of voting and passing bills for the benefit of the commonwealth. After this was accomplished, he said, then the House of Commons should spend the remaining time vindicating its liberties and privileges.[57] In the Parliament of 1629 Pym took a similar position, and in so doing broke with the more radical parliamentarians in the Commons. During the debate on tonnage and poundage he quietly scolded Eliot for putting the privileges of the House of Commons before the liberties of the nation. To determine the privileges of the Commons before those of the kingdom, Pym declared, "is but a meane matter," for the liberties of Parliament were "inferior to the liberties of the Kingdom." Above everything else, Pym reasoned, individual public freedoms of the nation must be determined and maintained.[58]

Pym was, however, as strong and unyielding in his hatreds as any member of Parliament in the 1620s, he was as opposed to arbitrary rule and incompetent government as Sir John Eliot and Sir Robert Phelips, and he was as thoroughly versed in the law of the rights, usages, and privileges of Parliament as Sir Edward Coke and Sir Edwin Sandys. But he was neither so rash nor so impetuous as those parliamentarians. Pym was responsible and decisive in thought and action. He was at his best in combining opposites, and in directing toward one end, one goal, ideas and policies and movements which were decidedly remote from one another. His statesmanship was consistently constructive; it was rarely destructive. His importance in the House of Commons during the 1620s was a result of his influence, not his eloquence, for he had none of the fire, none of the poetic imagination, and none of the emotional fervor of an Eliot or a Phelips.

John Pym was a man of phenomenal drive and resourcefulness, the type who, once he had committed himself to an enterprise, would carry it through to the utmost bounds of possibility. In any given issue he knew just how far he could go and the way to go about it. He always gave his whole heart to the tasks and projects he had set for himself. Personal considerations never entered his mind. The interests of his family were of secondary importance to him; he died in debt and as late as 1665 Pym's creditors were still seeking reimbursements.[59] He did everything thoroughly. He combined determination with moderation, practical ability with political insight, and moral and religious fervor with unflinching opportunism. He had none of Bacon's philosophy about him, and his mind teemed with the thoughts, the beliefs, the prejudices of his age. He was strong with their strengths and weak with their weaknesses. It has been said, and said well,[60] that Pym's overwhelming strength and importance lay chiefly in his faculty of appreciating the ideas and prejudices of the ordinary man, and of transmitting them into such logical and practical presentations that each man could feel in them kinship, if not paternity. But even if Pym's ideas were the ideas of ordinary men, he gave to them the logic and intellect of a far brighter glow. Englishmen were delighted to hear Pym converting their crude and tangled thoughts into well-reasoned arguments. John Pym was one of the greatest members of Parliament because he had the quality of speaking and interpreting the temper of the times and of translating that temper into noble words and actions. He never possessed the rhetorical brilliance of Coke or the emotional fervor of Eliot; he never possessed the magical fire of Phelips or the godly righteousness of Cromwell. What John Pym possessed was common sense, and he made the most of it.

With quite deliberate steps he far outdistanced all his competitors—the learned Selden, the temperamental Eliot, the quiet Hampden, the fiery Phelips, and the ambitious Wentworth—in the long, steady ascent toward power. With his indefatigable industry and his power of application, Pym became more knowledgeable than any parliamentarian in the very specialized technique of conducting the numerous and complex business of the House of Commons. His name appeared on countless committee lists during the 1620s, and it seemed as if it were impossible for any important issues to be transacted in the Commons without the detailed assistance of John Pym. And in the process of those activities, in the course of those uninspiring and arduous matters, he was not only gaining a thorough knowledge of the House of Commons but also acquiring a firm understanding of the institution of Parliament.

John Pym started his parliamentary career as a man devoted to conservation; he began with seeking to preserve rather than to destroy. He stood forth as a member of the House of Commons during the 1620s to vindicate the ancient and inherited freedoms and liberties of England and the Protestant religion. He occasionally set himself against the crown and countless times set himself against some Arminian bishops, because he sincerely believed that they had somehow endangered those very great and wonderful treasures. But he was never in any other sense the determined enemy of English kingship or of the Established Church. Indeed, John Pym was a parliamentary friend of lawful, constitutional monarchy in politics, and a religious comrade of moderate Protestantism in religion. He was against the despot, but not against the English crown; he was against all forms of Arminian innovations and toleration of Roman Catholics, but not against the Established Church. Pym was a moderate, a traditionalist, a conservatively minded member of Parliament who strongly believed in the rule of law. In the Parliament of 1628 Pym declared that every Englishman enjoyed the "plain," fundamental right of liberty under the law. He believed that the rule of law was the basic foundation of all nations. No king, or council, or judge, Pym said, employing either God's law or man's law could ever break the law, for the law of the land must always be followed.[61]

John Pym's reputation as a member of Parliament during the 1620s was founded upon hard work and timely debate. But he never led the House of Commons during the 1620s as Coke led it in 1621, or as Eliot led it in 1626, or as Wentworth led it in 1628. Indeed, Pym's early parliamentary career was solid rather than brilliant. In the Parliaments of the 1620s John Pym labored as a mason. Brick by brick and Parliament by Parliament he created for himself, by influence and by personal contacts, and established for himself, by knowledge and by incessant work, a thorough understanding of the machinery of the House of Commons, which enabled him in the 1640s to challenge successfully the powerful Stuart monarchy.

Notes

1. D. H. Willson, *The Privy Councillors in the House of Commons, 1604–1629* (Minneapolis, 1940), pp. 82–98.
2. See Mark H. Curtis, *Oxford and Cambridge in Transition* (Oxford, 1959), chapter 3; Mark H. Curtis, "The Alienated Intellectuals of Early Stuart England," *Past and Present* 23 (1962): 39.
3. See R. W. K. Hinton, "The Decline of Parliamentary Government Under Elizabeth I and the Early Stuarts," *Cambridge Historical Journal* 13 (1957): 116–32.
4. See Wallace Notestein, *The Winning of the Initiative by the House of Commons* (Oxford, 1924); D. H. Willson, "The Earl of Salisbury and the 'Court' Party in Parliament," *American Historical Review* 36 (1931): 274–94.
5. Wallace Notestein, Francis H. Relf, and Hartley Simpson, eds., *Commons Debates 1621* (New Haven, 1935), 4:14, 40, 444—hereafter cited as CD 1621.
6. Pym. In the preparation of this book extensive use was made of unpublished diaries of the Parliaments of 1624, 1626, and 1628. These are listed in the bibliography. I am using an abbreviation for each diary cited in the text, usually the last name of the author. As the folios in the typescript copies of the original manuscripts are not always given, all folio references have been omitted. References to the diaries can be found from the day cited.
7. CD 1621, 2:46–64, 5:222–23, 6:200, 322, 4:447–48; T. Tyrwritt, ed., *Proceedings and Debates of the House of Commons in 1620 and 1621* (London, 1766), 2:228–30—hereafter cited as P.D.; *Journals of the House of Commons* (London, 1803–63), 1:650.
8. Nicolas, March 19, 1624; Pym, March 19, 1624; Holles, March 19, 1624.

9. Borlase, April 11, 1628; Mass., April 11, 1628.

10. Borlase, May 6, 1628; Mass., May 6, 1628; Grosvenor (2), May 6, 1628; Harl. 5324, May 6, 1628. Harl. 1601, May 6, 1628.

11. *A Short View of the Life and Activities of the Late Deceased John Pym Esquire* (London, 1643), p. 13.

12. *Historical Manuscripts Commission, Seventh Report* (London, 1879), p. 557—hereafter cited as *H.M.C.*

13. Borlase, May 21, 1628.

14. CD 1621, 2:461–64.

15. CD 1621, 2:461–64, 4:447–48, 5:222–23, 405, 6:200, 232; P.D., 2:228–30; C.J., 1:650–51.

16. S. R. Gardiner, ed., *Debates in the House of Commons in 1625* (Westminster: Camden Society, 1873), pp. 18–25—hereafter cited as CD 1625; Sir John Eliot, *An Apology for Socrates and Negotium Posterorum*, edited by A. B. Grossart (London, 1881), 1:74—hereafter cited as *Neg. Post.*; Grosvenor (2), June 6, 1628; Borlase, June 6, 1628; Nicholas (2), June 6, 1628; Wallace Notestein and Francis H. Relf, eds., *Commons Debates for 1629* (Minneapolis, 1921), pp. 20–21—hereafter cited as CD 1629; John Rushworth, *Historical Collections of Private Passages of State, 1618–1649* (London, 1721), 1:647—hereafter cited as Rushworth; Thomas Cobbett, ed., *The Parliamentary History of England* (London, 1820), 2:446–47—hereafter cited as *Parl. Hist.*

17. CD 1621, 2:461–64, 5:222–23; P.D., 2:228–30; C.J., 1:651.

18. CD 1625, pp. 18–25.

19. CD 1625, p. 141.

20. Borlase, May 9, 1628; Grosvenor (2), May 9, 1628; Mass., May 9, 1628; Harl. 5324, May 9, 1628.

21. Borlase, June 6, 1628.

22. CD 1625, pp. 18–25.

23. CD 1629, pp. 20–21, 111–12.

24. C.J., 1:788.

25. CD 1625, pp. 47–49; C.J., 1:802, 805; Rushworth, 1:209–12; Whitelocke, April 17, 1626; Rich, April 17, 1626; Borlase, April 28, 1628; Mass., April 28, 1628; Grosvenor (2), April 28, 1628; Harl. 5324, April 28, 1628.

26. Rushworth, 1:595–604; *Parl. Hist.*, 2:390–402; *Journals of the House of Lords* (London, 1846), 2:845—hereafter cited as L.J.

27. Whitelocke, May 5, 1626, May 7, 1626; Grosvenor, May 5, 1626, May 7, 1626.

28. Rushworth, 1:209–12; Whitelocke, April 17, 1626; Rich, April 17, 1626.

29. CD 1621, 4:62–64; P.D., 1:51–52; C.J., 1:524.

30. CD 1625, p. 49.

31. CD 1629, pp. 20–21, 111–12; Rushworth, 1:647; *Parl. Hist.*, 2:446–47.

32. CD 1629, pp. 20–21, 111–12; Rushworth, 1:647; *Parl. Hist.*, 2:446–47.

33. CD 1625, pp. 18–25.

34. Ibid., pp. 96–101.

35. Whitelocke, February 27, 1626.

36. Rushworth, 1:335–39; L.J., 3:610–12.

37. Whitelocke, June 13, 1626.

38. Rushworth, 1:596–97.

39. CD 1621, 4:63–64, 447–48.
40. Rushworth, 1:602.
41. Whitelocke, June 13, 1626.
42. Grosvenor (2), June 10, 1628.
43. Rushworth, 1:335; L.J., 3:610.
44. P.D., 2:297–98; CD 1621, 6:229.
45. Grosvenor, June 9, 1626; Whitelocke, June 9, 1626.
46. CD 1621, 3:353.
47. Rushworth, 1:525; Borlase, April 4, 1628.
48. Grosvenor (2), April 22, 1628.
49. Holles, March 1, 1624.
50. Whitelocke, February 14, 1626; Rich, February 14, 1626.
51. CD 1621, 3:30.
52. Rushworth, 1:600.
53. Ibid., p. 596.
54. CD 1629, pp. 20–21, 111–12.
55. CD 1621, 3:30, 2:303, 5:83, 340; P.D., 1:283; C.J., 1:583.
56. Grosvenor (2), June 5, 1628.
57. CD 1621, 6:337.
58. CD 1629, pp. 156–57.
59. *Calendar of State Papers, Domestic, 1665–1666* (Charles II), p. 168.
60. S. R. Gardiner, *History of England from the Accession of James I to the Outbreak of the Civil War, 1603–1642* (London, 1883–84), 4:244.
61. Borlase, March 25, 1628, April 29, 1628; Grosvenor (2), April 29, 1628.

Bibliography

Bibliographies and Reference Works

Godfrey Davies, ed. *Bibliography of British History: Stuart Period, 1603–1714*. Oxford: Clarendon Press, 1928.

James T. Gerould, ed. *Sources of English History of the Seventeenth Century, 1603-1689*. Minneapolis: University of Minneapolis Press, 1921.

Eleanor S. Upton and George P. Winship, Jr., eds. *Guide to Sources of English History from 1603–1660 in Reports of the Royal Commission on Historical Manuscripts*. Washington, D.C.: Scarecrow Press, 1952.

Robert Walcott. *The Tudor-Stuart Period of English History (1485–1714): A Review of Changing Interpretations*. New York: Macmillan Company, 1964.

Perez Zagorin. "English History, 1588–1640: A Bibliographical Survey." *American Historical Review* 68 (1963): 364–85.

Parliamentary Sources

General

Cobbett, Thomas, ed. *The Parliamentary History of England*. 36 vols. London, 1806–20.

Journals of the House of Commons. 117 vols. London, 1803.

Journals of the House of Lords. 64 vols. London, 1846.

Rushworth, John. *Historical Collections of Private Passages of State, 1618–1649*. 8 vols. London, 1721.

Parliament of 1621

Notestein, Wallace; Relf, Francis H.; and Simpson, Hartley, eds. *Common Debates 1621*. 7 vols. New Haven: Yale University Press, 1935.

Tyrwritt, T., ed. *Proceedings and Debates of the House of Commons in 1620 and 1621* . . . 2 vols. London, 1766.

Gardiner, S. R., ed. *Notes of the Debates in the House of Lords, 1621*. Westminster: Camden Society, 1870.

Villiers, Evangeline de, ed. *The Hastings Journal of the Parliament of 1621*. Westminster: Camden Society, 1953.

Parliament of 1624

Gardiner, S. R., ed. *Notes of the Debates of the House of Lords, 1624, 1626*. Westminster: Camden Society, 1879.

(Nicolas) Edward Nicolas' Parliamentary Note Book, February 19 to May 29, 1624. State Papers, Domestic Series, James I, 166.

(Holland) The Diary of Sir Thomas Holland for 1624. Bodlein Library: February 25 to April 9 in Tanner, 392; April 10 to May 15 in Rawlinson D., 1100.

(Holles) The Diary of John Holles for 1624. Harleian MS. 6383.

(Erle) The Diary of Sir Walter Erle for the Parliament of 1624. Additional MS. 18597.

(Gurney) The Gurney Diary for 1624. At Keswick Hall near Norwich belonging to the Gurney Family.

(Pym) The Diary of John Pym for the Parliament of 1624. Additional MS. 26639.

(Harl. 159) An Anonymous Diary for the Parliament of 1624.

Parliament of 1625

Eliot, Sir John. *An Apology for Socrates and Negotium Posterorum*. Edited by Alexander B. Grosart. 2 vols. London, 1881.

Gardiner, S. R., ed. *Debates in the House of Commons in 1625*. Westminster: Camden Society, 1873.

Parliament of 1626

(Whitelocke) Bulstrode Whitelocke's Journal of the Parliament of 1626. Cambridge University Library, D.D. 12, 20–22.

(Rich) Sir Nathaniel Rich's Diary for the Parliament of 1626. Duke of Manchester's MS. at Kimbolton Castle, St. Neots, Huntingdonshire.

(Grosvenor) Sir Richard Grosvenor's Diary for the Parliament of 1626. Dublin, Trinity College Library, 611.

Parliament of 1628

Fuller, Thomas. *Ephemeris Parliamentaria*. London, 1654.

(Grosvenor [2]) Sir Richard Grosvenor's Diary for the Parliament of 1628. Dublin, Trinity College Library.

(Borlase) The Borlase Manuscript. Stowe MS. 366.

(Nicolas [2]) Notes of Sir Edward Nicolas for the Parliament of 1628. State Papers, Domestic Series, Charles I, 96.

(Mass.) The True Relation. Manuscript in the possession of the Massachusetts Historical Society. Notes by ———.

(Harl. 2313) Harleian MS. 2313, 5324.

(Harl. 5324) Notes by ———.

(Harl. 1601) Harleian MS. 1601. Notes by ———.

(Lowther) Notes by Mr. Lowther. *Historical Manuscripts Commission, Thirteenth Report*, Appendix 7, pp. 33–60.

Parliamentary Session of 1629

Notestein, Wallace, and Relf, Francis H., eds. *Commons Debates for 1629*. Minneapolis: University of Minnesota Press, 1921.

Printed Collections and General Printed Primary Sources

Acts of the Privy Council, 1613–1625 (James I). 7 vols. London, 1921–1933.

Acts of the Privy Council, 1625–1629. (Charles I). 5 vols. London, 1934–1958.

A Damnable Treason by a Contagious Plaster of a Plague Sore. London, 1641.

A Short View of the Life and Actions of the Late Deceased John Pym Esquire. London, 1643.

A Narrative of the Disease and Death of the Noble Gentleman John Pym Esquire. London, 1643.

Cabala . . . London, 1691.

Calendar of State Papers, Domestic Series, 1603–1625 (James I). 5 vols. London, 1857–1859.

Calendar of State Papers, Domestic Series, 1625–1647 (Charles I). 15 vols. London, 1858–1891.

Calendar of State Papers, Domestic Series, 1665–1666 (Charles II). London, 1864.

Calendar of State Papers, Venetian, 1603–1625 (James I). 9 vols. London, 1900–1912.

Calendar of State Papers, Venetian, 1625–1647 (Charles I). 9 vols. London, 1913–1926.

Carew, Richard. *The Survey of Cornwall*. London, 1602.

Edward, Earl of Clarendon. *The History of the Rebellion and Civil Wars in England*. Edited by W. D. Macray. 6 vols. Oxford: Clarendon Press, 1888.

Clark, Andrew, ed. *Register of the University of Oxford*. Oxford: Clarendon Press, 1888.

Coke, Sir Edward. *The Reports of Sir Edward Coke*. 7 vols. London, 1738.

Colby, Frederick T., ed. *The Visitations of the County of Devon in the Year 1620*. London: Harleian Society, 1872.

Collins, Arthur, ed. *Historical Collections of the Noble Families of Cavandise, Holles* . . . London, 1752.

Crisp, F. A., ed. *Abstracts of Somerset Wills*. 6 vols. London: Privately Printed, 1887–1890.

D'Ewes, Sir Simond. *The Journals of all the Parliaments during the Reign of Queen Elizabeth*. London, 1682.

Eliot, Sir John. *The Letter Book of Sir John Eliot*. Edited by Alexander B. Grosart. London, 1882.

———. *De Jure Maiestatis*. Edited by Alexander B. Grosart. London, 1882.

Fitzgeffrey, Charles. *Elisha, His Lamentations for His Owne, and all Israel's losse in Elijah*. London, 1622.

———. *Death's Sermons Unto the Living, Delivered at the Funerall of the Religious Ladie Phillipe, late Wife unto the Right Worshippfull Sr. Anthonie Rous of Halton in Cornwall*. London, 1620.

Foster, Joseph, ed. *Alumni Oxoniensis: The Members of the University of Oxford*. 4 vols. Oxford: Parkes and Co., 1892.

Fuller, Thomas. *Anglorum Speculum, or The Worthies of England in Church and State*. London, 1684.

Gardiner, S. R., ed. *The Constitutional Documents of the Puritan Revolution, 1625–1660*. Oxford: Clarendon Press, 1951.

Hakluyt, Richard. *The Principal Navigations, Voyages, Traffiques and Discoveries of the English Nation . . .* 3 vols. London, 1598–1600.

Halliwell, James O., ed. *Autobiography and Correspondence of Sir Simond D'Ewes*. 2 vols. London, 1845.

Historical Manuscripts Commission, Second Report. London, 1874.

Historical Manuscripts Commission, Third Report. London, 1875.

Historical Manuscripts Commission, Fourth Report. London, 1875.

Historical Manuscripts Commission, Sixth Report. London, 1877.

Historical Manuscripts Commission, Seventh Report. London, 1879.

Historical Manuscripts Commission, Bath Manuscripts. 3 vols. London, 1904.

Historical Manuscripts Commission, Hastings Manuscripts. 4 vols. London, 1930.

Historical Manuscripts Commission, Laing Manuscripts. 2 vols. London, 1914.

Hopwood, Charles H., ed. *Middle Temple Records*. London: Butterwood and Co., 1904.

James I. *The King's majesties declaration to his subjects, concerning Lawful Sports to be used*. London, 1618.

Kellison, Matthew. *The Gagg of the reformed gospell*. N.p., 1623?

Knowler, William, ed. *The Earl of Strafforde's Letters and Dispatches*. 2 vols. London, 1739.

Laing, David, ed. *The Letters and Journals of Robert Baillie*. 3 vols. Edinburgh: R. Ogle, 1841.

Laud, William. *Works*. Edited by W. Scott. 7 vols. London, 1847.

Luders, A.; Tomlins, T. E.; and Raithly, J., eds. *Statutes of the Realm*. 11 vols. London, 1810–1828.

Manningham, John. *Diary, 1601–1603*. Edited by John Bruce. Westminster: Camden Society, 1868.

Marshall, Stephan. *The Churches Lamentation. A Sermon of the Two Houses of Parliament a the Funerall of John Pym*. London, 1643.

Maynwaring, Roger. *Religion and Allegiance*. London, 1627.

McClure, N. E., ed. *The Letters of John Chamberlain*. 2 vols. Philadelphia: American Philosophical Society, 1939.

Montague, Richard. *A Gagg for the New Gospell? No. A New Gagg for an Old Goose*. London, 1624.

————. *Apello Caesarem: A Just Appeale from Two Unjust Informers*. London, 1625.

Moore, Sir Francis. *Cases Collect and Report*. London, 1663.

Noy, William. *Reports and Cases, King's Bench and Common Pleas, Taken in the Time of Queen Elizabeth, King James and King Charles*. London, 1656.

Overall, W. H. and H. C., eds. *Analytical Index to the Series of Records Known as the Remembrancia of the City of London*. London: E. J. Francis and Co., 1878.

Return of the Names of Every Member Returned to Serve in Each Parliament. 3 vols. London, 1878.

Roberts, George, ed. *The Diary of Walter Yonge, M.P.* Westminster: Camden Society, 1882.

Rymer, Thomas, ed. *Foedora*. 20 vols. London, 1735.

Spedding, James, ed. *The Letters and Life of Francis Bacon*. 7 vols. London: Longmans, Green, Longmans and Roberts, 1861–1874.

Steele, Robert, ed. *Tudor and Stuart Proclamations*. 2 vols. Oxford: Clarendon Press, 1910.

Stubbs, William, ed. *Select Charters and Other Illustrations of English Constitutional History*. Revised by H. W. C. Davis. Oxford: Clarendon Press, 1921.

Townshend, Heywood. *Historical Collections: Or an Exact Account of the Proceedings of the Four Last Parliaments of Queen Elizabeth*. London, 1680.

Welwood, Jr. *Memoirs of the Most Material Transactions in England for the Last Hundred Years to 1688*. 8 vols. London, 1700.

Williams, R. F., ed. *The Court and Times of James the First*. 2 vols. London: H. Colburn, 1848.

————. ed. *The Court and Times of Charles the First*. 2 vols. London: H. Colburn, 1848.

Secondary Authorities

Adair, E. R. "The Petition of Right." *History* 5 (1920): 99–103.

Akrigg, G. P. V. *Jacobean Pageant: Or the Court of King James I.* Cambridge: Harvard University Press, 1962.

Aylmer, G. E. *The King's Servants: The Civil Service of Charles I, 1625–1642.* London: Routledge and Kegan Paul, 1961.

Berquist, Goodwin F., Jr. "Revolution Through Moderation: John Pym's Appeal to the Moderates in 1640." *Quarterly Journal of Speech* 41 (1963): 23–30.

———. "John Pym: New Evidence on an Old Parliamentarion." *Notes and Queries*, New Series 5 (1958): 101.

———. "The Parliamentary Speaking of John Pym, 1621–1643." Ph.D. dissertation, Pennsylvania State University, 1958.

Brett, S. Reed. *John Pym, 1583–1643.* London: John Murray, 1940.

———. "John Pym." *Fortnightly* 154 (1943): 405–6.

Burke, John. *A Geneological and Heraldic History of the Landed Gentry; or Commoners of Great Britain and Ireland.* 4 vols. London: H. Colburn, 1837–1838.

Capes, W. W. *Scenes of Rural Life in Hampshire Among the Manors of Bramshott.* London: Macmillan and Co., Ltd., 1901.

Curtis, Mark H. "The Alienated Intellectuals of Early Stuart England." *Past and Present* 23 (1962): 25–43.

———. *Oxford and Cambridge in Transition.* Oxford: Clarendon Press, 1959.

Davies, Godfrey. "Arminian Versus Puritan in England, Ca. 1620–1640." *Huntington Library Quarterly* 5 (1934): 157–79.

———. "The Character of James VI and I." *Huntington Library Quarterly* 10 (1941): 33–63.

———. *The Early Stuarts, 1603–1660.* Oxford: Clarendon Press, 1959.

D'Israeli, Isaac. *Eliot, Hampden and Pym, Or a Reply of the Author of a Book entitled 'Commentaries on the Life and Reign of Charles I' to The Authors of a Book entitled Some Memorials of John Hampden and his times.* London, 1832.

Eliot-Drake, Lady. *The Family and Heirs of Sir Francis Drake.* 2 vols. London: Smith, Elder and Co., 1911.

Farnham, E. "The Somerset Election of 1614." *English Historical Review* 46 (1931): 579–99.

Forster, John. *Lives of Eminent British Statesmen.* 7 vols. London: Longman, Rees, Orme, Brown, and Green, 1831.

————. *Sir John Eliot*. 2 vols. London: Longman, Green, Longman, Roberts and Green, 1864.

Foster, E. R. "The Procedure of the House of Commons against Patents of Monopolies." In *Conflicts in Stuart England*. W. A. Aiken and Basil Henning, ed. New York: New York University Press, 1960.

Fraser, I. H. C. "The Agitation of the Commons, 2 March 1629, and the Interrogation of the Leaders of the Anti-Court Group." *Bulletin of the Institute of Historical Research* 30 (1957): 86–95.

Gardiner, S. R. "An Alleged Notebook of John Pym." *English Historical Review* 10 (1895): 105–6.

————. *The Thirty Years War, 1618–1648*. Boston: Estes and Lauriot, 1874.

————. *History of England from the Accession of James I to the Outbreak of the Civil War, 1603–1642*. 10 vols. London: Longmans, Green and Co., 1883–1884.

Gibb, M. A. *Buckingham*. London: Jonathan Cape, 1935.

Glow, Lotte. "Pym and Parliament: The Methods of Moderation." *The Journal of Modern History* 36 (1964): 373–97.

Greenleaf, W. H. "James I and the Divine Right of Kings." *Political Studies* 5 (1957): 36–48.

Hatsell, John. *Precedents of Proceedings in the House of Commons*. 4 vols. London: J. Dodsley, 1785.

Havran, Martin J. *The Catholics in Caroline England*. Stanford, Calif.: Stanford University Press, 1962.

————. "Parliament and Catholicism in England, 1626–1629." *Catholic Historical Review* 44 (1958): 273–89.

Hexter, J. H. *The Reign of King Pym*. Cambridge: Harvard University Press, 1941.

Higham, F. M.G. *Charles I: A Study*. London: Hanish Hamilton, 1932.

Hill, Christopher. *A Century of Revolution, 1603–1714*. Edinburgh: Thomas Nelson and Son, 1961.

Hinton, R. W. K. "The Decline of Parliamentary Government Under Elizabeth and the Early Stuarts." *Cambridge Historical Journal* 13 (1957): 118–31.

————. "Government and Liberty Under James I." *Cambridge Historical Journal* 11 (1953): 48–64.

————. "Was Charles I a Tyrant?" *Review of Politics* 18 (1956): 69–87.

Hughes, Edward. "A Durham Manuscript of the Commons Debate of 1629." *English Historical Review* 74 (1959): 672–73.

Hulme, E. W. "Elizabethan Patents of Monopolies." *Law Quarterly Review* 16 (1900): 45–56.

————. "History of the Patent System Under the Prerogative and Common Law." *Law Quarterly Review* 12 (1896): 141–54.

Hulme, Harold. "The Winning of Freedom of Speech by the House of Commons." *American Historical Review* 61 (1956): 825–53.

————. *The Life of Sir John Eliot*. New York: New York University Press, 1957.

————. "The Leadership of Sir John Eliot in the Parliament of 1626." *The Journal of Modern History* 4 (1932): 361–86.

————. "Opinion in the House of Commons on the Proposal for a Petition of Right, 6 May, 1628." *English Historical Review* 50 (1935): 300–306.

————. "The Sheriff as a Member of the House of Commons from Elizabeth to Cromwell." *The Journal of Modern History* 1 (1929): 361–77.

Keeler, Mary F. *The Long Parliament, 1640–1641: A Biographical Study of Its Members*. Philadelphia: American Philosophical Society, 1954.

Kirby, E. W. "Sermons before the Commons, 1640–42." *American Historical Review* 44 (1938): 528–48.

Maitland, F. W. *The Constitutional History of England*. Cambridge, England: University Press, 1920.

Mallet, Charles E. *A History of the University of Oxford*. 3 vols. London: Methuen and Co., 1924.

Marsh, A. E. W. *A History of the Borough and Town of Calne*. Calne, England: Robert S. Heath, 1903.

McElwee, William. *The Wisest Fool in Christendom: The Reign of King James VI and I*. London: Faber and Faber, 1958.

McIlwain, Charles H. "The House of Commons in 1621." *The Journal of Modern History* 9 (1937): 206–14.

————. *Constitutions Ancient and Modern*. Ithaca, N.Y.: Cornell University Press, 1940.

Moir, Thomas J. *The Addled Parliament of 1614*. Oxford: Clarendon Press, 1958.

———. "The Parliamentary Election of 1614." *The Historian* 16 (1954): 176–205.

Montague, F. C. *The History of England from the Accession of James I to the Restoration, 1603–1660*. London: Longmans, Green and Co., 1907.

Mosse, George L. *The Struggle for Sovereignty in England: From the Reign of Queen Elizabeth to the Petition of Right*. East Lansing, Mich.: Michigan State College Press, 1950.

Neale, J. E. *Elizabeth I and Her Parliaments*. 2 vols. London: Jonathan Cape, 1953–57.

Newton, A. P. *The Colonizing Activities of the English Puritans*. New Haven: Yale University Press, 1914.

Notestein, Wallace. *The Winning of the Initiative by the House of Commons*. London: Oxford University Press, 1924.

Nugent, Lord. *Some Memorials of John Hampden, His Party and His Times*. 2 vols. London: John Murray, 1832.

Oman, Carola. *Henrietta Maria*. New York: Macmillan Company, 1936.

Pearl, Valerie. *London and the Outbreak of the Puritan Revolution: City Government and National Politics, 1625–1643*. New York: Oxford University Press, 1961.

Price, W. H. *The English Patents of Monopoly*. Cambridge: Harvard University Press, 1906.

Ranke, Leopold von. *The History of England Principally in the Seventeenth Century*. 6 vols. Cambridge: Clarendon Press, 1875.

Relf, Francis H. *The Petition of Right*. Minneapolis: University of Minnesota Press, 1917.

Richardson, C. F. *English Preachers and Preaching*. New York: Macmillan Company, 1928.

Smith, Goldwin. *Three English Statesmen: Pym, Cromwell and Pitt*. New York: Harper and Brothers, 1867.

Snapp, Henry F. "The Impeachment of Roger Maynwaring." *Huntington Library Quarterly* 30 (1967): 217–32.

Snow, Vernon L. "The Concept of Revolution in Seventeenth Century England." *The Historical Journal* 5 (1962): 167–74.

Tanner, J. R. *English Constitutional Conflicts in the Seventeenth Century, 1603–1688*. Cambridge, England: University Press, 1961.

Tawney, R. H. *Business and Politics Under James I: Lionel Cranfield as Merchant and Adventurer*. Cambridge, England: University Press, 1958.

Tayler, Ida A. *Revolutionary Types*. London: Duckworth and Co., 1904.

Trevelyan, G. M. *England Under the Stuarts*. London: Methuen and Co., 1954.

Trevor-Roper, H. R. *Archbishop Laud*. London: Macmillan and Co., Ltd., 1940.

Vivian-Neal, A. W. *The Story of Brymore*. Taunton, England: Hammett and Company, c. 1951.

Wade, C. E. *John Pym*. London: Sir Isaac Pitman and Sons, Ltd., 1912.

Wedgwood, C. V. *The Thirty Years War*. New York: Doubleday and Company, 1961.

———. *Thomas Wentworth: First Earl of Strafford, 1593–1641*. London: Jonathan Cape, 1961.

———. *The King's Peace*. New York: Macmillan Company, 1956.

———. *The King's War*. London: Macmillan Company, Ltd., 1958.

Weston, C. C. "The Theory of Mixed Monarchy under Charles I and After." *English Historical Review* 75 (1960): 426–43.

Williamson, H. R. *John Hampden*. London: Faber and Faber, 1933.

Willson, D. H. "The Earl of Salisbury and the 'Court' Party in Parliament." *American Historical Review* 36 (1931): 274–94.

———. "Summoning and Dissolving Parliament, 1603–1625." *American Historical Review* 45 (1940): 279–300.

———. *The Privy Councillors in the House of Commons, 1604–1629*. Minneapolis: University of Minnesota Press, 1940.

———. *James VI and I*. New York: Henry Holt and Co., 1956.

Wingfield-Stratford, Esme. *King Charles and King Pym, 1637–1643*. London: Hollis and Carter, 1949.

Wright, Louis B. "Propaganda Against James I's 'Appeasement' of Spain." *Huntington Library Quarterly* 6 (1943): 149–72.

Zagorin, Perez. "The Court and the Country: A Note on Political Terminology in the Earlier Seventeenth Century." *English Historical Review* 77 (1962): 306–11.

INDEX

[The following abbreviations are used: MP = Member of Parliament; PC = Privy Councillor]